Pègúnrun Ikúdẹtì Kútelú Ọṣun
(Four Plays)

Ahmed Yerima

ALPHA CROWNES PUBLISHING LTD

First published in 2020 by Alpha Crownes Publishing Ltd
107 Windmill Street
Rochester, United Kingdom
Copyright © Ahmed Yerima, 2020

Ahmed Yerima is hereby identified as author of the plays in this collection in accordance with section 77 of the Copyright, Designs and Patents Act 1988 of the United Kingdom, and in accordance with the Nigerian Copyright Act, Cap 28 Laws of the Federation of Nigeria, 2004. The author has asserted his moral rights.

All rights whtsoever in these plays are strictly reserved and application for performance, etc. should be made before commencement of rehearsal to ahmedpyerima@yahoo.com. No performance may be given unless a licence has been obtained, and no alterations may be made in the title or the text of the play without the author's prior written consent.

You may not copy, store, distribute, transmit, reproduce or otherwise make available this publication (or any part of it) in any form, or binding or by any means (print, electronic, digital, optical, mechanical, photocopying, recording or otherwise), without the prior written permission of the publisher.

A catalogue record for this book is available from the British Library.
PB ISBN: 978-0-9935781-8-2
Cover Photography by Ahmed Yerima
Cover Design & Book Layout: Tokunbo Esho

PÈGÚNRUN, IKÚDẸTÌ, KÚTELÚ, ỌSUN.

FOUR PLAYS

by

AHMED YERIMA

Author's Note

Towards the end of 2018, there was so much anxiety and worry on my mind. Yet I foresaw and felt the coming of a majestic dawn. I longed to leave Ẹdẹ for a while. Four years was near enough. The place had been kind to me…but I knew it was time to leave. I wanted to return to another home of mine… Ilé-Ifẹ̀. I wanted to shut my eyes once again in the land of the gods. I wanted to see how much of modernity had affected what Ifẹ̀ implanted in me when I was growing up. I wanted to find deeper meanings to ideas that I had come across in my many years of travels.

The four plays in this collection are products of the new subconscious reality…a subtle process of grappling with old wounds against new reconstructed ideas and reality.

Pègúnrun remains a parody of an older and religiously inclined story. I wondered how it drifted there. But when l arrived at what you will read, I was satisfied. In this play, I examined the issues of sacrifice, belief and doubt within my imagined universe. *Ikúdẹtì* is the play where I tried to see if I could punish the erring character. The issue of destiny and man's continuous attempt to change his destiny is my preoccupation in *Kútelú*. And *Ọ̀sun* is the final confirmation of Èṣù as the arbiter in the conflict which projects man within his contrived machinations of the "playwright as little god" in his imagined world… mirroring man's contradictions, suggesting alternative human reactions and finding answers to questions whose answers are often swept under for fear of what one would discover if good attempts were made to ask and answer man's actions. The plays are set in my fictitious village, Ìjèkùn Odò. And they span the reigns of more than ten Kings and the repercussions of their actions, especially when tested against the cultural laws, beliefs, religions, traditional boundaries and phasing thoughts and discourses on the openings and closures within socio-political and historical realities.

Yet for me, it is the presence of the gods who exist as spiritual force and characters in the four plays that power my imaginative consciousness. Èṣù fascinates me here not as figure for personal worship but as inspiring figure that propels the flaws of my protagonists and invariably men. One that inspires man's intrinsic dependence on him. This is what Èṣù shares with man's sensibilities. As I wrote, I found Èṣù as trickster god (Èṣù Ọ̀dàrà), an embittered god (Èṣù Èbìtà), a black stone god, fearfully created demon god, a jealous god, a Scorpion stinging god, a Cactus pricking god, and gradually, a dual sexual god-like being, who sits at the Crossroad, emerged. Why? I don't know. This is the multiplicity and duplicity of the nature of Èṣù. Èṣù remains a roaming deity who inhabits man's universe with him, and therefore it is difficult to avoid clashing into him, meeting him by accident or embracing him willingly. Because of this, I have however come to the conclusion that man projects Èṣù's character ugliness by imbibing Èṣù's spiritual ugliness. In these plays man is the projected as the supreme protagonist. The self-destructive animal who blames his Aristotle's tragic flaws and human frailties on the sometimes less interested Èṣù about man. Man has therefore chosen Èṣù because of the flexibility of his nature as his life partner in order to overcome; constructively or destructively, what he considers as insurmountable trials and tribulations of his existence. What then is the humanity of Èṣù? Tóyìn Fálọlá in his edited book, *Èṣù: Yorùbá God, Power, and the Imaginative*

Frontiers, notes that Èṣù's humanity is based on his hegemonic nature. "...his complex devices and styles are to keep him in a permanent state of control. Whether he stays at the margin of discourse or at the center of sacrifice and rituals, Èṣù retains a hegemonic presence". (Carolina Academic Press, 2013, p. 10) A hegemonic presence which allows him to have a deeper understanding of man and his nuances and be able to return the embrace which man in despair, is ready to offer him. You can only imagine how excited I was when I found the photograph of a West African carved Èṣù Cult Dance staff or Wrist ornament with plaited hair in a top blouse and skirt of 1800-2000 (Finch & co). I have chosen to use it as my cover photograph. This time with a sword not the usual club as in the typical Yorùbá mythology. For me, this was a further confirmation and extension of Èṣù's humanity. And why man finds it so easy to embrace him or her, and share with him or her, certain deceitful characteristics which lead man, most times to a definite downfall. In these four plays, I expanded the "fiend-ship" of Èṣù's reverberating spirit and then highlight the partnership of Èṣù has with Ọ̀rúnmìlà and the other gods. I identify the position of Ọbàtálá, and re-identify man as a self deified acolyte of *Èṣù* himself or herself. The three worlds of the living, unborn and dead allowed me to transverse the magical sphere of my imagined worlds. I deconstruct history and action in order to reconstruct my refracted universe and to serve my story telling purposes, and yet I believe that I wrote the kind of plays I intended to write because within the ancient ambience of Ilé Ifẹ̀, the pounded yam and ẹ̀fọ́ rírò of "Yèyé Ẹ̀gin and Ìyá Pupa". And in the presence of my now elderly friends from yore, there will be a form of purgation, a continuous process of rethink, and a rebirth of the wondering souls of the audience. The audience who are intrinsic representations of the characters, I create here, must also surrender themselves to the process of purgation. They are the ones whose fears my characters portray in the four plays. It is their stories that are told in the three plays, and yet even though it may be easy for them to draw a line of disowning, between their destinies and those of my spent protagonists, they remain one and the same people. My characters are the extension of them, they are a mirror of them, and they share in their predicaments. I want them…the audience to identify themselves within these characters, and consider themselves lucky for having not fallen yet, but must learn from them. These are those whom these plays were written for. Those who must be aware of the overpowering essence of Èṣù and can choose to embrace him or avoid him. The benevolence of Èṣù which is part of his contradiction as a core Òrìṣà, is when he turns away from the seeker or spent protagonist, or better still, when one is able to blur his sight momentarily, with fervent prayers. And those who must find a way of seeking such a refuge in faith, the true God that sets the broken protagonist, free. This may be why I found an internal peace after writing these four plays from the spiritual relationship, which enriched my trust in the fulfilment of my desires and aspirations. Because like the prospective audience, I too was purged of falsified illusions, defeating social realities and now very few suffocated unachievable dreams and a stream of never-ending aspirations of man…still lingers.

This was exactly why and what I came to do at Ilé Ifẹ̀ for my sabbatical year (2019-2020), to edify myself up, to relearn and retouch base with where my creative "Muse" was born, was identified, was haunted, and ironically, still resides.

I thank God, Wọlé Ṣoyínká, Yẹmí Ògúnbíyí, Bridgette Yerima, Anthony Akínlọ, Èyítọ́pẹ́ Ògúngbénró Ògúnbọ́dẹdé, Akínṣọlá Adéjùwọ́n, Gbémisọlá Adéọtí, Segun Adekoya and Adéyẹmí Victoria Ọmọ́wùmí, my colleagues at the department of Dramatic Arts, and all those who met me between 1977-2020. To Láídé Adéwálé, Gbóyèga Àjàyí, Peter Fátómilọ́lá, Kọ́lá Oyèwọ̀, and to the bearded, wise Àwíṣẹ, Wándé Abímbọ́lá, your Ifá prophesy of a delayed return, is fulfilled. Once again, this is done.

Ahmed Yerima.
Visiting Professor, of Theatre and Cultural Studies,
Ọbáfẹ́mi Awólọ́wọ̀ University,
Ilé-Ifẹ̀. 2019-2020.

Professor of Theatre and Cultural Studies
Redeemer's University, Ẹdẹ.

Foreword

Another product of his well-acknowledged prodigious energy in dramatic compositions, Ahmed Yerima is offering four plays in this collection. The plays are connected in the main by their exploration of the tragic mode from Yoruba cultural performance, the people's beliefs about human fate and their faith in the gods. They also have a common spatio-temporal setting – Ìjèkùn-Odò in the interface of tradition and modernity.

In 2008, Yerima published a collection of four plays under the title: "The Ifẹ̀ Quartet". These were plays written and performed when he was a student in the Department of Dramatic Arts, University of Ifẹ̀ (now Ọbáfẹ́mi Awólọ́wọ̀ University), Ilé Ifẹ̀. The plays in that collection are: *The Assylum, The Flood, The Movement*, and *An Inspector Calls* (an adaptation of J. B. Priestley's *An Inspector Calls*). In a way, this collection is another "Ifẹ̀ Quartet" as the four plays here are also written whilst the playwright was in Ifẹ̀, not as an undergraduate, but as a Visiting Professor in his former department. The plays in the collection are *Pègúnrun (The Cactus), Ikúdẹtì (Cannot be Trapped by Death), Kútelú* (nickname for hunchback or deformed people) and *Ọ̀ṣun (River Goddess)*. The plays therefore mark the return of Yerima to his *alma mater*. They also provide another opportunity to explore the rich ambience of mythological, artistic and performance heritage of a people that nurture the dramatic oeuvre of frontline African literary dramatists such as Wọlé Ṣóyinká, Ọlá Rótìmí, Wálé Ògúnyẹmí, Olú Ọbáfẹ́mi and Fẹ́mi Òṣófisan on the one hand, and itinerant folk theatre heroes such as Hubert Ògúndé, Kọ́lá Ògúnmọ́lá, Dúró Ladípọ̀, Ìṣọ̀lá Ògúnṣọlá, Lérè Pàímọ́ and Akin Ògúngbè among others.

Yerima has explored Yorùbá culture and cosmology as the background of earlier plays especially in *The Silent Gods, Adé*

Ìrè, Yemọja, Erelú Kútì, Abóbakú, Mojágbè, Àjàgùnmàlè and Òrìsà Ìbejì. He gives attention to the deities as human beings, supernatural powers and, more importantly, as artistic muses that inspire creativity in different realms. Prominent and recurring divinities include Ọbàtálá, Ọ̀rúnmìlà, Ògún, Ṣàngó, Ọ̀ṣun, Yemọja and Èṣù. The last has featured the most because his life entwines with those of other gods and human beings. The Deities in this collection and as experienced in his previous plays are depicted in their ugliness and beauty. They are invested with great capacity for good and evil in their exertion of influence over human affairs.

In the collection, there is a fluid intersection between the human world and the world of super nature as the affairs of humans conjoin with those of Deities in Ìjèkùn-Odò, the fictional human community that hosts the Divinities as "guests" and also, as "house-owners". In spite of European inspired modernity, the hands of the Deities are not totally severed from human affairs. In particular, Yerima interrogates the persona of Èṣù in religious, literary and cosmological contexts. Èṣù Ẹlẹ́gbárá, Èṣù Láàlú or Èṣù Èbìtà, as variously encountered in his dramaturgy, is the many sides of the same coin, representing the Yorùbá trickster God that also dispenses retributive justice. He is fingered in the heat of conflicts generated by options available to humans at every situation and the anxiety that attends choices made by them. He is also implicated in the final resolution of conflicts and conflicting inter-personal relations. In some of Yerima's earlier plays, especially those in the mode of "pro-Pentecostal proselytism" such as Òwìwí and The Sacred Mutter, Èṣù is invested with much negativity. However, in this collection, the human will and the ability to make right choices push negativity more to the doorstep of human beings. When people are blinded by ambition and impatience, they enlist Èṣù in achieving rapid results to fulfill their ambition. Such human beings end up in a fiasco, regardless of their investment in securing the nod of Èṣù, because the Gods works with other Deities whose genial dispositions often frustrate inordinate desires. The Divinity Èṣù is, in a way, existentialist in orientation as he extracts pleasure from tension and impels humans to bear the consequences of their action or inaction, positive or negative and Sàùrá is his human manifestation as a Priest. Èṣù is praised as a contrarian who is sad when others are rejoicing and derives delight from the misfortune of others. He is a muse to be further considered in African tragic epistemology beyond Ògún and Òrúnmìlà as enunciated in the works of Ṣóyínká and Ọ̀ṣọ́fisan respectively.

Ìjèkùn-Odò reminds us of Ọlá Rótìmí's Ìjẹ̀kùn-Yemọja in *The Gods are not to Blame* (1968). Both are not located anywhere on the map of Yorùbá world. The setting is, therefore, as fictional as the central characters of the plays – Káróunwí, Ikúdẹtì, Adéyímiká and Ògìdán. They are monarchs who are somewhat created in the image of Aristotelian tragic heroes. There is also a concern with gender relations and gender discourse in each play from which one can glean the playwright's position. His argument is clear, consistent and audible enough in that regard.

Pègúnrun, the first play, presents Ìjèkùn-Odò experiencing Pègúnrun's anger under the reign of Ọba Káróunwí. Pègúnrun (Put an end to damnation or curse) is an invented Deity. Like many other Deities in the African world, she once lived as a human being, but later got deified on account of her altruism. There is a messianic archetypal dimension to her personality as she volunteered to lay down her life as sacrifice to save her community from ruin in the face of onslaught of slavery and colonialism. That was during the reign of Ọba Ọ̀mọ̀lé. In return, she demanded that her mother should be taken care of, she should experience the prosperity and plenitude of Ọbàtálá, and she should be deified thereafter, so that every year, the Ìjẹ̀kùn community would worship her in a festival where gender differences would be cast aside and everybody would dress as a woman. The latter obligation has been observed and is being preserved for over a century. Things turn sour during the reign of Ọba Károunwí who, not only holds Pègúnrun in contempt, but also wants to abolish the annual festival as he abhors it in totality particularly because of the primacy accorded women. The king's hostility coincides with the time of Pègúnrun's anger and her desire to avenge her ignominious treatment by the king and his supporters. She also wants to re-manifest in human form a hundred years after.

Ìjèkùn-Odò has just lost the Ìyálóde who is the leader of women and the human link between the Deity and her worshippers. A replacement, Abídèmí Àbẹ̀bí, is already selected and has the blessing of all the Deities (Ifá, Ṣàngó, Ògún) except Èṣù Èbìtà, who, according to the Chief Priest, is furious on account of a sacrilege committed by Abídèmí. Èṣù's service has been enlisted by an ambitious rival, Jowúọlá, who also aspires to the position of Ìyálóde. Jowúọlá is making a frantic claim to the position, backed by some elders in the family. All efforts to secure reconciliation within the family and make Jowúọlá give up her claim to the title fail. Ọba Károunwí seizes the opportunity of the division to propel his anti-tradition agenda in the garb of modernity and development. He also has a patriarchal war to wage against a humbling tradition that will make him "lower" his royal image by dressing like a woman during the celebration like every commoner. However, he seductively argues for a new gender order that frees the woman from silence and passivity, using Ẹfúnṣetán Aníwúrà and Queen Amina as the new role models for women in the new dispensation. He disagrees with his ancestor, Ọba Ọ̀mọ̀lé, who gave assent to the deification of Pègúnrun. Unfortunately, he fails to realise the trope of Mórèmí in the heroic altruism of Pègúnrun to recommend her as a model too. Thus, the insulting treatment of Pègúnrun sets him on collision course with the women. He earns the anger of the Goddess in that step and he is struck dead with his wife on his lap. He ends in disgrace, worse than what he plans for Pègúnrun and her acolyte.

The dominant confusion, however, is a physical manifestation of Pègúnrun's dissatisfaction. She is the godhead behind the Ìyálóde title. She seeks to return to the world after a century, ostensibly to reinvigorate social ties in Ìjèkùn-Odò and to redeem her desecrated persona in the hands of a bigoted monarch. Not only has Ọba Káróunwí cast a heavy shadow on her authenticity, he also struggles arduously to wipe her from the community's collective memory. The pleasant song of yesterday turns to rubbish in his ears. In all this, the hand of Èṣù is boldly held aloft, as confusion reigns in the family, the palace and the entire community.

Adélù, his son who succeeds him, wants to unravel the cause of his father's death. He is advised to tread with caution. He and the audience later learn about the reason and process of Pègúnrun's deification. In order not to die shamefully like his father, who dismissed the self-sacrifice of the Deity, he decides to go along with the community in pursuing the path of atonement, as advised by the priests. Jowúọlá, Òṣínnúbi and other conspirators are afflicted with ailments for their treachery, while the remaining members of the community recognise Abídèmí as Ìyálóde. The people, dressed like women, erupt in dance and ululation to celebrate the annual festival and the installation of a new representative of the Deity. Coincidentally, Pègúnrun makes a concrete manifestation of her return in Abídèmí, as the new priestess becomes the Goddess.

The ending of the play follows the mode of resolution of conflicts in many plays of the Yorùbá travelling theatre and the contemporary video/film tradition where there is always a reason to rejoice and celebrate in spite of preceding adversity, since there is a relief from tension and an opportunity is provided for a new order. There is a white lining after the dark cloud of disaster is dispelled, sometimes through *deus-ex-machina*. At the end of the play, the community regains its violated stability. This pattern is also adopted in the other three plays in this collection.

The mystery of Èṣù in explaining human action is a crucial element in this and other plays. Yerima uses suspense, foreboding and flashback to illuminate the mystery as he shows clearly that many problems of the world are consequences of human actions and people are designers of their own destiny and architects of their own (mis)fortune.

Ikúdẹtì, like *Kútelú* and *Ọ̀ṣun* derive their titles from major characters in the plays. In naming the characters, Yerima is witty and proverbial. The characters' names are tied to their roles just as one has a better understanding of their roles from the names they bear. Pègúnrun indicates a messianic archetype that saves a community from ruin on account of an old curse. Ikúdẹtì is someone who has outwitted death and is now immortal. He can no longer be struck by the arrows of death. Kútelú is a popular nickname for a hunchback especially the awkward upper spine that creates a "load" on the back. It is a derogatory reference to kyphosis, an abnormal backward curvature of the vertebral column. Ọ̀ṣun is the river Goddess associated with fertility and purity, therefore, her acolytes dress in all white.

Ikúdẹtì, ironically opens with the rumoured death of Ọba Àjàntálá Arábámbí, nicknamed "Ikúdẹtì". He is in a state of coma, "half dead, half living". From his astounding recklessness, he reminds us of Àjàntálá, the weird child in D. O. Fágúnwà's *Ògbójú Ọdẹ Nínú Igbó Irúnmọlẹ̀*. His mother, Yèyé Ọba, is apprehensive that her son will die without fulfilling the traditional rites of passage like previous Kings. This portends ignominy for such a king and his lineage. She suspects that the rival royal family of Ògúnbádéjọ Adéjọwà is behind the King's ordeal. However, Arábámbí's fate, like that of Ọba Ògìdán Arógunmásàá in Ọ̀ṣun, has earlier been sealed by a covenant already entered by his mother with the coven of witches and Èṣù Ẹlẹ́gbárá.

Here, Yerima continues his dialogue on the concept of "abọ́bakú" in some parts of Yorùbá land, a phenomenon that he has visited in a play of that title where he joins issues with Wọlé Ṣóyínká's *Death and the King's Horseman*, Dúró Ladípọ̀'s *Ọba Wàjà* and Moses Ọláìyá's *Abọ́bakú*. This is a practice that stems from the people's belief in life after death. It extends the life of royalty beyond the present physical realm to the ethereal as the king in transition is "accompanied" by loyal wives, horseman, slaves and relatives. *Abọ́bakú* means "he who dies with the king". The tradition demands that when the king joins his ancestor, some designated members of the royal household will "transit" along with the king to the next world. For this role, they would have been socially, psychologically, and (spi)ritually prepared as they demonstrate unflinching loyalty to royalty while the king is alive and when he dies.

However, Yerima explores the concept of *Abọ́bakú* from a more pragmatic and material angle. In the case of Ọba Arábámbí, he faces the dim prospect of dying unaccompanied by any aide as his death is not sure. He is not being accorded the necessary traditional rituals and transitional pageantry. A king that dies unaccompanied in Yerima's fictional world of Ìjèkùn-Odò dies like a pauper. It is this shameful death of a pauper that disturbs Yèyé as the body of her son, the king, is left alone in the dark room, a fate that has not befallen any king of the town in the last four centuries. The Head messenger and the Horseman who are expected to accompany the king in death are still alive. While the king's death is inconclusive, a new one cannot be enthroned.

The situation of suspended animation is believed to be a trick being played by Èṣù Ọ̀dàrà, the trickster God. The rest of the play is devoted to the unraveling of the mystery, using suspense and quest motif. As a result of the king's inordinate ambition, arrogance, pride and reckless exercise of power, he is being punished along with his mother for her ambitious scheming, deceit and adultery. Both of them are blinded by ambition as they become willing victims of witches with active support from Èṣù. Èṣù, in this context, acts directly and through proxies.

In presenting the characters and the consequences of their actions, Yerima allows a free interplay of freewill and determinism. An earlier prediction has shown that the King will rule for only seven years and the mother will outlive him. Not comfortable with such a short life as a Queen mother, she seeks to spiritually elongate her son's tenure and that brings her into a union with the witches and Èṣù. She undertakes a spiritual pilgrimage to the land of Ikú (Death) to get her son off the hook of death so that he can live a life of royalty for many more years. But the solution as found through divination is that the ordeal of the king is embedded in a palace secret that must be revealed. It is the consequent *anagnorisis* that will free the dying from his arrested transition and the community from the benumbing impasse.

The former king (Yèyé's husband) was impotent and could not produce a successor. By a special arrangement which remained a palace top secret, Yèyé was impregnated by Ẹlẹ́ṣin Àdèlé, but the product, Arábámbí Àjàntálá, was raised as a Prince in the palace. Through the scheming and manipulation of vital forces by Yèyé who knows the secret, Arábámbí was crowned with a mutual understanding between her and the vital forces that he would rule for only seven years. The crux of the matter is that the community is being ruled inadvertently by an impostor, the son of the horseman who ordinarily should succeed his father as the tender of the royal stable.

As the plot unfolds, it becomes clear that Yèyé weaves a tapestry of tragedy for her son on account of her Machiavellian acts. To guard the palace top secret, she poisons Ẹlẹ́ṣin Àdèlé who "fathered" her "Prince", because Àdèlé has not only revealed the secret to Balógun Abógunlóko, he is seeking a continuation of the affair with her and at a point, he wants to claim his son because he has only daughters from his marriage. She is not comfortable giving her son to a common horseman, who is rude to the King and another concubine of hers, Apáòkági. To permanently bury the secret, she kills Apáòkági and her husband, the King, because he wants to marry another wife, the 13th, and the bride is like a daughter to her. She then secures the support of the witches and Èṣù to enthrone her son. The witches physically eliminate thirty-seven qualified princes to pave the way for Arábámbí, who by blood, is not qualified. He is to rule for seven years, but for each year, five maidens are demanded as sacrificial objects.

While on the throne, unfortunately, Ọba Arábámbí rules tyrannically and recklessly, thinking that his life and reign have no expiry date. Surrounded by sycophants, he becomes rude to the witches; he defies every check. He boasts that he has conquered death and calls himself "Ikúdẹtì" or "Gbékúdè" (he who manacles death and renders it powerless). He is rude to other benefactors.

Because they have claimed so many lives all in a bid to be king and queen mother, Arábámbí ends up being a disaster in the saddle with his arrogance and recklessness. He also dies a miserable death, not like a king, but like a commoner that he truly is. He ends up like a bastard son, much hated by the people of Ìjèkùn-Odò for his recklessness and highhandedness. Yèyé too suffers as her late husband, in spirit, blames her for destroying the life of her son. Instead of allowing the will of God to prevail in the son's life, she turns herself into a mini-god, manipulating and scheming, moving and changing destiny. She is rejected and asked to leave the palace. She loses the throne, the glamour, the riches and the influence. She alone bears the fruits of her misfortune, just like the son.

Though he is seen to be ruled more by Èṣù in his thought and actions, *Arabambi is* denounced by Esu for his sordid deeds on account of his intoxication with power. The play ends with Arábámbí Ikúdẹtì left alone on stage waiting to finally and conclusively expire, to pave the way for a new era in Ìjèkùn-Odò.

From the King's fate, the playwright shows that if someone is destined to be great, living a life of virtue is necessary to accomplish the greatness and sustain it. Living recklessly in vice can cut short the joy of success as it effectively does for Ọba Arábámbí, an epitome of tyranny. "He was a bad King", declares Òjẹ̀. Arábámbí is an enduring metaphor for people who are trusted with transient power in transient offices, but who suddenly allow their unregulated or malformed ego to take full control of them. They turn themselves into vindictive monsters and dreadful demi-gods, generating tension and anxiety with each step they take. They consequently become alienated and isolated from the social realm into the arid enclave of the anti-social. As is often the case, they leave such offices prematurely and with ignominy on account of their aberrations and end up bearing the consequences of their cruelty. In this sense, Arábámbí has predecessors in *Adé-Ìrè, Mojàgbé* and *Àjàgùnmàlè*.

Yerima pursues a schema of didacticism in the plays. Through the presentation of characters, he preaches the values of tolerance, patience, humility, contentment, respect, altruism, unity and courage, among others. He denounces pride, arrogance, selfishness, greed, immoderacy and wickedness. This much is true of *Kútelú,* the third play in this collection, a character which also takes on the role of Èṣù in the manifestation of people's greed and excesses. It is about death and the King's hunchback. The part of Èṣù in the drama of life is foregrounded in *Kútelú,* when Apènà and the royal hunchback Kútelú in the presence of Apena at the shrine of Èṣù invokes the wrath of the god against the king by offering Èṣù its most abhorred element – àdí (palm kernel oil). The aim is to provoke Èṣù and direct the anger against the king so that he is punished. Apart from setting off the conflict in the play, it creates suspense and sustains it.

Olorì Ìwátáyọ̀ is asked to swear an oath of fidelity before the shrine of Ògún and Ṣàngó. She is allegedly caught in adulterous relationship with the king of a neigbouring town – Ọba Àdámórí Òkùgbàdà of Ìlosì Ilé. Kútelú reports the incident and the aggrieved Ọba Adéyímiká insists that the Olorì should swear an oath. If she is innocent, she lives on. If guilty and lying, she will die within seven days. Though there is opposition to the oath by Ìyálóde and other chiefs as it will hurt the royal family whichever way, she takes the oath and the conflict begins to unravel. The seed of the discord is watered with the invocation of Èṣù by the hunchback supervised by the Apènà, the priest of Ifá.

Coincidentally, the alleged lover, Ọba Òkùgbàdà dies, to fuel the suspicion of infidelity and affirm the veracity of Kútelú's claim. Ọba Adéyímiká also has a rough encounter with the District Officer, as he rebuffs his intervention in his domestic affairs. The tension is heightened by the Aláàfin who sends through Balógun, a coded message, àrokò, in white calabash to the King to abdicate the throne and commit suicide for withholding tributes from Aláàfin for three years, installing a new king without the consent of Aláàfin, and romancing with the colonialists represented by the District Officer and accepting his leadership over and above Aláàfin. He is also accused of embracing Christianity and giving the missionaries a piece of land on which to build their church. Rather than giving in easily and committing suicide as requested by Aláàfin, Ọba Adéyímiká decides to confront the paramount ruler. In the scheme, he enlists the support of another antagonist, the District Officer. He presents himself to the DO as a victim of Balógun's overbearing posture as he wants to punish him for his loyalty to the DO. He also alleges that Balógun is contesting the DO's power by instigating local chiefs to defy his authority.

Kútelú, because of his literacy, decides to intervene in the matter by approaching the DO. The DO suddenly reconciles with the King and his "sins" of arson and attempted polygamy are curiously forgiven. For his demonstrated loyalty, Ọba Adéyímiká installs Kútelú as "Bọ̀bajírọ̀rọ̀" (the King's close confidant). This act stirs jealousy and hatred among other chiefs as the king now trusts his counsel more than that of any other person. The priest describes him as a "glorified tale bearer" who has the master key to the thoughts of the king and controls his brain.

In a twist, Ọba Adéyímiká urges the chiefs not to enthrone Ọlágùnsóyè, widely believed to be his heir, as the king after him. He would rather want Adérójú, his nephew as his successor. His request complicates the plot further and unsettles the palace as Adérójú is from the lineage of a woman and cannot be king. This is another palace top secret similar to the one in *Ikúdẹtì* and it soon comes out. Ọba Adéyímiká is impotent. By a special arrangement which remained a sealed secret within the royal family, the hunchback impregnated Olorì Ìwátáyọ̀, and the product is Ọlágùnsóyè. Thus, Kútelú the hunchback is the father of Prince Ọlágùnsóyè, the heir apparent while Apena is the father of Kútelú and the grandfather of Ọlágùnsóyè. That is why Ọba Adéyímiká will not want him to become the king after him, moreso, as he is a product of a promiscuous mother who also had affairs with the District Officer, apart from Kútelú and Ọba Òkùgbàdà. He would not want her to be Queen mother.

Having sworn falsely on oath, Olorì Ìwátáyọ̀ tries to ward off the tragic consequences of her perjury. She decides to direct the curse on Ọba Adéyímiká so that the king will die instead. She secures the support of the witches to achieve this and to also secure the throne for her son, Ọlágùnsóyè, after the death of Ọba Adéyímiká. She will then become the Queen mother. Aggrieved by Kútelú, the hunchback, for reporting her "awful deed", she wants him ruined along with the King as they both bring her to public shame. The witches, working in concert with Èṣù, promise to assist her, but at a cost which they did not disclose. She agrees and immediately pays with her pregnancy.

The witches, led by Ìyá Mọ̀pó accost the King in his sleep and accuse him of treating them with contempt. From the encounter, the palace secret is further revealed: Ọba Adéyímiká sacrificed his manhood to become king. So for him to procreate, Olorì has to sleep with the hunchback, a trusted aide. They beget three sons and three daughters. Unfortunately, she becomes sexually insatiable and greedy for power as she allows other men to sleep with her. Kútelú feels betrayed by the Olorì and the King. The King betrays Kútelú and the Olorì. He seeks to take another wife despite his impotency. Olorì betrays both men in her lechery and greed for power. She lives like an unconscionable harlot, hoping to gain the DO to herself when the DO's wife dies. She also schemes to make her son king even when she knows that the royal blood does not in any way flow in his veins. The king has seen through her evil scheming and deceit. She is another Machiavellian schemer; a deceitful dissembler like Yèyé in *Ikúdẹtì*. Apènà describes her as "a fool... the promiscuous effigy of foolery".

In the end, she dies in Kútelú's arms as she embraces him. It coincides with the seventh day after taking the false oath of fidelity. Kútelú dies shortly, shot by some soldiers of the DO whilst engaging them in an argument. Because his life is tied to that of Kútelú, his *Abọ́bakú,* the King also dies within seven days of the oath. The harvest of death, however, clears the path for a new beginning. The royal drum symbolically signals a departure and, simultaneously, a new entrance reminiscent of Ṣóyinká's *Death and the King's Horseman.* Ọlágùnsóyè is installed as the new monarch of Ìjèkùn-Odò. Apènà is pleased that his grandson is made king while he blames Èṣù for the catastrophe that engulfs the town.

As the sun is setting on the misfortune of Ọba Adéyímiká, Kútelú and Olorì Ìwátáyọ̀, the sun rises in *Ọ̀ṣun,* the last play, with Ìjèkùn-Odò in a peaceful atmosphere of ritual cleansing associated with the annual celebration of Yèyé Odò Ọ̀ṣun. But the atmosphere turns suddenly sour. There has been a despicable violation of its overall ambience of purity, chastity, and tranquility symbolised by the maiden who carries the ritual calabash. The source of the violation, a well-guarded secret that must be unravelled, is what oils the wheel of conflict and propels its resolution in the end.

The current King of the town, Ọba Ògìdán Arógunmásàá, undergoes a ritual that will prolong his life and reign by three decades. The ritual is superintended by priest Ikúsanrí. Ògìdán has just reigned for three years and all seems set for his end; an unpalatable fate that he tries to ward off with the ritual. Unknown to him, he is under a curse placed on his father because whilst alive on the throne, the father violated a maiden and enslaved members of her family. The curse is that no descendant of his will reign more than two years on the throne. Ògìdán decides to enlist supernatural forces to ward off the curse sanctioned by the same supernatural forces. Expectedly, contrary to the assurance by the priest that the ritual has succeeded, all the affairs of the town become awry, including the festival of Òrìṣà Odò Ọ̀ṣun, an annual festival during which Ìjèkùn-Odò cleanses itself of evils of the old year and regenerates itself for the new-year ahead.

As a way out, the intervention of the deities are sought and secured. What follows, in a flashback, is the revelation of another firmly-guarded royal secret. Ọ̀tún's daughter, Ọ̀ṣúntáyọ̀ Bídèmí, a maiden, is raped to death. But contrary to official reports pointing at the people of a neighbouring town, the palace of Ọba Ògìdán is suspected. Because of his proven lechery and reckless use of power, he might have used the maiden as one of the "white doves" requested by Ikúsanrí for sacrifice to concretise the ritual of immortality and tenure-elongation. Ṣàmù, one of the Chiefs close to the King, is an accomplice. There is much anger in the pantheon, which reverberates across Ìjèkùn-Odò. First, a sacred tree is consumed by fire. Second, Ṣàmù drowns in the Ọ̀ṣun river. He is suspected to have been pushed towards his tragedy by invisible spiritual hands. Third, after the celebration, the sacred calabash that contains the cleansing ritual items is returned by the Goddess and is seen floating and drifting aimlessly on the river. The rejection of the sacrifice shows that the year ahead is full of danger. Through the use of multi-media, a device often associated with Brechtian epic theatre technique, Yerima reveals the source of the town's calamity. The votary maiden (Arugbá) of Ọ̀ṣun has been defiled. Consequently, she compromises the sanctity of that year's celebration with her impurity. That places a curse on her, the person responsible for her defilement and the town.

A peaceful social order returns after the revelation and peripeteia is secured for the eminent culprit. It takes the trio of Kórì, Iyemọja and Ọ̀ṣun to thwart the spiritual fortification that Ọba Ògìdán embarked upon at the beginning of the play. They also unmask him as "a crooked man with the crown... an epitome of evil" for exposing the Arugbá to defilement, instead of protecting her. Consequently, Ọ̀ṣun presents the monarch with the white calabash of death and he is reportedly executed in a shameful manner, by Ìlàrí, like a dog for Ògún's sacrifice. As clearly underscored in Yerima's schema of didacticism, "what will kill a king always lives within him". The play ends with a procession of Òṣun worshippers all dressed in white attire and dancing through the streets to celebrate the beginning of a new era, washed clean of infirmity, impurity and impunity of Ògìdán's reign.

Òṣun philosophically underscores the ephemerality of human existence and the need for constant regeneration. It also reinforces the concepts of leadership, power and social responsibilities. Ògìdán is another character presented in the image of an Aristotelian hero. He forfeits his high esteem in the society as a result of lechery and unconscionable exercise of power. He is implicated in the defilement of Arugbá, a kind of hamartia that sets him against the society and the supernatural realm. He tries to conceal the secret, using supernatural means, but he cannot hide from the Gods. He, therefore, crashes irredeemably from greatness to ignominy and death. The moral lesson is not lost on the audience. Leaders who are given to power abuse are likely to end up in ignominy like Ọba Ògìdán and Kúdẹtì, his predecessor, who suffers suspended animation for two years before he is finally strangled to death by Kingmakers to pave the way for a new era.

In this collection as in his other plays, the creative writer in Yerima is revealed in the presentation of the Deities and their actions in the human world. The rituals are largely invented, just like the settings and the characters. Consequently, a *caveat* is necessary. The rituals and the Deities encountered in his plays are primarily fictional. They are invented to score artistic and didactic goals. He creates rituals, manipulates Deities and tinkers with mytho-historical representations to serve his fancies as a playwright who needs to constantly communicate with his people in order to seek a better organised and well-governed society; a place where peace, security, happiness and fulfillment are guaranteed. There is, therefore, a limit to which one can see the plays as realistic representations and workings of Yorùbá cosmology as it concerns the affairs of the Deities, beyond the realm of artistic imagination.

In some plays, Yerima lifts Èṣù straight from the pages of the Bible and the Deity comes across vilified and disparaged. In another breath, he recognises his image in Yorùbá mythology and admits his ambivalence as a benevolent being that is committed to retributive justice. The Deity, according to myth, often weeps more than the bereaved. In pursuit of justice, he can impel men to their doom on account of their greediness, gullibility, recklessness and indiscretion. He is hot, he is gelid. He is both at the same time. That is why he can be enlisted in a cause by opposing parties while the party favoured on the side of justice will win. For instance, Ògìdán in extending his years on earth seeks the support of Èṣù. At the same time, Òtún who seeks revenge on the person that defiled and murdered his daughter also enlists the support of the same Deity.

Still on Yerima's musing on Èṣù, he contends that the Deity does not change destiny, but speeds up time for human actions. In the end, the playwright puts at the doorstep of humans, the consequences of their actions since they are the arbiters of their own destiny. Èṣù sits quietly and it is the human beings that approach him with their troubles. They are expected to be patient with him to act as he is sure to pursue the cause of justice and in doing so, sometimes grants requests far in excess of demand According to Ṣàùrá, his archetypal acolyte, Èṣù is "an Òrìṣà who knows how to pamper and yet bite". He is a Deity of binaries, kind and cruel, amiable and hostile. He radiates duality that governs human existence in the universe, and he cannot be ignored as he is in concert with other deities.

In summary, the four plays in the present collection contribute to the epistemology of tragedy as a dramatic mode in contemporary African literature. With this collection, Yerima has further enriched the discourse of tragedy with vital primary texts that are open to various hermeneutic anchors. He dramatises the vanity of inordinate quests for material things as they often destroy their blind seekers. Like Bunyan and Fágúnwà, Yerima serves in the same plate, the menu of wisdom and folly, contentment and greed, patience and haste. The choice is left to the individual, but Èṣù lurks around the corner as the choice is made and processed.

Certainly, the four plays will continue to excite critical interests, not only among teachers and critics, but also among practitioners of the theatre in Africa and beyond.

Professor Gbémisọlá Adéòtí
Department of English
Ọbáfẹmi Awólọ́wọ̀ University
Ilé Ifẹ̀, Nigeria.

PÈGÚNRUN, IKÚDẸTÌ, KÚTELÚ, ỌṢUN

FOUR PLAYS

PÈGÚNRUN

Dramatis Personae

ÌYÁ
PÈGÚNRUN
ABÍDÈMÍ
OLÚÁWO
KÉKERÉ AWO
ÒṢÍNNÚSÌ
JOWÚỌLÁ
ỌBA KÁRÓUNWÍ
ỌBA ỌMỌLE
PRINCE ADÉLÙ
ÒTÚN
ÌLÀRÍ ÀGBÀ
ÌLÀRÍ
IFÁKÍYÈSÍ
ÀDÙNNÍ
ÌBÍRÓNKẸ́
ÒWÒMIDÀ

PÈGÚNRUN

WHEN PLAY OPENS, THERE IS DARK STAGE, ONE LONE FIGURE THAT OF AN ELDERLY WOMAN BENDS BEFORE A SHRINE.

ÌYÁ: Cactus! Pègúnrun The unforgiven Viper of
   Ìjẹ̀kùn Odò, ọmọ òrukàn.
   Friend of Èṣù, the dreaded ones,
   Women of yore… who are as gentle as dew drops,
   But violent as a storm I greet both of you!
   Pègúnrun! Yèyé Obìrin.
   Ever starving Cobra, stand by us!
   It is the time of the year that we worship you.
   Yèyé Àjẹ́ ò, it is you I greet.
   Cactus! Soft within, but full of thorns.
   We can never ever forget your kindness,
   so turn to us with your ever endearing love.
   Soon, we shall dance for you. We have buried
   the last Ìyálóde as customs demand,
   her body lies in the sacred catacomb.
   It is time now to choose another… from your house.
   Adérónkẹ́ Abídèmí Àbẹbí is the one Ifá has chosen.
   She is young I know, but she is spirited like the
   woman who looms in the many tales
   about you. Once we receive your blessings,
   tonight, the Olúáwo as it is with our custom
   will prepare her for your throne.
   She will reign like you did, and like many
   after you… she will sit on the throne of mothers.
   The older women, who see your shadow in her,
   though now blurred with age, swear that
   she is the splitting image of your shapely dreaded
   self. Yèyé, Ògìdìgàdà! Pègúnrun! It is you I call!
   Yèyé, if I get the usual sign to affirm her

choice, then tomorrow, we shall take her to Kábíyèsí.
She will then lead us to your shrine on
the day of your festival.

(SHE TAKES KOLANUT. BREAKS IT AND THROWS THE PIECES ON THE FLOOR.)

> Ire o. Yèyé gives her nod. The land has a new mother.
> The women are blessed again. Ìbàdí ọmọ ẹkùn smiles at us again! (SHE SINGS SONG AND DANCES.)
> There are preparations to be made. Ìkàré Olówu, ọmọ Àdíríbótó.
> Kábíyèsí will hear our drums in the morning.
> Sleep Pègúnrun… prick no one, bite no one,
> lay calm in the four corners of the village boundaries, until we return to dance for you at the village square.

OLÚÁWO: HURRIES IN. Have you done it?

ÌYÁ: Yes.

OLÚÁWO: What did she say?

ÌYÁ: She is happy with our choice. She wants us to go to Kábíyèsí tomorrow and pick a date for the festival. Abídèmí is a lucky girl. All the gods of the land agree with her choice as the new Ìyálóde.

OLÚÁWO: WORRIED, GRUNTS. Except one.

ÌYÁ: Which one?

OLÚÁWO: Èṣù. Relationships are best maintained when truth is the basis of such a covenant, he said. Still foaming with anger, he promised to disrupt everything.

ÌYÁ: Èṣù kẹ̀? Méwàá rẹ̀ ò tó bẹ́ẹ̀!

OLÚÁWO: Èṣù mà ni ì! Apart from Olódùmarè it is him. It is Láàlú ògiri òkò I speak about. He can do millions.

ÌYÁ: Then appease him.

OLÚÁWO: How? He says the first sign of his anger will be found in the flames of wrath that will burn in Kábíyèsí's palace.

ÌYÁ: Flames of wrath kẹ? What have we done to warrant the burning of the palace? Please Olúáwo, give him what he wants. That is your task Olúáwo. Ours is to dance with nimble feet round the village in our one day of glory, when even the Kábíyèsí dresses like a woman, and we dance, singing swaying to the victory of mother over the tribulations against the village. Ó yá, hurry, go and try.

OLÚÁWO: I have tried.

ÌYÁ: Try harder. If the door is jammed, then force your way in through the windows or roof. Just make enough noise to get Èṣù to turn his face to you listen to our plea. The festival must go on.

OLÚÁWO: Woman have you not been listening to my rattles? Our useless banter wastes the value of the night. He refused bluntly, his back turned, I could read nothing else from his dead panned face, his half shaven head, and distant red eyes.

ÌYÁ: But why?

OLÚÁWO: I think Yèyé offended him. A covenant before she gave up her life for the village. Yèyé never kept her word, so his wound had time to forster. That is why I hurried here. Èṣù advised I did... so that we can stop everything.

ÌYÁ: IN A WHISPER. Stop everything?

OLÚÁWO: Yes.

ÌYÁ: A covenant? What covenant? We are human beings... weaklings all. What have we got to do with the anger of the gods? Èṣù should go to the land of the dead or little gods to sort it out with Yèyé. Anyway, it is too late now. Yèyé's spirit left us tonight.

OLÚÁWO: No. Summon her back. She had promised to come, each time we call. Three pulls at the chain, and she will arise. Call her; there may be fire on the mountain. I say call her Ìyá... we risk the desertion of her shrine. Tell her to come, just for a moment. Only her can find the soothing word for a livid Láàlú.

ÌYÁ: Why trouble her? She has given us the spiritual nod we asked for. Now her festival will go on tomorrow, flames or no flames.

OLÚÁWO: This is why I sent Kékeré Awo to Abídèmí to hurry to Èṣù throne at the Crossroads on the way to the market, during cold nights like tonight with the sacrificial needs of Èṣù. Èṣù looms Ìyá. His anger boils. I smelt the foam from his mouth.

ÌYÁ: Why? This year is the hundredth year after Yèyé's death. Why did Èṣù wait this long to foam in the mouth with anger? Why?

OLÚÁWO: Then you do not know Láàlú. This is why he is called Oníle-oríta, owner of the outside, and the inside. Seer of the crevices of man's inner machinations. The god of duality. Full of patience, because to properly understand man and his wild attitudes, the god of persuasion must be full of patience.

ÌYÁ: But he waited for too long.

OLÚÀWO: Too long is never long enough for Láàlú. Tonight, he emits bitterness. Even his eye pulsates with raw anger. I pray he accepts the sacrifices taken to him.

ABÍDÈMÍ: (RUNS IN WITH KÉKERÉ AWO). He did not Baba. As I climbed the steep steps to his shrine, I slipped, and down I fell.

ÌYÁ: Págà!

OLÚÀWO: Ṣàngbá fọ́! Now disaster will follow.

ABÍDÈMÍ: As the basket fell, the content still inside, Kékeré Awo caught it.

OLÚÀWO: Good.

ABÍDÈMÍ: But when I stood up, my left hand had started to bleed. The tips of the black stone did a little more than scratch the surface of my skin.

KÉKERÉ AWO: A small deep cut started to bleed.

ABÍDÈMÍ: A few drops of blood fell on *Èṣù's* black stone.

ÌYÁ: Èèwọ̀!

ABÍDÈMÍ: That was when we started to fear.

OLÚÀWO: Blood on Èṣù's black stone!

KÉKERÉ AWO: Bàbá quickly with the palm oil bottle we took, I rinsed it.

OLÚÁWO: Rinsed what?

KÉKERÉ AWO: Rinse the stone off the blood of the new Ìyálóde. I poured the oil, until the blood washed away. We then performed the ritual.

ÌYÁ: To whom? For whom?

OLÚÁWO: The blood. Èṣù abhors blood. You gave him a forbidden drink. Àdí is his oil that sooths him. What you did is forbidden in itself. You damned clumsy fool. WONDERS. Who do I go to now?

ÌYÁ: See who is talking. Olúáwo, you should tell us what to do. Do we go ahead and see Kábíyèsí tomorrow? Or do we simply say Yèyé has not spoken.

OLÚÁWO: Àgbẹdọ̀! A life started with a lie flows into disaster.

ÌYÁ: Maybe we should withdraw her as the new Ìyálóde; Èṣù will leave us alone in peace. Which Èṣù is after us?

KÉKERÉ AWO: Èbìtà.

ÌYÁ: Now even my feet tremble.

KÉKERÉ AWO: The one with hallowed red eyes. A club in hand, a pointed horn on his forehead. Happy when others are sad, sad when others are happy.

ÌYÁ: Quiet boy. We dread him, and here you are chattering songs of praise for the figure of our impending doom.

KÉKERÉ AWO: Ìyá as we left, I felt a warm wind follow us. A foul smell of death followed also. What does that mean father?

ABÍDÈMÍ: Bàbá, what do we do?

OLÚÁWO: Confusion reigns now. Èṣù has already started working. I hear a gentle rumble of an impending earthquake. Darkness everywhere. What do I do now? What do we do?

ÌYÁ: You go home Olúáwo. Abídèmí, go prepare yourself to meet the king in the morning. I shall wait here. If Yèyé tells me otherwise, I shall let you know. But if you see in the Courtyard of Ìyálóde's palace, then know that all is and will be well.

OLÚÁWO: I shall continue to try and calm Láàlú's restless nature. Even I begin to feel the foul warmth, here in our midst. If only we could predict him. Like an ill winded whirlwind, he looms, and we must cower in fear. HE TURNS TO LEAVE.

ABÍDÈMÍ: Why me? When did I ever offend this fearsome god. I don't even know the first Ìyálóde, even though I often feel I share a bond with her. But why me I ask? Why must her load fit my head so perfectly that I tremble in fear? And now Èṣù's unpredictable spirit push me... until I feel I will fall again... bleeding for a sin I did not even commit.

KÉKERÉ AWO: We really can't predict him. He seems set to choke us all. Hmm... again I feel a restless heat as if we are falling into snake pit. Its neck bent to bite us or swallow us whole.

ÌYÁ: Olúáwo take your clumsy fool away from here. Even the stench of his foul mouth begins to loom too.

OLÚÁWO: Ó yá Kékeré Awo, home. There is so much to do at the shrine tonight. Abídèmí... come to the shrine before you return home. There is an additional chant you will say before you set out tomorrow. He, who will stand like a rock, must first harden his heart like a rock. Tomorrow then Ìyá. EXIT OLÚÁWO.

ÌYÁ: May the day break.

KÉKERÉ AWO: Ìyá… sleep well. This will be an interesting game to play. We are after the devil, and the devil is after us. What a scary tale this is turning out to be.

ÌYÁ: A game did you say? Clasp your useless jaws together fool and shut your foul mouth! ANGRY. TURNS TO KÉKERÉ AWO SHARPLY. Go, stupid demented child, follow your master. You heard him. There are leaves to grind in your failed shrine tonight. I say disappear! Paré! KÉKERÉ AWO HURRIES AFTER OLÚÁWO. LEFT BEHIND, ABÍDÈMÍ KNEELS BEFORE ÌYÁ. I say go home. When up and down fail us, we find a safe place in the middle to hide our souls. Go home girl… I still hear the echoes of the kind gentle chuckle of Yèyé's voice. The fight of the gods does not concern mere mortals. First, we shall concentrate on your enthronement. The dance at the palace will be vigorous… go home and rest your young limbs. The task of the Ìyálóde ages the mind quickly. Go home girl.

ABÍDÈMÍ: Will that still take place. Will I still be?

ÌYÁ: Yes.

ABÍDÈMÍ: Then why am I afraid? PAUSE. IN A WHISPER. I am afraid Ìyá. I may become the pun… the plaything… the innocent reason for the impending gory godly cluster that will raise the hot dust. On one side there is so much expectant happiness, and on the other side, is this cold undiluted fear. Please help me mother.

ÌYÁ: Fear from you? Èèwọ̀! Nothing will happen to you, I swear! Our Yèyé is a hard nut to crack too. Èṣù will meet a different kind of woman when the cluster of dust heats up. I say go home. Hm. LOOKS UP. The morning light is set to rise, and tomorrow is about to come. But first, I must fly before the motherly birds flutter. Go home and await my return!

SLOWLY, LIGHTS FADE.

ÈṢÙ'S SHRINE. BÀBÁ ỌṢÌNNÚSÌ, ÌYÁ JOWÚỌLÁ AND ỌWỌ̀MIDÀ HURRY ONTO THE STAGE.

ỌṢÌNNÚSÌ: Hurry women, I fear they will soon beat the drums announcing that the choice of the new Ìyálóde has been confirmed by Ìyá Pègúnrun.

JOWÚỌLÁ: How? We did everything we were asked to do. This is Èṣù's shrine and there is nobody here. We can still stop them.

ỌṢÌNNÚSÌ: Stop whom? The sacrifice is always done at the same time. Ìyá goes to the shrine with the name of the candidate, and the candidate comes here to appeal to *Èṣù*, to hold the peace on the day of the announcement of her name as the new Ìyálóde of Ìjẹ̀kùn Odò.

ỌWỌ̀MIDÀ: WALKS TOWARDS THE SHRINE. Ṣọ̀npọ̀ná ò!

ỌṢÌNNÚSÌ: What now?

ỌWỌ̀MIDÀ: Someone has been here.

ỌSÌNNÚSÌ: Who? MOVES CLOSER TO THE SHRINE. It is true. And to crown it all up. Èṣù has been insulted. I see blood where the sacred oil of Èṣù should be. We must leave here. Now!

ỌSÌNNÚSÌ AND ỌWỌMIDÀ MOVE ABOUT TO LEAVE.

JOWÚỌLÁ: Stay where you are men. What has this world become? A hazy land of quenched dreams? I know what I heard from the lips of my dying sister... the former Ìyálóde. Take... she said to me as she handed over her Òṣùgbó. Wear it well on your shoulder. Let no stranger take it from you...she said. You were there Olórí Ẹbí. Bàbá Ọ̀sìnnúsì, you were there. And you my junior brother Ọ̀wọ̀midà was there. It is my legacy to inherit... why should I loss it all to a common child Abídèmí. Yes, the same blood runs in our veins... but when a dying spirit names a child, that word must be respected. I cannot walk away from my legacy because we see blood before the shrine of Èṣù. Common blood!

Ọ̀WỌ̀MIDÀ: But sister.

JOWÚỌLÁ: Not a word! Not even a breath of it. Not a whisper. If your manhood fails you, then hurry home. Go! I say hurry.

Ọ̀WỌ̀MIDÀ: I am afraid, we may be starting all wrong. Yes, we were there when the late Ìyálóde, our sister gave you the Òṣùgbó. She was old. I am not sure she remembered the tradition at the time. She was not even aware of who she was speaking to. She was too sick to comprehend sense. The family... our family... must stick together. Olórí Ẹbí, you know this, so why do you want it to happen? If we fall apart now and bring forth two candidates for the position of Ìyálóde, then the family is set to fall apart. And if a family falls apart, it will take a century to bring us back again. I fear the action of the dreaded Pègúnrun.

JOWÚỌLÁ: If I was not there the day you were born, and I saw you suckle my mother's breasts, I would have called you a bastard. Nothing... I repeat... nothing will stop me from leading the women of Ìjẹ̀kùn Odò. Not even the gods. I swear, brother.

ỌWỌMIDÀ: Dear sister...

JOWÚỌLÁ: Not one more word from you. Not one, until Èṣù is told our mission.

ỌWỌMIDÀ: I do understand that those with independent minds do things that amaze even the gods. But caution Sister... the jaws of death is always open for the blinded one. Caution.

JOWÚỌLÁ: Do you hear him, Bàbá Ọ̀sìnnúsì.

Ọ̀SÌNNÚSÌ: Yes... yes... hurry. Let us hurry with the offering to Èṣù. He is part of everything man sets out to do. So, it is right to please him, so that when he changes sides, his smile will still be turned to our side.

ỌWỌMIDÀ: What if the people hear that we did all these under the whim of my sister? That we allowed ourselves to be driven by her ambition against the very roots of our family. Pègúnrun selects the Ìyálóde, not you or Olórí Ẹbí.

Ọ̀SÌNNÚSÌ: So what do we do now?

ỌWỌMIDÀ: Go home. Wash our feet and hands and forget we ever came out tonight.

ÒṢÌNNÚSÌ: No! Our daughter has spent too much money already. We have taken expensive aṣọ òkè to the houses of the chiefs of the village. The women have collected food stuff and clothes from us. What does our daughter need to do? Build the Ọba a new palace?

JOWÚỌLÁ: Tell him Olórí Ẹbí.

ÒṢÌNNÚSÌ: Go home, wash our feet and embrace defeat. That is what you want. But what does our daughter want?

JOWÚỌLÁ: Sit on the throne of Pègúnrun, and reign as the queen of the women.

ỌWỌMIDÀ: I know that that is difficult to achieve. What has been decided as task for the gods cannot be handled by mere human beings. Sister let us go home.

JOWÚỌLÁ: I say no! Bàbá let us go ahead.

ÒṢÌNNÚSÌ: GOES TO THE SHRINE. Come closer both of you. THEY MOVE CLOSER. Èṣù Láàlú ògiri òkò. We three present are members of the Pègúnrun family. I am the Olórí Ẹbí of the family. We know that it is from our house that Ìyálóde of Ìjẹ̀kùn Odò must come, but we are tired that it is Pègúnrun our late mother who still choses the Ìyálóde. Many years have passed, and we want to change that tradition. We want... TO JOWÚỌLÁ. Call your name.

JOWÚỌLÁ: Jowúọlá...

ÒṢÌNNÚSÌ: No... no.... your full name. Èṣù needs to know.

JOWÚỌLÁ: Ọmọ ló jẹ́ kí wọn ó Jowúọlá mi. Daughter of Mórebá and Ọgúnbọ́dẹdé.

ỌṢÌNNÚSÌ: Yes, become the new Ìyálóde. When her name is mentioned to Ìyá Pègúnrun and Kábíyèsí let it be like honey to their ears. Let her be the choice. Let her be the one who adorns herself with the sacred treasured beads of the Ìyálóde.

JOWÚỌLÁ: Àṣẹ!

ỌṢÌNNÚSÌ: Ó yá... Ọwọ̀midà... say a word with Èṣù. Short and straight to our humble demand. Who you are first, Èṣù needs to know.

ỌWỌ̀MIDÀ: I am Ayé Ọwọ̀midà, the only son of Mórebá and Ogúnbọ́dẹdé, out of ten children. My sister wants to be Ìyálóde. It is her desire. I stand with her, but we do not want to offend our great great great grand mother, Pègúnrun. Let her choice prevail. But if there is room for a godly manipulation, so be it, enthrone my sister.

JOWÚỌLÁ: ANGRY. CUTS IN. Enthrone me Láàlú. Enthrone mi. Let me be the only choice, enthrone me when the names are mentioned. The only one. And anyone who stand in my way, remove the person Láàlú.

ỌṢÌNNÚSÌ: That will do.

JOWÚỌLÁ: Not yet. Out of the three of us, standing before you Láàlú, if any of us should break this bond of togetherness, let the person feel your cold hands of punishment.

ỌWỌ̀MIDÀ: Sister mi.

JOWÚỌLÁ: Let me finish.

ỌṢÌNNÚSÌ: You have finished. Láàlú has heard you. Not an evil word more. He heard everything. Let us hope he did not also take a pip into our hearts. Women! You always top up what we did not send you, and thus allow Láàlú to stretch your desires. Let us go. SOUND OF DRUMS.

JOWÚỌLÁ: I hear drums. Listen Bàbá. What do they say?

ỌṢÌNNÚSÌ: Pègúnrun has agreed to one of our women. LISTENS. They mention no name. They only say that one has been found and we should prepare to visit Kábíyèsí in the morning.

ỌWỌMIDÀ: Sister what if it is not you that has been chosen by our great mother?

JOWÚỌLÁ: Then we shall see how who is chosen lives to dance to the palace. All the gods are with me on this matter. Like your name, my respects and honour will be restored. I am the eldest woman in the family... my sister Títílọlá died in my hands handing over the Ọṣùgbó to me. I shall not return it. REMOVES THE ỌṢÙGBÓ FROM HER SHOULDER, AND TIES ON HER WAIST. I shall dance to the shrine this way in the morning. No one will reduce me. No one!

ỌṢÌNNÚSÌ: And no one will take your honour. Ògún will see to it. Èṣù Ọ̀dàrà will not let it happen. Let us go home.

ỌWỌMIDÀ: Then let us hurry home. Ìyá will tell us when we get home. My ears stretch already just to hear a word from Ìyá.

JOWÚỌLÁ: Why hurry the sunshine... when it must come... look at her... I stand announced as the new Ìyálóde. Pègúnrun must accept. Bàbá, the things I sent to Olúáwo, did you remember to send them?

ỌṢÌNNÚSÌ: I did. But he returned them back.

JOWÚỌLÁ: Why? He is the second voice of Pègúrun.

ỌSÌNNÚSÌ: He said he has heard. And he would send for them when all is well. He is my in law... he cannot fail me.

JOWÚỌLÁ: LETS OUT A WILD LAUGH. I feared this would happen, so I sent gifts to Kékeré Olúáwo. He promised to delay even the work of the gods if they don't go my way.

THE DRUMS BECOME LOUDER. JOWÚỌLÁ BEGINS TO DANCE.

ỌWỌMIDÀ: Sister you dance well. They must be at the door of Olórí Ẹbí to tell the good news.

ỌSÌNNÚSÌ: Yes. They must come to me. I am to lead the family to the palace. I just pray it is you Jowúọlá! Hurry!

AS THEY ALL LEAVE, SLOW LIGHTS FADE.

ABÍDÈMÍ'S ROOM. SHE IS ALL DRESSED UP FOR THE PRESENTATION AT THE PALACE. THE WOMEN FRET AROUND HER. SHE SITS CALMLY.

ÀDÙNNÍ: Where is Ìyá?

ABÍDÈMÍ: Gone up the hill to the shrine. To see if she forgot it there.

ÀDÙNNÍ: How can she forget it there when it was never taken there. Without it, you can never be Ìyálóde.

ÀDÙNNÍ: One hundred years, and now it is gone like the puff of smoke. This is a bad omen.

ABÍDÈMÍ: I know.

ÀDÙNNÍ: The women are almost all gathered. Where is Ìbírónkẹ́?

ABÍDÈMÍ: Gone to check the room of the new Ìyálóde. It has not been cleaned up since the death of the old Ìyálóde. If I am to sleep in it, it has to be clean. Ìbírónkẹ́ is at her chattering best, she was ranting so much, so I wanted her out of here.

ÀDÙNNÍ: The Òṣùgbó...

ABÍDÈMÍ: Another headache. It was wrapped round the late Ìyálóde. She won't let it go even after her death, says the women who were at her death bed. Ìyá Jowúọlá, her sister swears, that she never saw it.

ÀDÙNNÍ: I t was supposed to have been given to Bàbá Òṣìnnúsì, the Olórí Ẹbí, but he too swears he never saw it. That cloth is so old, it carries the story of the shoulders of all the Ìyálóde's that have been since the time of Pègúnrun. Why would someone take it?

ABÍDÈMÍ: I know it will be found. I can feel it. But we cannot go to the palace without it. I am worried. ENTERS ÌBÍRÓNKẸ́. What is going on Ìbírónkẹ́. Did you see it?

ÌBÍRÓNKẸ́: No, but a miracle of sadness and joy occurred here today.

ÀDÙNNÍ: Tell us what happened.

ÌBÍRÓNKẸ́: When I got there the elderly women who are to prepare the room had not arrived. I collected the key from Ìyá Jowúọlá and l went into the room. Then it happened.

ÀDÙNNÍ: What happened?

ÌBÍRÓNKẸ́: We opened the room, and found it made. The once sacred and rickety bed had been mended…new red soft sheets were spread on the bed. It looked set to receive even the aged bones of a sage. Then rich clothes everywhere… Sányán, Ẹtụ, Aṣọ òkè, shoes, and old rich cosmetics and ointments as our grandmothers use to have them, all laid out in the room. The smell of death had been washed off, just new smell of life. I screamed and people came. No one not even Jowúọlá, the eldest woman in the family knew what was going on. No one knew who made up the old room of Pègúnrun. No one! We all agreed that a group of spirits came to do this. A pure miracle. Abídèmí, the gods love you.

ABÍDÈMÍ: Then, where is my Òṣùgbó? Where is the veil that will cover my face from the world, until the Kábíyèsí unveils me. Where is it? I pray the spirits continue their miracle?

ÌYÁ RUNS IN. Ìyá!

ÌYÁ: The gods be praised. It was there, I found it there… a new Òṣùgbó. Pègúnrun has a hand in this. I ran first to Títílọlá's old room. The Olórí Ẹbí must have spent a fortune. It is transformed.

ÀDÙNNÍ: Ìbírónkẹ́ told us Ìyá. Now what next?

ÌYÁ: The women are gathered. We must leave. SHE COVERS THE HEAD OF ABÍDÈMÍ WITH THE ÒṢÙGBÓ. Yes, see how beautiful our new Pègúnrun looks. Ready to carry the problems, the goodness and coming prosperity on her shoulders.
Ìyá mi ti de o! Pègúnrun dé o!
Ẹ yàgò lọ́na.
Lọ kánkán!

ÌYÁLÓDE'S WOMEN GATHER, ALL GAILY DRESSED AND BEGIN TO SING IN HER HONOUR. BÀBÁ ÒṢÌNNÚSÌ JOINS. ÌYÁ JOWÚỌLÁ ALSO. DANCES AND DRUMINGS TAKE PLACE.

ÌYÁ: RAISES A SONG:
   À ń gbé Yèyé relé Ọba
   Yèyé!
   Rọra máa tẹlẹ múyẹ múyẹ
   Yèyé!
   Ìyálóde ń relé Ọba
   Yèyé!
   Abídèmí ń relé Ọba
   Yèyé!
   Rọra máa tẹlẹ múyẹ múyẹ
   Yèyé!

THE WOMEN BEGIN TO DANCE AND SING

SLOWLY, LIGHTS FADE.

OUTSIDE ỌBA KÁRÓUNWÍ'S PALACE. HE STANDS WITH HIS CHIEFS AS HE WATCHES THE WOMEN LED BY ÌYÁ DANCE IN WITH ABÍDÈMÍ DRESSED AND COVERED FOR HER PRESENTATION TO THE KING.

ÌYÁ: RAISES A SONG: À ń gbé Yèyé relé Ọba
  Yèyé!
  Rọra máa tẹlẹ̀ múyẹ́ múyẹ́
  Yèyé!
  Ìyálóde ń relé Ọba
  Yèyé!
  Abídèmí ń relé Ọba
  Yèyé!
  Rọra máa tẹlẹ̀ múyẹ́ múyẹ́
  Yèyé!

THE WOMEN CONTINUE TO DANCE AND SING.

KÚRUNMÍ WATCHES THEM IN AMUSEMENT FOR A WHILE BEFORE ORDERING THEM TO STOP. THE ÌLÀRÍ STOP THE WOMEN AND MOVE THEM TO A SIDE OF THE STAGE.

KÁRÓUNWÍ: Henceforth, this is how it will be. The pleasures of the new life, not noise. The new chasing out of my palace the old forgotten traditions of useless deaths and forced glorification of womanhood. On that note since the King has come to grace your welcome to my palace by meeting you at the gate of the palace, what do you want? And who is the covered wimp of a masquerade with a veil who stand before me?

ÌYÁ: Our new mother. The one chosen by Pègúnrun herself. The new Ìyálóde to be. We have brought her for your blessings.

KÁRÓUNWÍ: I will not bless a new Ìyálóde based on traditions and an old stale story. Who leads you here?

ỌSÌNNÚSÌ: STEPS FORWARD. I, Kábíyèsí. I am the Olórí Ẹbí of the Pègúnrun family.

KÁRÓUNWÍ: LETS OUT A WILD LAUGH. This world must really be going upside down... a man leads a family of women for a royal blessing to enthrone a woman. Does this make sense to you?

ỌSÌNNÚSÌ: It has been the practice we inherited, Kábíyèsí. My father's mother was the...

KÁRÓUNWÍ: Please save us another story. We have heard enough. LOOKS ROUND. Before us, we see people trapped in a cocoon of fermented lies, not one single Ìyálóde, not one.

ÌYÁ: COMES FORWARD, PULLING A COVERED ABÍDÈMÍ ALONG. Here Kábíyèsí... there is one Ìyálóde, and she stands before me, waiting to be uncovered.

KÁRÓUNWÍ: Then uncover her yourself.

ỌSÌNNÚSÌ: The family covered her Kábíyèsí.

KÁRÓUNWÍ: I say uncover her yourself. Well that is not what we heard. Last night, two people came to see me. They claimed that this covered woman cannot find the sacred veil. They said that she was not the one chosen by the immediate late Ìyálóde. Where are the people? I cannot see them. Their voices sounded so firm and rich last night, but by this morning they have disappeared.

ÌYÁ: There is only one Ìyálóde chosen by the family... and she stands here. Supported by Yèyé Pègúnrun and followed here by the whole family.

KÁRÓUNWÍ: I will close my eyes... when they are open, each one of you must have returned home. I say go! Leave here.

ÌYÁ: Why? You dig a moat around yourself Kábíyèsí. The earth will cave in.

KÁRÓUNWÍ: Yes. It will and it will swallow you and your lot up. I say leave the palace grounds.

ÌYÁ: Why? I say why appear so resolute in stripping us naked in front of the whole world? What have we done Kábíyèsí?

KÁRÓUNWÍ: Not you, but the times have changed. No one picks an Ìyálóde now based on stories peddled by women gossips to keep their prominence intact? These days, the ladder of merit has grown. The woman like a man must climb higher than a pretty face and waist.

ÌYÁ: Climb the ladder? Which ladder? From where? To where?

KÁRÓUNWÍ: You dare ask me old woman? Mark my words, the effect of water will not change even if the name of water is changed. Omi lomi yóò máa jẹ́!

ÌYÁ: Yes. Bàbá Ọṣinnúsì come closer... you stand aloof, and this makes me very worried. Where is Jowúọlá... we are about to be stripped of our honour and covered in shame. Kábíyèsí... this is the eldest woman in the family. I only keep the shrine of Pègúnrun.

KÁRÓUNWÍ: Fool.

ÌYÁ: Fool? Me?

KÁRÓUNWÍ: One's load is always carried on the shoulder… why do you push your neck forward for the hangman's axe at the shrine of Ògún? Why? A common visitor decides to speak for the family who do not even know her. One more word from you, and I shall cut your tongue. LOOKS AROUND. Where are they? The owners of the family of dreamers? I say who leads these pack of women?

JOWÚQLÁ: STEPS FORWARD. I am here.

ỌSÌNNÚSÌ: Me too Kábíyèsí.

KÁRÓUNWÍ: Good. The old Owls are gathered. Last night when the people came to see me, I said that I will clear the air of doubt by asking each of you to bless the purported covered choice of the family. So, go one by one, and show me that your blood line is pure and together. Bless her.

ỌSÌNNÚSÌ: ỌSÌNNÚSÌ GLANCES AT JOWÚQLÁ WITH FEAR. We have already done it at home Kábíyèsí.

JOWÚQLÁ: Yes…yes. We have Kábíyèsí.

KÁRÓUNWÍ: I say do it again. There is no overdose of prayers, is there? LETS OUT A LAUGH. This is the first time that I will see people afraid to bless a child about to go to war. See how you tremble with fear. I say your family is not one. Greed and ambition have set in. You soil the tradition. That is why I want to moderate it. Change it a little. This is not an advice, but an order. Henceforth…

ÌYÁ: RUNS BEFORE HIM. Kábíyèsí please!

KÁRÓUNWÍ: LOOKS AT HER. The Àtókàn, afraid of losing her job runs to beg. Leave my presence old woman… you begin to irritate me. Even if death were to appear before me now, I will not change my mind.

ÌYÁ: Why?

KÁRÓUNWÍ: The old woman speaks again. PAUSE. Now let me tell you. Pègúnrun, if she really existed once, gave her life to stop the war coming to our land. She stopped the Whiteman coming to make us and our children slaves. But now times have changed, we need the Whiteman's ways to grow, to develop. The song of yesterday has turned to the rubbish of today. Do you hear me now women?

ÌYÁ: RAISES A SONG. À ń gbé Yèyé relé Ọba
Yèyé!
Rọra máa tẹlẹ̀ múyẹ̀ múyẹ̀
Yèyé!
Ìyálóde ń relé Ọba
Yèyé!
Abídèmí ń relé Ọba
Yèyé!
Rọra máa tẹlẹ̀ múyẹ̀ múyẹ̀
Yèyé!

THE WOMEN BEGIN TO DANCE AND SING AGAIN.

KÁRÓUNWÍ: I say shut them up. THE ÌLÀRÍ'S MOVE TOWARDS THE WOMEN. THEY KEEP QUIET. Good. The gifts I got yesterday were not sent by peasant farmers. The man gave me money. The wanted to buy vote to pick another. Your family has become divided and rotted. Yet the world moves forward, and we must move with it. That is all I am saying. Ìyá tell Pègúnrun that. This year we shall not dance for her. This year men will be men, and women will remain women. This year, her made up past glory will be laid to rest forever. We even need the space her shrine lies to build a new befitting Ọjà Ọba. TO THE CHIEFS. Do I speak your mind? THE CHIEFS NOD THEIR HEADS. You see my own family is together.

ỌṢÌNNÚSÌ: We are one Kábíyèsí. The family is together.

KÁRÓUNWÍ: Then each of you should take a pinch of sand, place it on her palm and pray for her. ỌṢÌNNÚSÌ AND JOWÚỌLÁ STAND, UNABLE TO MOVE. Your feet got stuck? Pity.

ÌYÁ: ON HER KNEES. Kábíyèsí do not perform the task of the gods. Let it be them who perform the act of judgment. You push Pègúnrun.

KÁRÓUNWÍ: Oh woman! Can't you hear my voice... Pègúnrun is dead and buried. Even Kings die once.

ÌYÁ: I know what you said. But please let them be. We have brought before you the choice of the goddess.

KÁRÓUNWÍ: You push me old woman.

ÌYÁ: I know. But you trample on our every inch of pride. We begin to gather a stench of profound repulsion. We, the once prized family of importance, are not worth a cowry shell any more. Please Kábíyèsí be kinder.

KÁRÓUNWÍ: That power bestowed on you by a story gives you lot a false sense of importance. That is why you have chosen to confront the King. That you now drag your tails behind you and come to make noise in my palace with demands.

ÌYÁ: May we know what is so important that you have decided to look down on the death of our great mother Pègúnrun? Why do you belittle her so? Why does she mean so little to you now when each blood she shed on that day saved the village which you now rule? Kábíyèsí Káróunwí, speak well about her, and do not utter this awful rubbish about a great daughter of Ìjẹ̀kùn Odò. Why do you look so confused now? I am sure you understand what I mean to say Kábíyèsí. Don't rub yourself with the mud of shame, remember, the slip of a King is difficult to rise from. How do you want us to remember your reign?

KÁRÓUNWÍ: A king who foresaw the future. One who removed the blindfolds from the eyes of his people and made them see better. Mother the world has moved.

ÌYÁ: To where... I still see Ìjẹ̀kùn Odò the way it was the very day I was born into it... through my mother's bowels.

KÁRÓUNWÍ: My very problem. Women no longer sit and wait like the women in your family. These days, they strive and they too sweat. Have you not heard of the great woman of Ìbàdàn, Ẹfúnṣetán Aníwúrà. Her wealth is untold, her slaves numberless, and her power, equal to that of the Olúbàdàn. That is the new woman. The kind of woman, I want you all to be. I don't want an Ìyálóde who will beautify my palace and say nothing but agree with the male chiefs. No! I want one that will contribute to what we say and do, and also lead discussions.

ÌYÁ: If that is why we have failed you, then we have really failed. Women let us go home.

KÁRÓUNWÍ: I am happy that you realize that the lowest of you cannot step here anymore. Yes. Go home!

ÌYÁ: See how he gloats. We are finished. The lasting reputation of our Yèyé is destroyed today.

KÁRÓUNWÍ: Yes. And henceforth, the Pègúnrun festival where men become women is stopped. No more. Ever!

ÌYÁ: Ever? When we dance to greet you Kábíyèsí, we say you are second to the gods, not a god. Our mother Pègúnrun was a heroine… and now a goddess. Why do you now ignore her honourable death and sacrifice? Why?

KÁRÓUNWÍ: A heroine? Just because she died? She was going to die one day anyway. She was just a woman, and nothing more. And my great great great grand father Ọba Ọmọ́lẹ was a fool by agreeing too quickly to her every wish. I overturn all his agreements, today. Ọba mẹ́wàá, Ìgbà mẹ́wàá! This is my time, and I overturn them all. This is a new period. A new beginning. Fathers of the land, have I said your minds?

ỌTÚN: Every word Kábíyèsí!

KÁRÓUNWÍ: Did you hear them women?

ÌYÁ: Then we too still have the weapon that will reject the King on behalf of the land. KÁRÓUNWÍ AND HIS CHIEFS LET OUT A BIG LAUGH. SHE STEPS FORWARD AND UNFOLDS HER WRAPPER.

KÁRÓUNWÍ: What craziness is this?

ÌYÁ: Women!

THE OTHER WOMEN FOLLOW. THE CHIEFS GRAB KÁBÍYÈSÍ AND TAKE HIM INTO THE PALACE.

ÌYÁ: THE WOMEN LAUGH. There! The king runs from us… like a bad child. Look at him flee, and he called us common women. RAISES A SONG:
Yíò tẹ́ o,
Yíò tẹ́ o,
Káróunwí fojú di Yèyé,
Yíò tẹ́ o.

Wait let us reveal the Orò of the woman to you Kábíyèsí. Wait and bite the dust of motherhood... come back and behold the nakedness of your life!
Àní
Yíò tẹ́ o,
Yíò tẹ́ o,
Káróunwí fojú di Yèyé,
Yíò tẹ́ o.
Shame and disgrace await you!

SLOWLY LIGHTS FADE.

DIM LIGHTS WHEN PLAY OPENS. PÈGÚNRUN'S SHRINE.
ÌYÁ HURRIES IN. RUNS TO THE EDGE OF THE SHRINE.
PULLS A CHAIN.

ÌYÁ: By the gods, I call you Yèyé Pègúnrun. Rise. You gave your word that if we ever need your help, we should pull at the chain. This is the second time. Arise Yèyé... step out! Your daughters are washed in shame, help us before the stench becomes even too hard to bear. Ọba Káróunwí pours, and we like play dolls are held captive in the mist of your dedicated love and promise. What do we do? Ọba Káróunwí turned your truth into just a lie. A common smelly lie! I say arise before a more massive tragedy hits your beloved Ìjẹ̀kùn Odò. I say rise, I pull for the third time.

PÈGÚNRUN: STEPS INTO THE DARKNESS. Do not bother. Your cries came earlier with each step of your heartbeat. Welcome.

ÌYÁ: SHOCKED, FALLS TO HER KNEES. Yèyé you are up!

PÈGÚNRUN: I had to. When no one came for me, I knew something was wrong. And as I see you all covered in smudge, I know better.

ÌYÁ: I wanted to stop at the edge of river Ìjẹ̀kùn Odò and clean myself. But where do I start? I asked myself... the legs or the head, so I decide to come the way I am. Forgive me mother.

PÈGÚNRUN: You sound distracted, what is the matter?

ÌYÁ: Plenty went wrong Yèyé. Ọba Káróunwí mocked your heroic deeds. He even claims that you are a made-up story... an old myth which must be swept away into the forgotten bush. He mocked the loss of our mother. He said we were crying fools, who only like children seek a place of importance and attention. And to pour salt on an open wound, he drove us like flies in search of rotten food... he swept the feet of all of your children from the very palace you saved from shame. Cactus, what do we do?

PÈGÚNRUN: They betrayed my trust.

ÌYÁ: Trust? They killed over and over again mother. Your blood flowing at the bank of the river once again

PÈGÚNRUN: The pain you feel touches me.

ÌYÁ: Why have you stayed too long to return to us? I kept asking myself. Why?

PÈGÚNRUN: I have to wait for the right time.

ÌYÁ: I chose to be your Priestess because I was told you will soon return. I told myself, I would serve her for only a while. I never knew you would be this difficult to follow... when will you return to us as your story fore tell?

PÈGÚNRUN: Soon. But tell me what happened at the palace. Why was I not summoned at the shrine?

ÌYÁ: It was KÁRÓUNWÍ... all the villagers were ready to grace your name, KÁRÓUNWÍ barred us. The whole village. He refused to dance in your name... not even a finger to the rhythm of the drums.

PÈGÚNRUN: And the men... the rest of them... what did they do?

ÌYÁ: Nothing. They were dressed as women, but none of them felt the fear of a goddess. Not one.

PÈGÚNRUN: Nothing. Not one felt a layer of fear in their eyes.

ÌYÁ: You have stayed away for too long Yèyé. Men only fear what they see. As Károunwí spoke, I remembered the words of Ifá and felt sorry for them. Let no one pursue power in a haste. Let no one embrace the search for wealth with impunity. Issues that can be settled with maturity, ought not to be treated with a rashness of the mind. Downfall is imminent for the fool who negates these words of wisdom.

PÈGÚNRUN: But did Károunwí negate these words of wisdom... today?

ÌYÁ: Today. Yes Yèyé. Like a baboon he jumped from tree to tree... howling ...shrieking... boasting... and puffing.

PEGUNGUN: What do you want me to do to him?

ÌYÁ: He is a king... only his left ear Yèyé. Pull it gently. The rich and powerful cannot bear much pain. Kíkẹ́ là ń kẹ́ Ọba.

PÈGÚNRUN: (CHUCKLES SARCASTICALLY). I see Èṣù's hand in this. Did you send him his gifts?

ÌYÁ: Yes. REMEMBERS. Há hà! earlier...

PÈGÚNRUN: Yes...earlier.

ÌYÁ: We sent Abídèmí to his shrine, and a mishap occurred.

PÈGÚNRUN: A mishap?

ÌYÁ: We begged him. RECALLS. Há hà...could it be...

PÈGÚNRUN: Could it be what, woman? Why are you stuttering?

ÌYÁ: The young Abídèmí fell at Èṣù's shrine and wounded herself. It bled and poured on Èṣù's black stone. A taboo!

PÈGÚNRUN: I know. And when he foamed in the mouth with anger, I pledged the use of my three children to him.

ÌYÁ: Even I do not understand.

PÈGÚNRUN: Do not bother or you might lose your mind.

ÌYÁ: Cactus!

PÈGÚNRUN: Where is Abídèmí at this moment?

ÌYÁ: At home. I left her lying on the bed. Like all the Ìyálóde's before her, she fell on the way back home. But today, she fainted twice by the time we got home.

PÈGÚNRUN: That must have been when I felt the jolt.

ÌYÁ: Hm Yèyé?

PÈGÚNRUN: Never mind. Continue.

ÌYÁ: Yes. Twice she fainted mother. The women carried her in exhausted... it was as if her spirit was ebbing. Her flesh softens as if ready to separate itself from the bones. Like all the other new Ìyálóde's before the walk to your shrine. This is when I started to worry and why I came here straight from the house. Yèyé her eyes are sunk in as if she was preparing to take a long trip.

PÈGÚNRUN: IN A WHISPER. Home. Her kindness fully paid... her case no longer needed. She was to go...

ÌYÁ: To go? To where mother? For what? Mother... tonight, you speak in a tongue that eludes me. As if I am a stranger to your thoughts. When I should know... but even now, I am lost.

PÈGÚNRUN: Never mind. Soon it shall find you. HOLDS OUT A CLOTH. Take this... cover Abídèmí as she lies on my bed. You handle it yourself woman. As always.

ÌYÁ: And Ọba Káróunwí. Will he go only with a part on the hand? Remember Yèyé, a woman's reputation is weak, it is like glass, once it shatters nothing can bring it back again. Ọba Káróunwí shattered your image today. Even like looked Ṣìgìdì... a clay doll fit for the game of fools. This is why I ask again... what will happen to Ọba Káróunwí now? Will he go without a pinch from the Cactus?

PÈGÚNRUN: BRINGS OUT HER LEFT HAND, AND AS IF WATCHING A MIRROR. There he sits, his Olorì on his feet. SHE CLAPS BOTH HANDS, AS IF CRUSHING A FLY. Go home. It is done.

THE SOUND OF THE PALACE DRUMS ARE HEARD.

ÌYÁ: The drums from the palace. Há hà!

PÈGÚNRUN: What do they say?

ÌYÁ: Kábíyèsí Oyètọ́lá Káróunwí is gone... climbed the roof of the palace to a greater world. The drums play a dirge in his honour. Cactus... what have you done? We only wanted his left ear pulled, not his head cut off.

PÈGÚNRUN: Then he should never have played with the pain from the very pith of a woman. TURNS HER BACK. I say it is done. I have work to do. Go! ÌYÁ HURRIES OUT.

PÈGÚNRUN: SLOWLY SHE TURNS TO THE AUDIENCE. Was I in the wrong in this matter? Am I in the wrong? Ọba

Káróunwí abused my devotion and resolution to keep my people alive, and in one word, he rubbished the essence of my sacrifice. CHUCKLES. To the third generation, the Káróunwí family shall feel the angered pinches of my prickly thorns. I have spoken.

SLOWLY LIGHTS FADE.

THRONE ROOM, THE CHIEFS ARE SEATED. THE CROWN AND ROYAL HORSE TAIL ARE ON THE THRONE CHAIR. ADÍFÁLÀ SITS ON THE FLOOR. HIS EYES ON THE ÒPÈLÈ. ALL ARE EXPECTANT AS ADÉLÙ ENTERS.

ADÉLÙ: I saw him... what used to be my father... and King of Ìjèkùn Odò. Òtún what happened here?

ÒTÚN: No one knows... Obalóla.

ADÉLÙ: Then what are we doing here? Keep kings alive as long as we want them, and then kill them when we have had enough of him?

ÒTÚN: No Obalóla. The late king's fingers were on too many issues, one or too could have dragged him along to the royal roof of the palace.

ADÉLÙ: And why was he seated, dead, with his youngest wife on his laps. NO ONE SPEAKS. Is this a palace of mute killers? I say why was a dead woman sitting on the laps of my late father?

ADÍFÁLÀ: Aroko.

ADÉLÙ: Who spoke?

ADÍFÁLÀ: I did Prince Adélù.

ADÉLÙ: Yes Bàbá. Aroko you say.

ADÍFÁLÀ: A message from the killer or killers. Ifá says it is a woman.

ADÉLÙ: A woman. Kills the king and allows the late Olorì to sit on his laps? This is an insult.

ÒTÚN: Mind what you say Obalóla?

ADÉLÙ: What if I don't? What more can she do? At least remove her from him so that we make arrangements to bury her.

ADÍFÁLÀ: CONSULTS THE IFÀ. It is the message of the strength of a woman. Even in death she sits on men. CHUCKLES. What a strong woman. A goddess indeed. The mother of the village of Ìjẹ̀kùn Odò. It is you I greet.

ADÉLÙ: Pègúnrun.

ÀDÍFÁLA: Yes. She swells. She foams. Her teeth grit. And her cheeks twitch. Your father dared her. He refused to accept Pègúnrun's choice for the new Ìyálóde, and so she bit him.

ADÉLÙ: And she killed a king? In a twinkle of her thought? Just like that?

ÒTÚN: Just like that Ọbalọ́la. A privilege of a goddess.

ADÍFÁLÀ: Yes. The question is what will the new King want from Pègúnrun? I mean... will he embrace his late father's new ideas or accept our old stories about a woman who gave us her life?

ADÉLÙ: What does Ifá say?

ADÍFÁLÀ: Kí là ń fún àgbà... kílẹ̀ tutù? Owó... owó là ń fún àgbà kílẹ̀ tutù, owó.

ADÉLÙ: When the elders have spoken, and Ifá has concurred, who will go against the words of the god of wisdom?

ÒTÚN: Our very thought indeed.

ADÉLÙ: I don't want to die.

ÒTÚN: A wise decision my king to be.

ADÍFÁLÀ: A wise decision indeed. Five days.

ADÉLÙ: Five days.

ADÍFÁLÀ: That is all she has given us to adopt her choice as Ìyálóde or the earth would shake. Five days.

ADÉLÙ: Five days? Even before I sit on my father's throne?

ADÍFÁLÀ: Five days my Prince.

ADÉLÙ: Then this very minute, let us go to the shrine of Pègúnrun and worship her. Let us go with gifts and all. Let us touch the once gentle woman in her.

ADÍFÁLÀ: At the crack of dawn. She will come.

ADÉLÙ: Crack of dawn?

ADÍFÁLÀ: She will come. Ọtún, there is work to be done. We need to prepare the Ọbalọ́la for this visit.

ÒTÚN: And it is not as simple as that Ọbalọ́la. We hear rumours, rumble of a break in the family. Another candidate has been chosen for the title.

ADÉLÙ: For the person of Ìyálóde?

ÒTÚN: Yes.

ADÍFÁLÀ: A smoke that will be settled when she arrives.

ADÉLÙ: At the crack of dawn.

ADÍFÁLÀ: Yes. At the crack of dawn. But there are preparations to be made.

SLOWLY LIGHTS FADE.

WHEN DIM LIGHTS COME ON, IT REVEALS THE INNER CHAMBERS OF THE KING'S CHAMBER. ADÉLÙ LIES ON THE BED ASLEEP. A DARK SHADOW OF PÈGÚNRUN STANDS OVER HIM AS HE SLEEPS.

PÈGÚNRUN: Ọbalọ́la. I have come. See him sleep like a child that he is, searching for mysteries in the wind which he will never understand. A mere village fool about to be robed and crowne. A sacrifice. Wake up man.

ADÉLÙ: Who calls me in my sleep, a spirit or a goddess?

PÈGÚNRUN: Cactus. Soft with life on the inside, full of thorns on the outside. Burning... fired up by an un-soothing anger... woman. That is me.

ADÉLÙ: I don't know you.

PÈGÚNRUN: I knew you long before you were born. I am she... the revolving spirit of life. Young prince, you fight two spirits.

ADÉLÙ: Two spirits?

PÈGÚNRUN: Which one do you want to meet? It depends on you. Which one young prince. The hand of time clicks.

ADÉLÙ: I don't understand.

PÈGÚNRUN: Then give me the answer I seek, or else tonight your father who is on the sudden journey to the land of the spirits will wait for you at the crossroads of life and death.

ADÉLÙ: My father?

PÈGÚNRUN: Yes. Ọba Adébánmówó Károunwí. His fresh body begins to gather moist… from the damp wetness of river of Ìjẹ̀kùn Odò. Talk to me. I have no time to waste.

ADÉLÙ: You know him?

PÈGÚNRUN: Answer me man. I have little time for memories. Talk to me. Face the whirlwind and let it blow out the caste of blurred blindness which envelopes your sight right now.

ADÉLÙ: Where are the fools who call themselves palace guards? How did you enter my room?

PÈGÚNRUN: I say leave stories alone. You sent for me.

ADÉLÙ: Me? When? Where? Who are you?

PÈGÚNRUN: I am Pègúnrun. The Cactus… the woman whose life you doubt.

ADÉLÙ: You? Yes. HE PROSTRATES. Mother!

PÈGÚNRUN: Rise. You sent for me. I am here.

ADÉLÙ: Indeed, I sent… wished to have you before me, just a wish… but I never knew you would come this way. Do I dream? RISES. Tell me about you. Is it true or is it a well woven tale? I mean life is too sweet to just let go so easily. My father the late King died because of you. Tell me, mother of the land, what really happened?

PÈGÚNRUN: Then watch and see.

LIGHTS SLOWLY FADE ON THE KING'S CHAMBERS. LIGHTS COME ON SLOWLY TO THE FRUGALLY SET THRONE ROOM WHICH DEPICTS A HUNDRED YEARS AGO. THE ELDERLY KING ỌMỌLE SITS WITH TWO OF

HIS CHIEFS AND PÈGÚNRUN. ADÍFÁLÀ SITS ON THE FLOOR.

ỌMỌLE: You have heard what Adífálà said. And I believe him. The Whiteman and his soldiers approach us. The bullying Ìlàrís of Aláàfin Abíọ́dún continues to harass us. Neighbouring villages have already started to scramble for survival with each other. Some have started to attack themselves. The slave market booms. The coral market competes for our daily lives. We cannot catch, kill our brothers or even sell them to the Whiteman or black slave dealers. We do not have the soldiers or the connection to survive in the midst of these madness. I am afraid that the end of Ìjẹ̀kùn Odò is approaching.

ỌTÚN: May the gods forbid!

ỌMỌLE: May the gods forbid indeed. But the mouth of the dreaded Lion is open. Its fangs foam, its teeth drenched, death approaches. Apènà what do we do?

APÈNÀ: What we can do Kábíyèsí? The weight takes words from my mouth. It makes me breath with fear?

ỌMỌLE: Was I here alone when Adífálà spoke? Am I a fool who hears voices in his head then? A big fat fool, sitting like a fat unripe pumpkin alone in a dried up farm? See how wild hawks gather and descend, and still sit here and jabber? You heard Adífálà, did you not? Adífálà, tell them one more time. What Ifá said?

ADÍFÁLÀ: The future is dark. Haze of smoke everywhere. Cries of dying children and women. Ìjẹ̀kùn Odò is about to be wiped out.

APÈNÀ: Kábíyèsí, I remember now.

ỌMỌLE: Shut your mouth and listen more. The real Dane guns are coming, you are talking of death. Continue, Adífálà.

ADÍFÁLÀ: Unless a sacrifice of a young woman is made, we shall not know peace.

APÈNÀ: What kind of sacrifice Bàbá?

ỌMỌLE: Now you are talking, our dance steps are in tune. Speak Bàbá Ifá.

ADÍFÁLÀ: The sacrifice needs a a daughter of Ìjẹkùn Odò in a position of power. A young woman who has not known a man. A virgin. She must give herself up willingly.

ÒTÚN: Where do we get such a woman?

APÈNÀ: My very thought Kábíyèsí. But... we can ask Balógun to go to neighbouring countries and kidnap an Olorì. The wife of a King should be important enough.

ỌMỌLE: Open your ears again Apènà. She should be a daughter of Ìjẹkùn Odò.

PÈGÚNRUN: RISES SLOWLY. I am the woman you seek. I shall do it.

ADÍFÁLÀ: Your death shall be painful. We shall strangle you with your wrapper. And then divide your body into four parts, each part at the corner of the village. Your head shall be buried at the central Market square.

PÈGÚNRUN: I say l am the woman you seek.

ỌMỌLE: Abídèmí. Indeed, you are your father's child. Exactly twenty years ago today, your brave father was killed at the Ẹdẹ Ilé junction on his way from Ìwó with a message for my late father. I went with him on that trip. The sword that went through his stomach was meant for me. We arrived with his body in evening to meet that you had been born a few hours earlier. And you pick his mantle of honour. You want to lay down your life for the village.

PÈGÚNRUN: KÁBÍYÈSÍ. I say I will do it.

ỌMỌLE: Adífálà, what does Ifá say about the willing choice?

ADÍFÁLÀ: CONSULTS HIS ADÍFÁLÀ. Ifá accepts the choice. Abídèmí, Ifá greets you. Ọrúnmìlà blesses you. Three things. Ifá wants you to say three things that your heart wants the village to do for you after your death.

PÈGÚNRUN: THINKS. Three things I desire.

ADÍFÁLÀ: Yes.

PÈGÚNRUN: My poor mother. I am an only child.

ỌMỌLE: That is not a wish. She will live with me in the palace, until she dies. I owe her for two kindness now. Name something else.

PÈGÚNRUN: I want to visit the shrine of Ọbàtálá before I die.

APÈNÀ: Again, that is not a wish, you can visit anywhere you want to go until midnight when the deed will be done.

PÈGÚNRUN: Then I want to be deified. I, Pègúnrun want to be a goddess, worshipped by the whole village all dressed like women, dancing around the village. And a sacrifice of my favourite food. Agìdì and Ewédú soup, with pure water from the stream.

ỌMỌLE: That will be done.

PÈGÚNRUN: To honour my mother and family, all the subsequent Ìyálódes of Ìjẹ̀kùn Odò will come from my family.

ỌMỌ́LE: Done.

PÈGÚNRUN: And I shall have the final say on who is chosen as Ìyálóde, the night before she dances to see Kábíyèsí on the day of my worship.

ỌMỌ́LE: That too is done.

LIGHTS GO OFF.

PÈGÚNRUN: From there I took my leave, left for the shrine of Ọbàtálá. He granted me my wish, and I returned alone to the Ògun shrine where the deed was done. And now my people forget everything. They question the very essence of my being. I bleed.

ADÉLÙ: And my father? He died. What bastardy act did he commit to die with a woman on his laps? What did he do mother?

PÈGÚNRUN: A fool! Hear his words that fired my tempestuous spirit into a fire spitting volcano. I foamed.

LIGHTS GO OFF, AND A SPOTLIGHT PICKS UP ỌBA KÁRÓUNWÍ ON HIS CHAIR THRONE.

KÁRÓUNWÍ How are we sure she even lived? A tale I tell you, an old grandmother's tale trapped within the broken rotted teeth of age. A myth... a mere myth to make the woman feel right. I hear she even said that she would return after a hundred years. Is a hundred years yesterday? Has she got the key to the heaven that Olódùmarè will allow her to "come and go, at will?" All I am saying is that we have moved on.

Ayé ń lọ, à ń tọ̀ ọ́. I shall no longer follow the concocted foul wind. I shall not tie a wrapper... or plait my hair just because a woman said so... a common old woman's myth.... which must now be forgotten. Èèwọ̀!

SPOTLIGHT FADE. LIGHTS BACK ON PÈGÚNRUN AND ADÉLÙ.

PÈGÚNRUN: ANGRY. Was that all? Was all my blood a myth? Did my act mean nothing at all? His words tore my sacrifice to a meaningless act, so I took him!

ADÉLÙ: But he was my father!

PEGURUN: With the brain of a child. ANGRY. He mocked me! The royal fool mocked me, so with gritted teeth, I let him down into the crypt of death, choked in his own saliva. PAUSE. That was it. Those very words killed your father.

ADÉLÙ: You killed a king and now you boast of it. Why?

PÈGÚNRUN: After a hundred years, men still use women. You have perfected the way of making our words sound like chippings of foolish birds who believe that because the morning is bright and beautiful, the whole day will be the same. Ọba Ọmọ́le gave me his word... and your stupid father rubbished it. That was why... that was why he had to die.

ADÉLÙ: How? A king? What happened to the praise chant that says a king is death itself?

PÈGÚNRUN: Mere words to broaden the inflated shoulders of a beaded fool.

ADÉLÙ: LOOKS AROUND. AFRAID. Where are they... the soldiers who are to guard me in the night?

PÈGÚNRUN: Why do you want them?

ADÉLÙ: To arrest you. You speak what you do not know.

PÈGÚNRUN: You sound agitated. Are you afraid my king to be?

ADÉLÙ: No. My men… I can't find them. Have you killed them too? I say, where are they? Answer, woman!

PÈGÚNRUN: Asleep… one step at the edge of death. Do you want them to trip over?

ADÉLÙ: No. What do you want woman?

PÈGÚNRUN: Nothing. Just listen like a king that you want to be. And when all appear hazy, call Adífálà from the village of Ìlú Àìgbàgbé. The present one is called Ifákíyèsí, son of Ifábámidélé.

ADÉLÙ: Does he still live?

PÈGÚNRUN: Again, you talk too much. I thought you were the one alive? Just ask to see the one with plucked eyes. I must leave, the sheet of darkness folds, the day will break soon. I never stay out this late, I must step over to my world.

ADÉLÙ. SNEEZES. A cold storm gathers, I hear there is another candidate in your family. What do I do, Yèyé?

PÈGÚNRUN: CHUCKLES. When the time comes, the cloud will clear.

ADÉLÙ: I don't understand…SNEEZES AGAIN. Suddenly the air is dusty and stale.

PÈGÚNRUN: Stale. I must leave.

ADÉLÙ: Shall we meet again then? SNEEZES.

PÈGÚNRUN: The cold night's dew has not even began to fall, and already you sneeze. Let the day break first, and we shall see if you will still recognize the colour of the night... but for now, let us clear the dry leaves from the moist grave, so that the dead may breathe once again! Until then, fear remains your only companion.

SLOWLY LIGHTS GO OFF. PÈGÚNRUN DISAPPEARS. ADÉLÙ ANGRY, SCREAMS.

ADÉLÙ: Where is she? Who really is she? Where has she gone? PAUSE. AGITATED. Where are they? Where are the fools whose incapable hands the people thrust my life? ÌLÀRÍ RUNS IN. Where have you been?

ÌLÀRÍ: Outside. We did not hear you call, except now our prince.

ADÉLÙ: Do you know Ifákíyèsí from Ìlú Àigbàgbé?

ÌLÀRÍ: The blind Seer. I know him. ENTER ÌLÀRÍ ÀGBÀ.

ADÉLÙ: Go before the day breaks. I want to see him. Carry him here if you have to. I hear only he may have the light to my father's death. Hurry!

HE WATCHES ÌLÀRÍ LEAVE.

ÌLÀRÍ ÀGBÀ: Ọbalọ́la, the Pègúnrun family will bring the chosen member of their family to the palace.

ADÉLÙ: What if I do not want to meet with them. My father has just died a mysterious death, and you all want me to celebrate.

ÌLÀRÍ ÀGBÀ: This is the serious matter Ọba Àgbà. We hear that the spirit of Pègúnrun gave us five days for her festival or she will wipe out the village. Already children and women are struck with mysterious sickness. Fear grips us all. Pègúnrun is not a spirit to play with. Let them come.

ADÉLÙ: Alright, not too long. I want to spend more time with the blind Seer of Ìlú Àìgbàgbé.

ÌLÀRÍ ÀGBÀ: Thank you Ọba Àgbà.

ADÉLÙ: What do I have to do?

ÌLÀRÍ ÀGBÀ: Simple. They present their choice, and you remove he veil, and we dance and sing. Then on the day of the festival, we dress like women.

ADÉLÙ: The whole village.

ÌLÀRÍ ÀGBÀ: The whole village, led by you. Then we go to the shrine of Pègúnrun, where you will pray for her and for the village. The Masquerades will dance, also dressed like women. And the next day, we will bury your father, and you immediately become the new Kábíyèsí of Ìjẹkùn Odò.

ADÉLÙ: And the death of my father?

ÌLÀRÍ ÀGBÀ: Many reasons kill a king, Ọba Àgbà. Let it be.

ADÉLÙ: Then I shall follow the words of the elders which say that a task left uncompleted by the father should be completed by the son. I shall complete this... and fill the gaping wound.

ÌLÀRÍ ÀGBÀ: With time the wind will blow away the leaves that cover the moist grave. Sleep my prince. One step at a time. With time, these seeming interlocking mysteries will unfold.

ADÉLÙ: They must. CHUCKLES SADLY. That proverb again. The wind will blow away the leaves that cover the moist grave. I hope this will be soon?

ÌLÀRÍ ÀGBÀ: Soon Ọbalọ́la... soon.

SLOWLY LIGHTS FADE.

ỌṢÌNNÚSÌ'S ROOM. HE EATS, DRESSED LIKE A WOMAN, WHEN JOWÚỌLÁ ENTERS.

JOWÚỌLÁ: Bàbá you eat?

ỌṢÌNNÚSÌ: Yes. Is there a rule where we are forbidden to eat now? You heard what happened to me last night?

JOWÚỌLÁ: No.

ỌṢÌNNÚSÌ: I had spoken with my son and the farmers working on my farm when suddenly, I felt a pain... excruciating... biting... holding me down on my seat. I screamed. It was Ìyá Tọ́pẹ́ Àgbà that came in with ointment.

JOWÚỌLÁ: Then it is true that the spirits are after us. I was pressed down on my bed when I woke three days ago. I could not rise from the bed. Until Bàbá Fìjàbí was called. He had heard about Ọ̀wọ̀midà's sickness, so he asked me to meet him here this morning.

ỌṢÌNNÚSÌ: I am here. And Ọ̀wọ̀midà... how is he?

JOWÚỌLÁ: I am fine, but Ọ̀wọ̀midà is not. I did not recognize my brother when I saw Him. His stomach was swollen. His tongue darkened, longer than his mouth. He looked more like a rejected effigy for sacrifice.

ÒṢÌNNÚSÌ: Did he say what happened?

JOWÚỌLÁ: No. But he remembers that the sickness started shortly after he returned from the palace. That night, an unseen hand beat him in his sleep. Ọba Káróunwí had given them back the gifts we sent to him. His wife boiled half the tuber of yam we sent. That was when it started.

ÒṢÌNNÚSÌ: Who went with him.

JOWÚỌLÁ: Ìbàdé. He fell from the top of the palm tree the second day. He died as he fell.

ÒṢÌNNÚSÌ: And now Ọba Káróunwí is dead.

JOWÚỌLÁ: His mouth killed him.

ÒṢÌNNÚSÌ: I hope ours do not kill us too.

JOWÚỌLÁ: Àṣẹ! That is why Bàbá Fijabi said we should meet with him here this morning.

ÒṢÌNNÚSÌ: So, where is he? That man moves like a snail. He will be close by at noon.

JOWÚỌLÁ: He feels we offended Pègúnrun. And that if we were not children of the great mother, we should have died by now.

ÒṢÌNNÚSÌ: Why does he feel that way?

JOWÚỌLÁ: Pègúnrun visited him. He was beaten to a pulp. That woman will hang a dead person.

ÒṢÌNNÚSÌ: If a great medicine man like Fìjàbí gets beaten by Pègúnrun, and a king dies while playing with his wife, I am now afraid. I do not want to die eating my breakfast. I woke up this morning grateful to Olódùmarè that I lived to see another day... the night before was a struggle. Death seemed so near. I wish we had not done it. I have been feeling very weak, since we returned from Èṣù's shrine.

JOWÚỌLÁ: I keep wondering what would have happened to us if we had blessed Abídèmí when Ọba Károunwí asked us to.

ÒṢÌNNÚSÌ: I was stiffened with fear. Just a word of blessing and I would have dried up there... still standing. Dead.

JOWÚỌLÁ: Me too. But Ìyá came at the nick of time. She saved our lives.

ÒṢÌNNÚSÌ: Raw death would have killed us in broad daylight. Even in death we would have been the dead laughing stuck of the village. The type that killed Ọba Károunwí. Rumour has it that his youngest Olorì died sitting on his laps.

JOWÚỌLÁ: CHUCKLES. Even in death, the royalty die like fools. CHUCKLES AGAIN. Rumour? The story is everywhere. Now his son Adélù is everywhere searching for what killed his father. Death may embrace him too. A son who digs for the reason of his father's death, often meets his own grave.

ÌYÁ: ENTERS. Good morning Bàbá Ọṣìnnúsì. Your wife told me that your body was warm last night. JOWÚỌLÁ today is good.

JOWÚỌLÁ: Yes. Good morning Ìyá.

ÌYÁ: It is good I met both of you. Soon we shall be called back to the palace by the Prince, and there are preparations to be made. I don't know why but Pègúnrun sends a message of warning to both of you. Nothing must go wrong she warned. Not even a thought of evil must follow the activities.

JOWÚỌLÁ: Our hands are innocent.

ỌṢÌNNÚSÌ: Yes.

JOWÚỌLÁ: But we are all ears, Ìyá.

ÌYÁ: A black chicken. A bottle of palm oil. And nine obì àbàtà... three for each of you... must be taken to the shrine of Pègúnrun, before noon today. Èṣù her best friend foams in the mouth with anger too. Her wrapper falls intermittently... a grave sign of pure undiluted anger.

JOWÚỌLÁ: Or...

ÌYÁ: Or you will all die, like the traitors that you are... all three of you will perish... drowned at the deep center of Ìjẹ̀kùn Odò river... trying to wallow in a pool of greed. And you Jowúọlá... you seem to be the typical woman who unwraps the wrapper that should tie her family in a sacred bond together. Ṣíọ̀!

ỌṢÌNNÚSÌ: The three of us.

JOWÚỌLÁ: But...

ÌYÁ: The fire you lit before Èṣù will soon consume you. Cover the fire now or the smoke will spread and choke you all.

ỌṢÌNNÚSÌ: We have heard. Ears are used to hear... we have heard... please go Ìyá.

JOWÚỌLÁ: But first Olórí Ẹbí, we shall wait for Bàbá Fijàbí.

ÌYÁ: He won't come today.

JOWÚOLÁ: How do you know that?

ÌYÁ: He died in his sleep this morning for his treachery. Èṣù strangled him. Her deadly claws all over his wicked fat neck. In fact, he lies, hands folded without his wooden foot, in a moist grave. Hurry fools… wash your rotten mouths from your cursed oath with water and salt… the sun begins to rise.

JOWÚOLÁ: We shall wash our mouths clean Ìyá.

ÒṢÌNNÚSÌ: Hurry woman go and do what Pègúnrun asked. Hurry!

ÌYÁ: While you argue whether the sun will set, I shall leave. There are things to be done. Do not forget what I told you. Do not let Èṣù use us to provide food for dogs. I leave for Abídèmí's house. Bring the Òṣùgbó along, we shall need to cover her feet while she sits. EXITS ÌYÁ.

ÒṢÌNNÚSÌ: You heard her Jowúolá. Three graves wait…

JOWÚOLÁ: Let them wait. By the gods I shall not return what the gods have given me. My late sister Títí Àgbà gave it to me on her death bed, and on my death bed I will release it to my own daughter.

ÒṢÌNNÚSÌ: Don't rewrite the story of our bloodline too. Remember, Ìyá said…

JOWÚOLÁ: Ìyá needs to know that Èṣù finds food for the dog on the streets. I share in Pègúnrun's blood. She cannot hurt me. The crown of Ìyálóde is mine to keep. Last night I beckoned on the spirits of the family, and they promised to stand by me. Let the sun rise a million times, I shall remain who and what I am.

ỌSÌNNÚSÌ: Mere boasts Jowúọlá. This is no longer a game of words. How are you sure you have the right Òṣùgbó? Jowúọlá, do not play with the Cactus... it has thorns. It pricks! And the prickly edge is poisonous, it kills. Please!

JOWÚỌLÁ: At the palace. When the eyes are open, we shall know the imposter. The bloodline of inheritance to the Ìyálóde throne will change today. The gods chose me, Pègúnrun must agree. Bàbá, I say nothing can touch us. Nothing!

ÌDẸRA RUNS IN.

ÌDẸRA: AGITATED. Mama come with me quickly! My father. He lies still! Not a blink! Not a word! But he breaths... slowly.

ỌSÌNNÚSÌ: I warned you Sister! If you scratch old wounds, one is bound to find smelly gushing glut. Just do what Ìyá said.

JOWÚỌLÁ: Èèwọ̀! What stupid trick is Ọ̀wọ̀midà up to now? This is no time for children's pranks. Come son. Take us there! ALL RUN OUT.

LIGHTS SLOWLY FADE.

COURTYARD OF THE PÈGÚNRUN FAMILY HOUSE. THE WOMEN ARE STILL GAILY DRESSED ALL WEARING THE SAME DRESS, INCLUDING THE MEN.

ỌṢÌNNÚSÌ: ON STAGE LOOKING OUT FOR JOWÚỌLÁ, WHO ENTERS, CARRYING THE ÒṢÙGBÓ IN A LITTLE BAG. You are here. What took you so long?

JOWÚỌLÁ: I went home to take it.

ỌṢÌNNÚSÌ: Good. Now that you have it, hand it over to Ìyá.

JOWÚỌLÁ: Never I shall hold it until we get to the palace. I shall wear it when we get to the palace. When the truth shall be revealed. ÌYÁ APPROACHES.

ÌYÁ: Have you got the Òṣùgbó?

JOWÚỌLÁ: No Ìyá. But I am still searching.

ÌYÁ: CHUCKLES. Death shows its face, and fool says it a friendly masque. Find it woman. We do not use powers beyond its limit. We need it to cover Abídèmí's feet when she is seated at the palace.

JOWÚỌLÁ: I say I do not have it.

ÌYÁ: Remember that traditions are not changed on whims or desires of village idiots. If you have it, give it up now.

JOWÚỌLÁ: I say I don't have it. Why would I lie?

ÌYÁ: Alright. How is your brother Ọwọ̀midà?

JOWÚỌLÁ: He is in a coma. He hangs between life and death. His wife is having to bask him in the warmth of boiled healing leaves. It must be high fever.

ÌYÁ: May it be as you wish... but the sun rises by the second. Soon we shall see the hidden crevices of moist graves. May he be healed if his hands are clean.

ÒṢÌNNÚSÌ: Àṣẹ!

ÌYÁ: But remember Bàbá Òṣìnnúsì, that a man who thinks he can outperform the jumping tricks of the monkey may, meet his maker before his time. Tell the eldest woman to call all the women together.

ÒṢÌNNÚSÌ: Yes...yes. SHOUTS OUT. Jowúọlá, tell the women to gather together. It is almost time to go to the palace. THE WOMEN GATHER.

ÌYÁ: RAISES A SONG. À ń gbé Yèyé relé Ọba
Yèyé!
Rọra máa tẹlẹ múyẹ múyẹ
Yèyé!
Ìyálóde ń relé Ọba
Yèyé!
Abídèmí ń relé Ọba
Yèyé!
Rọra máa tẹlẹ múyẹ múyẹ
Yèyé!

THE WOMEN BEGIN TO DANCE AND SING, WHEN ÌLÀRÍ'S AND SOLDIERS FROM THE PALACE ENTER.

ÌYÁ: What again? What does the Ọbalọ́la want from us this time? Has he decided to dance with the death steps of his father? The drummers of shame are never tired. Has he?

ÌLÀRÍ ÀGBÀ: No Ìyá. We have come with a message from Ọbalọ́la. He says only a handful of the women should come for now. Just four people with the Olórí ẹbí. There is still a matter to be cleared before the festival can start.

ÌYÁ: The remaining women? What happens to them?

ÌLÀRÍ ÀGBÀ: They should stay here for now, until we send for them.

ÌYÁ: You heard him, Olórí ẹbí. Jowúọlá, Abídèmí, Moróntódùn, Túnráyọ̀ and myself. Let us hurry women. Ọbalọ́la wants us. THEY ALL HURRY OUT. ABÍDÈMÍ IS STILL COVERED. Hold her on both sides. She must not fall. Not a song, not a word. Èṣù is at work. I know that we did not serve him with Àdí. Àdí is his mother's name. Èèwọ̀! It is palm oil that he takes and that is what we gave him. We shall surely overcome this contrived hiccups of pretentious fools. THE WOMEN EXIT. LEAVING JOWÚỌLÁ BEHIND.

JOWÚỌLÁ: Yọkọlú yọkọlú,
Kò a tán bí?
Èṣù gbé Ìyá ṣánlẹ̀
Ìyá yọké!!
LETS OUT A WILD LAUGH.
This dance gets only sweeter.
Èṣù láàlú, ògiri òkò,
lè kúrú, lè ga,
lè ga, lè kúrú,
Òdàrà,
You dazzle even the one with the heart of stone with suffocating excitement. Èṣù Èbìtà, the hard one, it is you I also call. I stand on your promised colours of red and black, for this, I assured. So, I am covered with your sisterly love, always. Embrace me with the assurance of love, do not play with me for I am not a toy for the pranks of children. LET OUT A CHUCKLE. TURNS TO THE AUDIENCE. Stare at

me if you like. To you, I am a common envious sinner. But who cares? Cheered on by Ẹlẹ́gbárá herself, my goal is my unwavering aim.

SLOWLY LIGHTS FADE.

THRONE ROOM OF THE PALACE. WHEN LIGHTS COME ON, BÀBÁ IFÁKÍYÈSÍ SITS ON THE FLOOR TENDING THE ADÍFÁLÀ. THE REST ARE SEATED ON THE FLOOR. ADÉLÙ SITS ON THE CHAIR. ALL EYES ON IFÁKÍYÈSÍ AS HE CONSULTS IFÁ.

IFÁKÍYÈSÍ: Olódùmarè made the moon,
    Olódùmarè made the sun
    Then he sat down and gave them each work to do.
    Both were to shine at different times.
    Then Èṣù Láàlú came and asked who was superior.
    Sprinkling the spirit of rivalry and deceit between them
    As always Olódùmarè sat back and watched Èṣù display his trickery.
    Unknown to them, Ọrúnmìlà, the god of wisdom also watched
    But when it was time to fight, Ọrúnmìlà stepped in.
    Why not bring half of your powers each, to the fight.
    So they brought half of their powers.
    Then the god of wisdom said, why don't you join the powers you
    Have brought to fight with, and mix them all up.
    And so the eclipse was born... and Olódùmarè enjoyed the spackle
    Of half light, and half moon. And the naïve men said the sun and
    Moon are at war. But what do they know? How can man measure the greatness of god?

ADÉLÙ: Bàbá Ifákíyèsí. I greet you. And welcome you to Ìjẹ̀kùn Odò.

IFÁKÍYÈSÍ: I greet you too. As soon as I was told you wanted to see me, I came. I knew your father well.

ADÉLÙ: Did you like him? My father... I mean?

IFÁKÍYÈSÍ: I knew him well. He had great spirits, and he could never hide his feelings. Even the gods did not understand him well. And when the gods do not understand a man, they take him away to live with them for a while. But who are we to understand a man? I am sorry my prince.

ADÉLÙ: Me too. Bàbá… I am in search of the reason my father died so suddenly. He still lies in his room unburied.

IFÁKÍYÈSÍ: Why do you search for tears? Each man his own head. Each head, his own destiny. Let him be. He has done his own. Search instead for a better tomorrow.

ADÉLÙ: I greet you Bàbá. I want to know…

IFÁKÍYÈSÍ: You want to know if Pègúnrun lived?

ADÉLÙ: Er… yes.

IFÁKÍYÈSÍ: Yes… she did. Your forefathers were afraid of the coming of the white men and their funny ways. They did not want wars or slavery in their land. The gods had wanted a total wipe out of Ìjẹkùn Odò. To avoid this calamity, Pègúnrun gave herself up as sacrifice.

ADÉLÙ: So, she lived?

IFÁKÍYÈSÍ: Some truths sound like stories when told for a long time. Pègúnrun's tale is like one of them now. She was real, I swear!

ADÉLÙ: I know what happened that day.

IFÁKÍYÈSÍ: I know. She has come to see you. She must have told you that night.

ADÉLÙ: How do you know she came?

IFÁKÍYÈSÍ: I know Kábíyèsí. You would not have sent for me, if you did not believe what you saw. Even now I feel her presence.

ADÉLÙ: Me too. One thing she did not tell me was what happened at the shrine of Ọbàtálá.

IFÁKÍYÈSÍ: From the mouths of my fathers, she told Ọbàtálá to grant her a return to earth after a hundred years. Ọbàtálá out of a sense of pity granted her wish. This year is a hundred years since she gave up her life for the people of Ìjẹkùn Odò. She wants to return home to rest, joined together once again after such a long time. This is why she will not forgive anyone who stands in her way. Your late father did.

ADÉLÙ: And see what happened to him. What does she want with me now?

ÌYÁ: Her dance.

IFÁKÍYÈSÍ: Dance for her.

ADÉLÙ: Me? Dance for a woman who killed my father?

ÌYÁ: Dance for here, Ọbalọ́la and end all these mysteries.

IFÁKÍYÈSÍ: Yes. Adorn yourself in her clothes, and dance for her. Accept her choice and dance for her Kábíyèsí, and all will be well. The birds of Ìjẹkùn Odò will chirp like birds, and the rats will run wild and eat, and burrow like rats. Ifá has spoken.

ADÉLÙ; Why? A woman…

IFÁKÍYÈSÍ: Do not make the mistake of your father Kábíyèsí. A woman is the pot of life. Men lick her to live but take her for granted. If a man breaks his pot, then he is finished. If the fluttering birds do not punish him, the spirt of the woman will. Save your people Kábíyèsí.

ADÉLÙ: Save my people. I do not understand.

IFÁKÍYÈSÍ: Why do you want to understand everything? Even the sky does not understand why the earth is so near and yet so far from it. What else do you want to know Kábíyèsí?

ADÉLÙ: ÒTÚN GOES TO WHISPER INTO HIS EAR. Yes. I have another problem Bàbá. Just one. Another claims the throne of Pègúnrun.

ÒTÚN: Yes Bàbá. A woman. From the family of Pègúnrun. She says that she is the rightful choice. She hides the real Òṣùgbó.

ADÉLÙ: My problem, is who do we enthrone as the new Ìyálóde.

ÌYÁ: One. The true one. Abídèmí.

IFÁKÍYÈSÍ: Is she here? The one who claims what she is not?

ADÉLÙ: I don't know. But the choice of the family is here.

ÌYÁ: Yes.

IFÁKÍYÈSÍ: Wait! I smell the two Òṣùgbó's in this room. One is new.

ÌYÁ: Given to me at the shrine. The other is a hundred years old. The one Pègúnrun, our mother wrapped round herself until she died. It was used to cover her feet as he was placed on her bed. We cannot find it now. And without it, the story is incomplete.

IFÁKÍYÈSÍ: TO NO ONE IN PARTICULAR. Woman why do you clutch what is not yours? You delay the arrival of the spirit. NO ANSWER. Answer woman.

ADÉLÙ: Do you speak with me Bàbá?

IFÁKÍYÈSÍ: No. Her. Death beckons, and the fool dances, her feet more nibble than they were when she was sane. Woman why do you clutch at the apron strings of death so willingly? Even if Èṣù dances with you, can't you see that he is ten steps ahead of you. All you see is his shadow. LOOKS UP. Há hà há! This fool is set to die. Speak woman.

JOWÚQLÁ: STRUGGLES WITHIN HERSELF. BUT LETS IT OUT. She gave me Bàbá.

IFÁKÍYÈSÍ: Who gave you woman?

JOWÚQLÁ; My late sister Títí Àgbà. The last Ìyálóde. On her death bed. She gave it to me. Take this, she said. It is yours, and then her eyes closed. In tears, I collected it, and it became mine.

ÌYÁ: Yours. Liar!

ADÉLÙ: ÌYÁ please.

IFÁKÍYÈSÍ: Are you not the eldest woman in the family?

JOWÚQLÁ: I am Bàbá. But...

IFÁKÍYÈSÍ: Then why did you reduce your age to play childhood pranks? Jealousy and envy thrive in the blood of a woman. You hated the youth of Abídèmí, and so you wanted to take away her shine which Olódùmarè had given her. As you kept her glory, you angered Pègúnrun. The end might be painful.

JOWÚQLÁ: Bàbá you reduce me.

IFÁKÍYÈSÍ: Why did you do it? What other reason is there?

JOWÚQLÁ: What?

IFÁKÍYÈSÍ: So if and when she said, take this, she could have also meant as the eldest woman in the family, take this and give it to the rightful owner when she arrives?

JOWÚQLÁ: Yes Bàbá... but I know what I heard. LOOKING AT ÒṢÌNNÚSÌ. He was there.

ÒṢÌNNÚSÌ: Yes.

JOWÚQLÁ: In her eyes, I saw a passover of love. She pleaded with me to take up the mantle of spiritual leadership. I could not but accept it. With humility of course.

ÌYÁ: Of course. Yèyé foamed in the mouth with anger. I warned her, but her ears were stuffed.

JOWÚQLÁ: Stuffed?

IFÁKÍYÈSÍ: See them... dangling on the pendulum of death.

ÒṢÌNNÚSÌ: JOWÚQLÁ!

IFÁKÍYÈSÍ: Three spirits await us at the market square when the new King dances with the people. Three spirits. Who is Òṣìnnúsì?

JOWÚQLÁ: He. POINTS TO ÒṢÌNNÚSÌ. My eldest brother. And the Olórí ẹbí of the family.

ADÉLÙ: Òṣìnnúsì... you heard your sister's claim.

ÒṢÌNNÚSÌ: Yes Kábíyèsí.

IFÁKÍYÈSÍ: Here is the he-goat of the sacrifice. Where is the Òṣùgbó? That is all she needs for the final transformation into being. Yèyé approaches, and your delay angers her.

ÒṢÌNNÚSÌ: With her Bàbá. The Òṣùgbó is with her. SLOWLY JOWÚQLÁ BRINGS OUT THE ÒṢÙGBÓ. ÌYÁ SNATCHES IT FROM HER, AND TIES IT ROUND THE WAIST OF ABÍDÈMÍ. AS IF IN A TRANCE, ABÍDÈMÍ NOW AS PÈGÚNRUN, WALKS TO ADÉLÙ.

PÈGÚNRUN: Kábíyèsí Adélù unveil me, and let me breath one more time.

IFÁKÍYÈSÍ: Do I hear Yèyé's voice?

ADÉLÙ: Yèyé kẹ?

ÌYÁ: Unveil her Kábíyèsí. Hurry!

ADÉLÙ: UNVEILS HER. It is you.

PÈGÚNRUN: Yes, me. I told you that we shall meet soon.

ADÉLÙ: And the leaves are still blowing from the moist grave?

PÈGÚNRUN: Not anymore. Not for now. The dead have crossed the threshold. I have returned.

IFÁKÍYÈSÍ: It is done then. My task here is done. Yèyé has returned.

ÌYÁ: VERY HAPPY. Yes.

PÈGÚNRUN: WALKS SLOWLY TO FACE JOWÚQLÁ AND ÒṢÌNNÚSÌ. You both tarried with death for a while. Are you still ready to go? Your brother Òwọmidà waits for you at the crossroads. RAISES HER TWO HANDS.

ỌSÌNNÚSÌ: Yèyé forgive your children.

ÌYÁ: HURRIES TO HER. Not again Yèyé. I have seen you snuff lives with those two hands. A mother remembers only the empty gaping mouth of a suckling child. I beg you.

PÈGÚNRUN: Ọba Adélù. It is your palace. What do I do? These three soil my blood. Their heart darkened... they led the dance of shame against the honour of my spirit. Pronounce!

ADÉLÙ: I beg you.

IFÁKÍYÈSÍ: Mother. Children are born to err. It is their right. Forgiveness and compassion is the cross of motherhood. We know you are a goddess...but when we turn to Èṣù and he sets in motion a music to our ears... our feet refuse to listen to our hearts... we dance until we fall into the deep sides of the river. Ẹ jèbùrẹ́, awo olùgbẹ́bẹ̀... Yèyé Ìlú.

ÌYÁ: Do you hear us?

JOWÚỌLÁ: Forgive us Yèyé. Till death... we shall allow no stray thoughts into our hearts again. This is the work of Láàlú, who dangled the deceitfully sweet àgbálùmọ̀ before our biddy eyes.

ADÉLÙ: Mother... we have waited a hundred years. Forgive them. Remember... this is my palace you said earlier. Forgive them.

PÈGÚNRUN. PONDERS FOR A WHILE. Rise fools. No more bloodshed. It is enough!

JOUWOLA AND ỌSÌNNÚSÌ: Thank you Yèyé.

IFÁKÍYÈSÍ: You see? Sweetness of love shall return to the land of Ìjẹ̀kùn Odò. Blinded once you see now. Your mother has been with you all along, and you did not even know.

ÌYÁ: I was blind. Watching out for bigger signs to come. I thought a lone bright star will lead us once again. We even thought this time a big wide moon would fall. I thought the water of Ìjẹ̀kùn Odò would dry up leaving ẹja àrọ̀ gasping for air all alone. I never knew. I never knew she had been with us all along. And Èṣù with folded arms, ate our sacrifices and laughed at us as we danced around in circles. Bàbá pray for us.

IFÁKÍYÈSÍ: Pègúnrun we greet you.

ALL: Welcome Yèyé!

IFÁKÍYÈSÍ: The men and women of Ìjẹ̀kùn Odò will multiply this new year.

ALL: Àṣẹ!

IFÁKÍYÈSÍ: Protect all women of Ìjẹ̀kùn Odò from the trials of Èṣù. May the pregnant women deliver their children safely.

ALL: Àṣẹ!

IFÁKÍYÈSÍ: Obeisance to you Pègúnrun. Protect also the new Ọba Adélù of Ijekun Ode

ADÉLÙ RISES.

ALL: Àṣẹ!

PÈGÚNRUN: Enough! I have had enough words for now. Ọba Adélù!

ADÉLÙ: What does she want now?

PÈGÚNRUN: Ọba Adélù give me my dance. Only you for now.

ADÉLÙ: Only me? Now?

PÈGÚNRUN: Yes. Now.

ÒTÚN: Go on Ọbalọ́la. She has agreed to your becoming the new Ọba. Dance.

SLOWLY ADÉLÙ REMOVES HIS AGBÁDÁ AND CAP TO REVEAL THAT HE IS DRESSED IN THE SAME COSTUME AS THE WOMEN AND PÈGÚNRUN. THE MUSICIANS JOIN AND THE OTHER WOMEN.

ADÉLÙ: Let the dance begin. Pègúnrun has returned to her home. The village will be well again. We shall find renewed peace and development. Call the women, let them join me.

AS THE DRUMS BEAT, AND ADÉLÙ SWAYS.

SLOWLY FINAL LIGHTS FADE.

THE END

IKÚDẸTÌ

Dramatis Personae

YÈYÉ ỌBA
OLORÌ KÉKERÉ
ÒṢÙGBÓ
OLÚÁWO
ÌYÁ MỌ̀PÓ
ADÍFÁLÀ
ẸLẸ́ṢIN
JAGÙNNÀ
IKÚ BÀBÁYÈYÉ
ỌBA ARÁBÁMBÍ IKÚDẸTÌ ÀJÀNTÁLẸ́
ỌBA AGÚNLÉJÌKÁ ÀJÀNTÁLÉ
CHANTER
DANCERS, SINGERS AND DRUMMERS.

IKÚDẸTÌ

WHEN PLAY OPENS YÈYÉ ỌBA LIES ON THE MAT IN THE MIDDLE OF THE STAGE. THE BATA DRUMS ANNOUNCE THE DEATH OF KING IKÚDẸTÌ.

YÈYÉ ỌBA: WAKES UP SLOWY AS THE SLOW GBẸ̀DU DRUMS SUBSIDE. AS ÒṢÙGBÓ, A SENIOR ÌLÀRÍ OF THE PALACE IN RED DRAPED CLOTH TIED AT THE RIGHT SHOULDER, ENTERS HURRIEDLY.

ÒṢÙGBÓ: Yèyé, ignore the drums. Kábíyèsí did not die. The drums lie!

YÈYÉ: Òṣùgbó, Ìlàrí what are you doing here? I heard the dying voices of the royal drums announce the passing of the king. It is done then? Ṣé Ọba ti wàjà?

ÒṢÙGBÓ: My queen.

YÈYÉ: You hesitate Òṣùgbó. Let me repeat myself. SLOWLY. PICKS HER WORDS. Has the Ọba... my son finally joined his ancestors? Did you recut his umbilical cord as the elders taught you to? I mean where is my son as I speak?

ÒṢÙGBÓ: Dead? Still. His back turned to our cravings. His ears turned off our noises, but he remains half-dead.

YÈYÉ: Half-dead? What does all that mean? All I want to know is did he go the way of the kings before him? Through the well laid out narrow sacred backyard behind the Palace, where he and his dedicated followers will dance to the land of the dead. Did he?

ÒṢÙGBÓ: No.

YÈYÉ: Sònpònà! Which of my enemies did this? I am sure it must have been the Ògúnbádéjo Adéjowà family. They could never wait. The seven years my son reigned was like hell to them. When we danced and dined, they wept all night. So, who accompanied my son to the land of the dead? Which part of the Palace accompanied Àjàntálé Arábámbí to see his forefathers? Who did he take then... beyond his shadow... who will see my son through the three deadly worlds of the wicked spirits? Who will mind his every need? I say who?

ÒSÙGBÓ: No one. Not even the whiff of dust or the fall of the morning dew followed his shadow. He died alone and left alone. And now he looms in the darkness of the bland world alone.

YÈYÉ: Looms alone? Now you frighten me. Adániwáyé, don't sleep. Iná kò ní jó mi!

ÒSÙGBÓ: I wish I was with him to serve him as I can. But the higher forces control our steps now.

YÈYÉ: Someone should have persuaded him. Tricked him... lured him. Were the drummers not lined out? Were rich sányán and etù not displayed for him to pick from? Háà... my son has been cheated in death. Corruption has entered the palace again. No king dies alone.

ÒSÙGBÓ: Corruption? By whom? To whom? No mother!

YÈYÉ: Then why do you speak nonsense? At least did he take those who should escort him to the land of the dead along?

ÒSÙGBÓ: No. That is why I have come to see you Yèyé. He left the retinue behind. Not a soul.

Not even a pinch of sweet life went with him.

YÈYÉ: Then he is not dead. He was brought up to love life to death. And live life even in death. He was a king, not an ordinary man. Then why do you want to visit the misfortune of the poor on a king? Speak in the language of our people. The language I will understand Òṣùgbó. How did my son die? We cannot punish you for the incomplete death of my son. Go on Òṣùgbó... Tell me that he lives. Tell me that this was all a joke.

ÒṢÙGBÓ: Ìyá wa, I saw him. I saw his pelted lips freeze. I saw his limbs... stretched. I saw the last wind of air exhale from his lungs. Now he lies set in death. Nothing moves. He is dead mother. He left alone.

YÈYÉ: I should have known this would happen yesterday.

ÒṢÙGBÓ: What Yèyé?

YÈYÉ: It was at the market, as I bought things for the celebration that would have happened today. The blind beggar's child kept pulling at my dress. It was a boy begging for me to carry her. Why, I asked myself. These beggars are dirty, I kept telling myself. So, when he persisted, I spanked him. Asked my slaves to drag them out of my sight.

ÒṢÙGBÓ: Hà! Ìyá. The Olúáwo told you to show kindness to everyone to help ease Kábíyèsí's path.

YÈYÉ: How was I to know that the woman was a witch. I fell into her trap, now she rubs her bad luck all over me.

ÒṢÙGBÓ: Yèyé, I think what has happened is beyond a blind witch and her poor son.

YÈYÉ: These things are linked Òṣùgbó. I did not help her son. So, who will protect mine in that deadly world of the dead? Without a mother. Who?

ÒṢÙGBÓ: I say this is why I have come. In four hundred years… this has never happened. I was born to follow him as the most senior Ìlàrí, it was my job also to follow him to the land beyond. But I am here.

YÈYÉ: How about the Ẹlẹ́ṣin?

ÒṢÙGBÓ: His task is to serve him… cater for his little needs, beyond. But he too lives. That is why we have come to ask you about what we have to do.

YÈYÉ: Ask me? About what? A feast made for men suddenly turns sour because of the dirty hands, now they search for wisdom from an old woman.

ÒṢÙGBÓ: Yèyé… maybe it is all a matter of destiny. Maybe he was born to die that way. His death has defied all ritual preparations.

YÈYÉ: Á yángà ẹnu rẹ! May destiny strike you like a spear straight into your damned heart. CHUCKLES. Òṣùgbó sometimes, 1 wonder if you are really worth every strand of grey hair on your aged head. Òmùgọ̀. Sometimes I wonder if indeed Ikú Bàbáyèyé ò, Ògìgídí Ọkùnrin really passed through your house before coming to the palace to take him.

ÒṢÙGBÓ: He did Yèyé. Three steps to the left and three feet to the right… head bent, still holding his kùmọ̀ on one hand, and the head of the owl of death in his right… he came to my house. I waited. I was supposed to be the first to die. I picked the two best drummers and the chief chanter to follow us. Dead, we were now to dance to the palace to take him. But death came as he was supposed to, danced in front of my house. We slept deeper. From a distance we thought we followed him, until the morning sun set, and we found death had fooled us.

YÈYÉ: You saw him, and he did not take you? Instead, he took my poor son.

ÒṢÙGBÓ: Yes.

YÈYÉ: Do you know what I was expecting to do this morning? Like custom demands, wake up, cry, pray and eat a little. Wear great clothes and then take my new position as the eldest and most respected mother of the village. When I was told that the gods would allow my son to rule for only seven years, I cried at first, then I was told that I would live beyond him, pampered, in royal splendor, I stopped my tears. But do you know what has been happening all day since you woke me up?

ÒṢÙGBÓ: No Yèyé.

YÈYÉ: Nothing. Sacrilege! A good mother should not rest. Àbí?

ÒṢÙGBÓ: No. And like you elders say, the filth of the child is the smell of the mother.

YÈYÉ: Um?

ÒṢÙGBÓ: Er... I am sorry.

MUSIC AS A RETINUE OF PEOPLE ENTER, RUNNING TOWARDS YÈYÉ ỌBA.

YÈYÉ: And who are these imbeciles? From which dark crevice have they emerged? Ìgbàyí làárọ̀! Human ghosts who are determined to mingle with the living, turning up for the leftovers of the world. Èèwọ̀! I shall not dance with those presumed dead. Each time the sun rises, it will not bring them light, but darkness. TURNS HER BACK ON THEM. What do you want from me, you shameless beings? My heart and my head are in conflict and this world is beginning to lose its meaning.

Away from me! Ó yá! Ẹ parẹ́!

OLORÌ KÉKERÉ: ON HER KNEES. Forgive me Yèyé. I drank the portion and laid still by his side. I waited, then a cool breeze blew and I slept off. When I woke up, Kábíyèsí laid still, his eyes open. He had left me alone.

YÈYÉ: Indeed, I see you are dressed, but not for the occasion we dressed you for. What do you still want?

OLORÌ KÉKERÉ: I am still ready to go and meet my husband. Help me.

YÈYÉ: And you Ẹlẹ́ṣin, you make me want to throw up all over your face.

ẸLẸ́ṢIN: You can do more than that and I will gladly live, rejoice and dance. I stayed awake by the footsteps of Kábíyèsí.

YÈYÉ: Yes… and what happened?

ẸLẸ́ṢIN: I saw it come.

YÈYÉ: What came?

ẸLẸ́ṢIN: Death. Ikú approached us angry. He ignored me and Olorì Kékeré, grabbed Kábíyèsí by the hand. I saw a small struggle, and then he went limp.

YÈYÉ: Who went limp?

ẸLẸ́ṢIN: After a gentle touch of his forehead. Kábíyèsí rose and followed Ikú. That was when I got confused.

YÈYÉ: Confused?

ẸLẸ́ṢIN: The person Kábíyèsí followed was a woman.

OLORÌ KÉKERÉ: Ẹlẹ́ṣin I swear if you lie, I will kill you myself. How can Kábíyèsí facing death, still follow a woman somewhere. To where? Where is sweeter than this life?

ẸLẸ́ṢIN: I am sorry, but that was what I saw. But what happened at the break of dawn was unbelievable.

YÈYÉ: What you say torture me.

ẸLẸ́ṢIN: The three elders came in with torches… it was then we noticed that the dead Kábíyèsí did not die.

YÈYÉ: He did not die. How? The drums said…

OLORÌ KÉKERÉ: Never mind what the drums said Ìyá. When I awoke and saw Kábíyèsí still. I screamed… Bàbá lọ! Kábíyèsí wàjà. And the drummers started beating the drums to announce his death.

ẸLẸ́ṢIN: When the elders came with Òṣùgbó Ìlàrí, they found him breathing, still, but dead. As if death changed his mind. As if death returned half of him to us. And took away his leftovers.

OLORÌ KÉKERÉ: We tried everything to wake him up. I even tried…

ẸLẸ́ṢIN: Olorì Kékeré, not everything must come out of your mouth. That was when Òṣùgbó was asked to call you. Bàbá Awo had arrived, and between Bạbá Awo and Apènà, it was agreed that you may be able to find a cure.

YÈYÉ: A cure? Me? How? I am just an old woman.

OLÚAWO: Yèyé, we are sorry that the rains did not fall as we expected.. The rivers dried unexpectedly. The impossible happened, so we turned back to the source.

YÈYÉ: The source? It is that bad?

OLÚAWO: Yes. Kábíyèsí has not joined his ancestors. We need you. TURNS TO THE RETINUE. Go to your different rooms. We must find a way to resolve this. You will be informed. THE RETINUE LEAVE. You follow me Yèyé Ọba.

YÈYÉ: To where?

OLÚAWO: Too see the wonders of Èṣù ọdàrà. Only he could have done this. Only Ẹlẹ́gbárá can dance leaving half of a king behind.

YÈYÉ: What wondrous powers indeed.

SLOW LIGHTS AS THEY EXIT.

WHEN LIGHT RETURNS. YÈYÉ ENTERS WITH OLÚÁWO. IKÚDẸTÌ LIES ON THE BED. HE IS COVERED WITH A RED CLOTH. HE DOES NOT MOVE, GRUNT OR SPEAK THROUGHTOUT THE SCENE.

OLÚÁWO: Enter. Here lies our once great king. YÈYÉ MAKES TEARFUL NOISES. Not a teardrop. Not a sound. I shall return.

OLÚÁWO TURNS AND LEAVES YÈYÉ BEHIND.

YÈYÉ: RUNS TO THE BED. SHE KNEELS BY THE BED. Arábámbí Àjàntálẹ́ Ẹnìtàn Ikúdẹtì. Why do you lie so still? What have they done to you? Who dares to turn you into a stone effigy. Who? Speak to me. This is your mother Ìfẹ́dayọ̀ Àbẹ̀bí... I am here. Where are you son? PAUSE. How can loneliness and sadness envelope you in my time? What audacity! See how they have crippled my once lively son and turned him into a stuffed doll fit for children to play with. PAUSE. Arábámbí... sleep gently son for it was my fault. I looked elsewhere while they came and scattered my trap, and I shall now go home with nothing... not even a bush rat. I was the one who went to the backyard to play, while my treasure was stolen. I swear I shall remedy this. Your mother will give you the vigour to rise again and be your old self. Nothing will touch you now. Not even when the moon refuses to shine, not when the sun refuses to set. Nothing can stop me. Nothing. Sleep well, until I return. ENTER OLÚÁWO. What did you say I have to do to save my son?

OLÚÁWO: Go to the world of the dead and speak to Ikú. Beg him to forgive your son, and Kábíyèsí will rise without a scratch. Not a thing more. Will you go?

YÈYÉ: Why are women born with such ill luck? Why must they carry even the crosses of their son... all in the name of motherhood? Now all his wives are gone and since I am the mother, I shall carry him one more time. Wash his vomit from my body, and his shit from his anus. Here I am Olúáwo. I am ready to suffer once again.

OLÚÁWO: Yèyé, be strong.

YÈYÉ: I was born strong. All women are.

OLÚÁWO: You will go then?

YÈYÉ: I say, I will.

OLÚÁWO: Then prepare yourself to go.

YÈYÉ: I am always prepared. I feared this would happen, so I told my servants to come. It will be a long and tedious journey, so I asked them to prepare. SHE CLAPS HER HANDS.

A RETINUE OF SLAVES WITH HUGE BOXES COME ON STAGE SINGING

Ibi tí Ìyá bá rè là ń lọ
Ẹ yàgò fún Yèyé Ọba
Ibi tí Yèyé bá ń lọ, là ń lọ.

OLÚÁWO: VISIBLY ANGRY. Who are these, Yèyé?

YÈYÉ: Royal Escorts. Those to remind me constantly of my sweet life. They carry water, food... the type a king's mother should eat... and my soft matress and pillow. And of course, the many sányán and aṣọ òkè clothes to be more regal when I meet and dine with the gods! ÒṢÙGBÓ is the antelope meat well-seasoned the way I like it?

ÒṢÙGBÓ: Soft and tender. The way you like it. I am sure the gods will lap it up.

YÈYÉ: Good.

ÒṢÙGBÓ: And the laundry man brought the new aṣọ òkè beaten and tender. I have picked the best. The gods will be so impressed. On your looks alone they will release Kábíyèsí to you. Ta ní tó yájú sí Yèyé? Èèwọ̀! Tani to lodi si Yèyé? Aṣọ òkè!

OLÚÁWO: Òṣùgbó Ìlàrí panu dé. These are the deceitful songs that led us to the state we are in now. ANGRY. Woman are you ready?

YÈYÉ: Here ready as always, Olúáwo. But wait I see anger on your brow. Why?

OLÚÁWO: This trip... the trip we talked about is not one of seasoned meals or change of clothes. It is a ritual trip of life. Are you ready woman?

YÈYÉ: I am sorry. Ó yá ẹ jáde. Clear the room. I shall send for the ones I need soon. Go out for now. THE RETINUE LEAVE THE ROOM. I am sorry Olúáwo.

OLÚÁWO: Yèyé... this is serious. What do you want from me before you leave?

YÈYÉ: Nothing. I have questions to ask.

OLÚÁWO: Ask them when you get to where you are going.

YÈYÉ: Thank you. But I need an acolyte for this trip.

OLÚÁWO: Call the supreme friend of all men. Call Láàlú ògiri òkò!

YÈYÉ: Èṣù láàlú! Come and let us go. There is fried àkàrà on the stone top of your shrine, there is palm oil on the stone top of your shrine. Come with me. Be with me and let us be one. Let shame not be my cloak. TURNS TO OLÚÁWO I am ready.

OLÚÁWO: Good, but before you go, remember that if you return without appropriate answers to our question concerning Kabiyesi, the kingmakers will have to take his life as the elders have taught us. Do you understand?

YÈYE: Yes. But I assure you, I will return with positive answers. Nothing will happen to my son. I am his mother... I should know best.

OLUAWO: Good Then say after me. And when we finish, you shall embark on the trip. Wear this. HE GIVES A BEADED BANGLE. The spirits will be able to see you and help you, when they see the beaded bangle. And it will bring you back here to the palace when your task is accomplished. Hit your left foot when we finish this incantation. CLEARS HIS THROAT. Now repeat after me.

Ìrìnàjò, mo dé,
Ìrìnàjò mo fẹ́ lọ.
Orí gbé mi pàdé aláwo're .
Agbe gbé mi lọ sí ibi tí mo fẹ́ rè.
Now!

YÈYÉ HITS HER LEFT FOOT, SHARP LIGHTS GO. THE STAGE IS DARK WHILE MUSIC PLAYS.

WHEN LIGHTS COME ON YÈYÉ ỌBA IS SEATED ON A STOOL, AND BÀBÁ ADÍFÁLÀ SITS ON THE MAT. ADÍFÁLÀ CONSULTS THE ỌPẸ̀LẸ̀.

YÈYÉ: Démọkẹ́ sat, hands set. My eyes fixed. I was not going to let it happen to me... so I kept my eyes wide open Bàbá. I was the daughter of a poor family and I had sworn when my mother died of hunger that I was going to live beyond her. I would rob my lips with honey and pierce my feet with crooked stones in the farm. Démọkẹ́ was going to be Ẹlẹ́ṣin after his father, so I gave him my heart.

ADÍFÁLÀ: And then what did the bright future Ẹlẹ́ṣin boy do?

YÈYÉ: My feet tightly entwined, he climbed down, hissed and left the room.

ADÍFÁLÀ: But here within the cleavage of the hidden rocks, Ifá shows me movements of lovers. The truth woman.

YÈYÉ: You see too much Bàbá. These are secrets of the palace. Every palace has a secret.

ADÍFÁLÀ: I know. But every palace secret reflects the happenings within such a palace. Tell me the truth, Ìyá, and let the gods decide. You wanted answers, so answer the questions first.

YÈYÉ: The truth Bàbá is bitter, and heavy.

ADÍFÁLÀ: Say it.

YÈYÉ: Alright, it was before you treated my late husband of his impotence, he could not impregnate a woman.

ADÍFÁLÀ: Háà... but you had a child.

YÈYÉ: Six years after, Bàbá. I waited to take in, but the child would not come. Woo it would come in, wáà it would wash out the next morning. Not an egg remained to do the job.

Ajagùnnà had just become king, as the young Olorì, I had to bless my king, or else my head would leave my neck.

ADÍFÁLÀ: So you did it?

YÈYÉ: Yes. It was for the honour of the throne.

ADÍFÁLÀ: Ẹléṣin did not hiss or close the door. He took what you gave him.

YÈYÉ: Bẹ́ẹ̀ ni Bàbá.

ADÍFÁLÀ: And you became pregnant?

YÈYÉ: Yes.

ADÍFÁLÀ: So, your son Àjàntálẹ́ was not the son of his father. He was the son of Ẹléṣin.

YÈYÉ: Er… yes… no. It was for the honour of the throne Bàbá. What else do you seek? Ask Ifá. But a woman always knows who owns the child. But right now I am confused. What matters is that he became a king after his father. Àbí?

ADÍFÁLÀ: Ifá I thank you. Um CHUCKLES. Kí lò ń wá ká? A son behaves like the father and you say he does not resemble the house where he was born. What happened to Ẹléṣin Àdèlé? The truth I beg you, Yèyé.

YÈYÉ: He died an untimely death.

ADÍFÁLÀ: Untimely death, indeed. He was poisoned.

YÈYÉ: Then why am I here if you know everything.

ADÍFÁLÀ: Ìyá!

YÈYÉ: Yes.

ADÍFÁLÀ: By whom?

YÈYÉ: I poisoned him. This time it was for the honour of the king.

ADÍFÁLÀ: Um Ifá you are so eloquent today. This was why he asked you why you came for the answers you know. CHUCKLES. You poisoned Ẹlẹ́ṣin Àdèlé?

YÈYÉ: I did. This time for my honour. He leaked our secret to Balógun Abógunlóko. I warned him. Then he started to make demands. He wanted our little game to continue.

ADÍFÁLÀ: He wanted another child from you. His only child had died when a tree fell on him.

YÈYÉ: Yes. I could not continue. I got my sister to marry him. But she had six daughters. Three set of twins like our mother. So he wanted his son back. Aṣọ òkè! Who would give a prince to a common Ẹlẹ́ṣin?

ADÍFÁLÀ: You refused vehemently.

YÈYÉ: Yes. It was wise to refuse. That was when he started to undermine the king. My dear husband. I could take any form of insult, but not my husband.

ADÍFÁLÀ: How?

YÈYÉ: He refused to go to war with the people of Ìrẹ̀sì. Or he would go to war and refuse to bring the tributes to the palace.

ADÍFÁLÀ: He died suddenly. How?

YÈYÉ: I... I killed him. This time for my son? On his own after a little brawl at the market square with Ajagun Apáòkági, he woke up the next morning and killed every member of Apáòkági's family. First, he fled, then he ran to me. Nothing is ever right or wrong in love. I had to kill him.

ADÍFÁLÀ: Apáòkági.

YÈYÉ: He was my lover. He replaced Ẹléṣin in my body. But Ẹléṣin owned my heart. Men are foolish. They never know when to draw the line between common sense and danger when it comes to women. I knew that one day they would carry their brawl to the palace.

ADÍFÁLÀ: And your husband the king?

YÈYÉ: He too died.

ADÍFÁLÀ: How?

YÈYÉ: First the gods killed him.

ADÍFÁLÀ: And then after the gods nudged him...

YÈYÉ: I killed him after he married my sister's daughter. What was he looking for? He had twelve wives already. I was a mother to that girl. I could imagine it, he plunging both of us at his pleasure. Then one day on top of me he called me her name. It was enough. No woman can take that. My stomach turned, and hatred brewed. So I paid Apènà to do away with him.

ADÍFÁLÀ: How did he die?

YÈYÉ: Apènà lacerated his head with poison as he prepared him for the Ojúmọ́ festival. He dried up in his sleep... not a trace. I killed him for me.

ADÍFÁLÀ: And when he died, you enthroned your son Àjàntálẹ́ Arábámbí as king. You laced him with so much power; he thought he was Ikú himself.

YÈYÉ: Yes.

ADÍFÁLÀ: You enthroned him within a pool of blood. So he lived a life of excesses, he played a game of survival with death and met a shameful end. A death stripped of the honour of an Ọba's death an empty death fit only for the son of a common Ẹlẹ́ṣin. A bastard son. Ọmọ òfò, ló kúkú òfò.

YÈYÉ: Why do you speak so harshly of my son? Was I wrong? Am I wrong to have been a mother? My child came first. I did everything to protect him. I am a woman. All I did was for the future of my son. Now like you, they all condemn him. They say he was a wicked soul. But he was a child. My only child. I see the soiled hands of jealous enemies in this. That is why I am here Bàbá, to find out what and who killed my poor son?

ADÍFÁLÀ: Ikú... Death.

ADÍFÁLÀ: I know it is death. Where do I meet him? I love my son. I am his mother. I must save him.

ADÍFÁLÀ: To the two worlds between life and death then. Only Ikú who took him, can release him now. But to which world will he be released. Ifá says there is no reason to bother.

YÈYÉ: No reason kẹ́? Not even death can stop me.

ADEFILA: Mother, did you check the àkọsẹ̀jayé of your son, when he was born?

YÈYÉ: Awo said he was going to be great.

ADEFILA: Then he did not tell you the secrets of the revelation. It is here. Ifá says he should enjoy how he wants, he should live how he wants to, because he is a man who goes to the market wàrà wàrà... a turmoil, and leaves in the haze of a whirlwind. A man who walks without watching his back will fall. That is why he fell. Do you remember now? Or have you forgotten? Did you forget, woman?

YÈYÉ: No. But I thought I could help.

ADÍFÁLÀ: Help who? Man or god? You should have listened to what Ifá said, but no... you decided to play god. Àbí?

YÈYÉ: HESISTATES. No... but this is not the empty hand of life Bàbá. I see envy here. A common chicken cannot throw away my food, and still live. I want a pint of blood.

ADÍFÁLÀ: Alright then... you have started well. Continue through the backyard of life. The same route Ọba Arábámbí took accompanied by death away from here. It will be a tedious journey Yèyé Ọba... go home and cry out the remaining tears in your eyes.

YÈYÉ: No! Even now my motherly nipples ache. But all the past which you now eloquently dig, I made sacrifices to wash my hands and head from the aftermaths.

ADÍFÁLÀ: Yes. but you and the late Olúáwo forgot that blood does not wash away that easy, it leaves stains in the cleft of little fingers. It is part of the stains which hunt your so-called innocent son now. Go home woman and forget all these ever took place. Besides, your son had a huge ego... and man's ego often offends the gods. Your son offended the gods... and the gods may have done this to teach him a lesson.

SLOWLY LIGHTS GO FADE.

WHEN PLAY OPENS, STAGE IS DARK. YÈYÉ ỌBA DANCES IN, ACCOMPANIED BY DRUMMERS. ANOTHER OLD WOMAN, RICHLY DRESSED, COMES AND STAND BY THE ENTRANCE OF THE HOUSE. SHE, ÌYÁ MỌPÓ, IS NOT IMPRESSED BY YÈYÉ ỌBA'S DANCE.

YÈYÉ: SINGS. Ìyá Mọpó mọ ohùn rẹ
Ìyá Mọpó mọ ohùn
Ohùn Ẹlẹyẹ.

ÌYÁ MỌPÓ: You can stop the charade now. We have seen these dance steps before. And what did they yield us? Ṣíọ̀!

YÈYÉ KNEELS. ÌYÁ MỌPÓ STILL UNIMPRESSED. SHE TURNS HER BACK ON YÈYÉ.

YÈYÉ: I expected a little more friendliness from the queen of the birds. I, myself, being one. Remember?

ÌYÁ MỌPÓ: Yèyé Ọba, do not let my eyes roll outwards towards you. I hear how you have gone all over the village to say that your son had been wronged. by us. Wronged Yèyé Ọba? Us?

YÈYÉ: Wronged kẹ? Aṣọ òkè! I only said…

ÌYÁ MỌPÓ: We know what you said. And we have taken our share from the basket of blame you carried everywhere in search for pity. You.

YÈYÉ: Pity kẹ?

ÌYÁ MỌPÓ: You lured us. We joined hands with you to make your son king. And after he wore the crown and became the bastion of the Òrìṣà of the village, no one could touch him. No one. Not even the birds.

YÈYÉ: Háà.

ÌYÁ MỌPÓ: He took a crowned fool of Jesters. He took us on. Then he took on death in a game of who dies first. That was when he added the name Ikúdẹtì to his other names. He even boasted that he had conquered death and called himself Gbékúdè. So when we heard last night that he died, we cheered with a sense of caution.

YÈYÉ: Háà Ìyá!

ÌYÁ MỌPÓ: Leave me alone, you great pretender. Our aims were clear to you from the start. When your mother Wúràọlá brought you to join us and to change your fortune, you knew what we stood for; Òté Owó, Òté Ọmọ and Òté Àlááfìà.

YÈYÉ: They sounded good to be until you kept asking... a goat, then a cow, and then human life. My father, my brothers, my cousins, my in-laws. It did not stop, and those who were to share the joy with me, were dwindling.

ÌYÁ MỌPÓ: That was when you decided to stab us in the back. And then you started your little game. You first placed a blame on one of us.

YÈYÉ: A blame? On who?

ÌYÁ: Me. I brought you the higher conclave after you came to my house before the first cock crow, asking for the impossible.

YÈYÉ: True.

ÌYÁ MỌPÓ: You wanted your son to be king. Your story was pathetic. We cried. We had known how difficult it was for the first wife of the King to have twenty miscarriages. We women too, and we knew what it meant not to have a child for the king, so we took pity on you. No, you say we are corrupt… and that we are liars.

YÈYÉ: Ha. They lied against me. I never said so.

ÌYÁ MỌ̀PÓ: Olori, we know what we heard. And saw how you behaved. How many princes wanted to be king?

YÈYÉ: Thirty seven

ÌYÁ MỌ̀PÓ: Because of the many contenders we had to remove, how many years did we tell you your son would reign for?

YÈYÉ: Seven.

ÌYÁ MỌ̀PÓ: Thank you, Yèyé. And those seven years, from where did I say that we will get for them?

YÈYÉ: Àwọn Òrìṣà méje.

ÌYÁ MỌ̀PÓ: Yes. The seven spirits of the land. Each gave a year, and each collected how many maidens for a year?

YÈYÉ: Five. But it was much to give.

ÌYÁ MỌ̀PÓ: Now you speak. How did we tamper with the thirty seven princes until your son was begged to become king (YÈYÉ ỌBA DOES NOT ANSWER). Answer! Has the cat stolen your tongue again? I say answer woman. How many did we blind?

YÈYÉ: Ten.

ÌYÁ MỌ̀PÓ: How many did we maim?

YÈYÉ: Ten.

ÌYÁ MÒPÓ: How many slept in their sleep? YÈYÉ ỌBA DOES NOT ANSWER. Let me remind you. Twelve. They had their smooth àmàlà paste made here on earth and collected their soup from their late forefathers in the land of the ancestors. And out of the five left whose lucky pebbles did Ifá announce as fullest enough to wear the crown?

YÈYÉ: My son's, Ìyá.

ÌYÁ MÒPÓ: And he became Ọba Àjàntálẹ́ Ẹnìtàn Arábámbí. But when he thought he had conquered the world. Did we cry?

YÈYÉ: No.

ÌYÁ MÒPÓ: What did we do?

YÈYÉ: You watched him dance like a fool, eat like a glutton and belch like an baboon to his grave.

ÌYÁ MÒPÓ: Good.

YÈYÉ: But Ìyá, a child is still a child.

ÌYÁ MÒPÓ: And a fool, a fool.

YÈYÉ: He was a fool, a big stupid one. A goat, but he was my son. Your son. I brought him here and you embraced him… remember? I hear he is only suspended between life and death. You can forgive him. Blame his sins on a poor mother and give him a second chance.

ÌYÁ MÒPÓ: Mother… the conclave of the birds can only be fools once. After Èṣù, we come second. We are senior to man on earth. So why should a man we made king call us fools. Go to him woman, let him suckle the last few drops of your withered breasts, and let him die in whatever state you find him. Go!

YÈYÉ: Háà Ìyá please… your words hurt.

ÌYÁ MỌPÓ: They should. You hurt us too. The day of the coronation was the last day we saw happiness. We danced to the palace and I was hoping that day to wear the ewé akòko on my head and I would become the Ìyálóde. But instead, he brought a crooked feet woman from the city… who was not one of us… and called her mother of the village. We hurt that day. I cried all night. I flew round the village ten times in anger, until I fell and had to be brought down by palm wine tappers in the morning. Your son hurt me… he hurt us.

YÈYÉ: Forgive us.

ÌYÁ MỌPÓ: Forgiveness is too easy a word to use here. A man who chooses to blind you easily can never be forgiven that easily. Let him bear the roast.

YÈYÉ: No. I call on the benefits of my membership. I call on a favour from one bird to another. Save my son.

ÌYÁ MỌPÓ: Too late. Go home woman. We even strip you of your wings. Go home soon the drums will beat and the husbands and children will sleep, and my acolytes will begin to perch. Go woman!

THE ÌYÁ MỌPÓ SONG CONTINUES. ÌYÁ MỌPÓ STANDS STILL. HER BACK STILL TURNED. SLOWLY YÈYÉ EXITS THE STAGE.

SLOWLY LIGHTS FADE.

WHEN THE SCENE OPENS, SOUND OF EGÚNGÚN MUSIC PLAYS. YÈYÉ ỌBA, NOW TIRED, DANCES INTO THE TO RHYTHM OF THE MUSIC.

YÈYÉ: Eégún Bàbá mi bọ́ óde!
Àwa ò kí ń ṣe Olòṣì,
Aṣọ òkè laṣọ tí a dá fÉgún.
Obìlì bílì
King of all Masquerades,
Father of us all.
It is you I call.
Flash with the speed of light
Father come out… father your daughter calls!

ỌJẸ̀, A CRUMPLED MAN, IN A WORN OUT EÉGÚN DRESS SITS ON A STOOL. HE SHAKES WITH COLD. A CHEWING STICK IN HIS MOUTH.

ỌJẸ̀: May the Gods of the land tear that mouth of yours on both sides till you cannot speak. May they tear the mouth until you cannot speak. Was that not the same song you sang when you came here with your son, begging us to take him on my back to see Ikú Bàbáyèyé, so that he could become King.

YÈYÉ: Háá Bàbá.

ỌJẸ̀: Shut that mouth and let me finish. We only asked two things from him. That he made me Odòrú of all the masquerades in the village, and secondly, that he sewed for our fathers a new gown. Look at me. See what this old fool looks like now. He deified me a full-blown clown and abandoned us.

YÈYÉ: He passed this way last night. Unsung.

ÒJẸ: He did? I was too sick to open the door. And to whom? It was a cold night. And besides, my drums are torn, and the master drummer has gone to the city to learn a better trade than waiting for the crumbs from the table of a stingy king which never came. So how did he pass without my notice?

YÈYÉ: Who, Bàbá? Your grandson?

ÒJẸ: No. Your son. The crushed king. His two feet stuck in the mud. CHUCKLES. Where was his salvation to come from? Where? He did not sprinkle cold water to wet the floor and so when it was time... the dryness of the earth was too harsh even for an eégún with nimble soft feet. Where is he now?

YÈYÉ ỌBA: Between the worlds, Bàbá.

ÒJẸ: And he shall remain there until death takes him finally. He was a bad king. And besides, it is the voice given to a mad man that he uses to portend his madness. He is the true son of his mother.

YÈYÉ: Ha... that is a stone thrown directly at me.

ÒJẸ: When I first set eyes on you as a maiden, I warned my son. This woman and her children to come will be bad for us. But no one listened. You had trapped my son with the witchcraft between your feet.

YÈYÉ: Háà Bàbá.

ÒJẸ: I told them that I did not sell pounded yam paste, so no one should make complaints on how I pounded mine. We were from the house of eégún not kings, but you were too full of ambition. See how you have ended us all. I say, see how far we went before the madness you planted, manifested.

YÈYÉ: He had only seven years Bàbá Òjè. Maybe a bit more years would have made him a better king.

ÒJÈ; Even if he had stayed a million years, he would have been a bigger worshipper of the great woman, Èṣù. CHUCKLES. Even Èṣù wondered at his manifestation. That thing... your son... I swear, he could transform into a monster in a flash. Seven years of neglect... that was all our family got... now it is all wasted.

YÈYÉ: He was not alone. Even his chiefs pushed him. Ọtún, Gbàmù the short fat toad, and Òsì, his official Tax Collector. They pushed him to the edge of the mountain. They were bad advisers.

ÒJÈ: And yàkàtà, he fell. Like a fool. I remember with tears how he made the masquerade come out to dance for the Governor. We broke tradition, and without a drop of hot drink and the black goat for the elders, we came out of the sacred grove, donned the sacred costume and danced all day. Until the costume stuck to my flesh as the threads undid each joint. The keepers of the land rejected me and cursed me. I am here on exile until death comes. Do you know he denied knowing a thing about the incidence? My own grandchild took me to the world, naked, abandoned for the rains to beat. Henceforth, nakedness shall be his cloth.

YÈYÉ: Ẹ jèbùrẹ́ Bàbá.

ÒJÈ: Between the worlds, can we even help him? If only he was dead. If only he had sewn us the new masquerade dress like we told him to. If only he had remained the grandson of a masquerade. Too many if onlys.

YÈYÉ: Bàbá.

ÒJẸ̀: CHUCKLES. I knew no drummer will play for him in death. The sound of the drums is to talk to him, persuade him to remain still... remind him of what he was... ease his feet as he climbs the ladder to the Àjà... the roof of the palace to join his ancestors.

YÈYÉ: It was the chiefs. They taught him to disregard the little things about our customs. They gave him the name Ikúdẹtì assuring him that he could defeat death in a game of fall. He allowed them to creep into his personae. It was his chiefs, Bàbá.

ÒJẸ̀: Woman!

YÈYÉ: Bàbá please.

ÒJẸ̀: I remember the jeers that day, as I swung my old bones to the tune and rhythm of the drums All of them will dance a dance of shame too. They will never find peace. The gods of the land will never smile on them. Their wives, their children will die one after the other in their very eyes. As they watch the sacred gown of the Eégúnlá wear and tear, so will their efforts in life wear and tear.

YÈYÉ: Háà Bàbá... the wound is fresh, but let patience seal the wounds.

ÒJẸ̀: Seal the wounds which still bleeds? Aṣọ òkè!

YÈYÉ: KNEELS. I call in the blood he shares with you. Ignore me. We started on a wrong foot. It will be difficult to retrace them now but forgive me all the same.

ÒJẸ̀: What do you want from me then?

YÈYÉ: Your blessings... your prayers.

ÒJÈ: Yèyé, you push me. Prayers you want? Prayers you will get then. First to his chiefs, his friends. I pray that they will misbehave in the morning... run mad in the day... and will be buried at night. All of them. TURNS TO YÈYÉ. And you... despicable woman... pity shall embrace you. Your shadow shall fall on worry. YÈYÉ RUNS OUT OF THE STAGE. You should have waited to hear your curse, you emptiness of womanhood.

SLOWLY LIGHTS FADE.

DIM LIGHTS. WHEN LIGHTS COME A BEAUTIFUL WOMAN, IKÚ ENTERS. YÈYÉ ỌBA IS LYING ON A MAT. THE MESSENGER THAT FOLLOWS IKÚ CARRIES A BASKET OF FRUITS. STANDING OVER YÈYÉ ỌBA, IKÚ SPEAKS.

IKÚ: Down the riverside, where the earth reverberates, people call my name with respect, Èṣù my sister, the only rival. But you, this woman calls me with so much impunity. Who are you?

YÈYÉ: TURNS ON THE MAT, SLOWLY SHE AWAKENS. For three days, I have waited in vain to see the one I seek. I am a mother.

IKÚ: From which world?

YÈYÉ: The one where people die.

IKÚ: People die in every world. That is why people fear Ikú, even animals run for their dear lives. A big puzzle... Why have you come to see Ikú?

YÈYÉ: My son. He hangs between both worlds. I have come to beg for a tilt.

IKÚ: A tilt to where?

Yèyé: The land of the living. SHE GETS UP ON HER KNEES. I don't want my son to die. I want him to live.

IKÚ: Why?

YÈYÉ: He is my son... the only one I have.

IKÚ: Not enough.

YÈYÉ: I love him more than anyone or anything in the world.

IKÚ: Not enough. Tell me. How old was he?

YÈYÉ: Fifty six.

IKÚ: Who was he?

YÈYÉ: A king. He had eight villages under him. He ruled mighty and strong.

IKÚ: Not important here. What did he do? How will be remembered? How many lives did he touch? Those answers will help him cross over. They will ease his way.

YÈYÉ: He was a king. He touched lives as a king. He will be remembered a king. He was my son. I know him well. I brought him up myself.

IKÚ: Were you yourself a good mother? Let me tell you. Not too long ago... Adániwáyé called me. Asked me to take a peep at the world he created. When I did, even I cried. The white garment of Adániwáyé was soaked. What is this? I asked him Man had turned the world upside down. Indeed, man had deified himself god. He would take his mother like you and cut off her head so that he would become rich. He would kill and maim others for a flimsy excuse. For a fulfilment of a desire, man would ramp and vamp, until all was destroyed. Man was no longer a beauty of Adániwáyé. He wrapped his arms around the deceitful being of Èṣù. He was now his own master, and Èṣù his ultimate companion. Man! Was your son like that woman? Or was he worse?

YÈYÉ: No. Mine was milder. He turned life, but not upside down… totally.

IKÚ: What do you want from Ikú?

YÈYÉ: STILL ON HER KNEES. SHE MOVES CLOSER. I want to meet Ikú. I want to beg him to spear my son's life.

IKÚ: CHUCKLES. Him? Who was your son?

YÈYÉ: Ọba Arábámbí Àjàntálẹ́ Ẹnìtàn Ikúdẹtì.

IKÚ: Um… I know of him.

YÈYÉ: Tell me please I beg you… tell your master to release him. Let me take him home. I will keep a better eye on him now. He will be a better man this time, and I, a better mother.

IKÚ: Too late. The dance of life is only once. As you dance round the three pillars, the lights begin to fade. No invention of man has changed that. PAUSE. Because you are a woman, I shall grant your wish, but I can say even now that the selfishness of man will prevail. LOOKS AT THE MESENGER. Give her fruits to eat. Then take her to Àjàntálẹ́. When she finishes, show her the way home.

YÈYÉ: Home?

IKÚ: Yes, home. It is good deeds which save men. Mother the nature of men is glaring, open your eyes and see. You don't need to search to be saved. You should have sat and watched the bundle of wrapped up surge unravel.

YÈYÉ: What did I know? I thought I could save my son.

IKÚ: With a lie? You forget that a poor man's wealth is his self-respect, while a rich man's wealth is how he can ride shoddy on the poor man and kill his spirit.

YÈYÉ: No one told me it was a lie... that he was a lie. They shielded the truth from me. That was why foolishly, I thought I could prove his truth.

IKÚ: If you started with a lie, then you must know that a lie is like quick sand... all plaited... all looking falsely well, but the truth has no falsity. It is plain. But it is solid like a rock.

YÈYÉ: But he is... was my son. By the gods see how I lose comprehension on what to call him. Where do I place him now?

IKÚ: Where he was born to be placed. Woman, nature's law must prevail. The day he left you, he was no longer a son... or a child

YÈYÉ: But he is. In my eyes... all I see is a child before me. Why won't people see him thus? Why?

IKÚ: No. He is a man who rose from your womb with a tinge of your blood in his veins. Let him be. He arranged the load his calabash carries. Let him bear the pain of his own stumble.

YÈYÉ: But he will fall.

IKÚ: Let him.

YÈYÉ: No! if only you know what I had to do to have him? What I had to give up to let him grow in the house of the king where everyone owned a space and a claim to the throne. If only you know. And yet in all this madness, I tried to make righteousness my guide… it was my purpose…

IKÚ: A LAUGH. Righteousness! What did you find, if you may tell?

YÈYÉ: Nothing.

IKÚ: Nothing?

YÈYÉ: Nothing. PAUSE. I needed an enemy… someone to point my crooked finger to. You must understand, it is difficult for a mother to accept defeat or accept the loss of his son so easily? I found it easier to lie to the village, than to tell the truth to myself.

IKÚ: Don't feel bad mother. Go home old woman. Your scratched feet, peeled with pain won't say a thing… they won't even say you are saved. They are just emblems of wasted efforts. Even as you speak… another life has just been born.

YÈYÉ: Your words sooth me. Thank you, kind woman. But please who are you? I could put in a good word on your behalf when I meet Ikú.

IKÚ: CHUCKLES. You came here to see Ikú… you found her.

YÈYÉ: Her kẹ? I thought he was a he! Such bold and heartless action should have been left to a rocky heart of man. I am happy though… only a woman can understand my sensitivity.

IKÚ: You will see him, I cannot dissuade you. If a true heart willingly gives up his or her life freely, I shall let him go. He will return to earth. But it must come from the being of the man.

YÈYÉ: Thank you. I will give up my soul I promise. But before I meet my son, I have a favour to ask.

IKÚ: Granted.

YÈYÉ: Háà... even before I ask?

IKÚ: Hush! Do not rush your lips. Your heart race, the beats push you. See the two men you seek first. Talk with them, and then your heart will know what you have decided.

YÈYÉ: Thank you once again. When will I meet you in my world, where I can throw a feast in your honour.

IKÚ: LAUGHS. A feast? We shall meet soon enough. Give her food... her feeble body yearns for it. Let her sleep, and the two people you want to see shall come to see you. Then you can see your son. EXIT IKÚ.

YÈYÉ SITS, AND FOOD IS SERVED.

YÈYÉ EATS.

SLOW LIGHTS FADE.

WHEN LIGHTS OPEN, YÈYÉ IS SPREAD ON THE MAT ASLEEP. LEFTOVER OF HER FOOD IS BY HER SIDE. LIGHTS MEET

CHANTER: Wà á jayé Ọba pẹ́
    Ọba Agúnléjìká Àjàntálẹ́
    Àní wà á jayé Ọba pẹ́
    Ọba tó bá tójú wa
    Tó tún hùwà dáadáa
    Á jayé Ọba lọ́run

THE DRUMMERS AND DANCERS JOIN. ỌBA AGÚNLÉJÌKÁ JOINS AND DANCES. YÈYÉ WAKES UP FROM THE SLEEP AND IS ENTHRALLED BY THE DANCE. SHE RECOGNIZES ỌBA AGÚNLÉJÌKÁ, JOINS IN THE DANCE. AT THE END OF THE MUSIC SHE KNEELS BEFORE HIM.

YÈYÉ: Kábíyèsí o.
    Ọba Agúnléjìká Àjàntálé
    Ọkọ mi o!
    K'ádé pẹ́ lórí
    Kí bàtà pẹ́ lẹ́sẹ̀

YÈYÉ: Days and nights have passed, but you remain like the last time I saw you. LOOKS AT THE REST OF THEM. All of you continue to be blessed with good health.

AGÚNLÉJÌKÁ: When one dies, one stops growing. And besides, here is more peaceful. But what we do for you Olorì Ìfẹ́bìyí? I know you did not come to dance and sing here.

YÈYÉ: Yes, I did not come to do that, Kábíyèsí.

AGÚNLÉJÌKÁ: Then what do you want? Have you exhausted the world of the living that you chase us here?

YÈYÉ: I came to see the life you live.

AGÚNLÉJÌKÁ: You have seen it. What else is there for you to see?

YÈYÉ: This is the life I wished for... and prayed for... for our son.

AGÚNLÉJÌKÁ: I have not seen him here. But I have heard of a king who hangs between both worlds.

YÈYÉ: Yes. That is him. Please Kábíyèsí KNEELS. Put in a word for him.

AGÚNLÉJÌKÁ: You see what you have done woman? You see how you have destroyed his life? I warned you. I begged you. Let the will of Adániwáyé be fulfilled in his life. But no. You had to become a life changer, a fate mover and a destiny changer. You became the goddess in your son's life. Now his life hangs.

YÈYÉ: I beg you Kábíyèsí.

AGÚNLÉJÌKÁ: LOUD LAUGH. She begs me. That was before my life ended. Kábiọ̀òsí. That was before. Now, here in this place... I live for ever in this enjoyment, I do not return. I just exist. Gúdú gúdú kì ń sẹgbẹ́ Dùndún.

YÈYÉ: I know that you are angry with me. I offended you when I took your life.

AGÚNLÉJÌKÁ: You? Are you Olódùmarè? Are you Adániwáyé? Or are you you Olùdándè? Why then do you take on the glory which is not yours to take? Offend me kẹ́? You did not kill me. It was my time, and you were used to fulfill my destiny. It was the head I picked. It was the end to the life I wanted. So do not kneel before me and wallow in self-pity. Please get up.

YÈYÉ: Kábíyèsí.

AGÚNLÉJÌKÁ: I say get up. If I knew that this was the reason why you wanted to see me, I would not have come.

YÈYÉ: How about our son?

AGÚNLÉJÌKÁ: Your son... not mine. The woman always knows... so sit down and know.

YÈYÉ: He is your loving son. At least he became king after you.

AGÚNLÉJÌKÁ: Yes, he became king after me. Do you think you made him king? When each of my thirty seven sons were born I checked their destiny. The Babaláwo said that your son was going to be king. That was àkọsẹ̀jayé. Again, you were just a tool. I swear by Odùduwà, if you had sat still, he would have been king. But again, your blood boiled and you could not wait, so you appointed yourself god.

YÈYÉ: So...

AGÚNLÉJÌKÁ: Even your trip here is not necessary. Whatever you find will not change his destiny. He was born to hang between the two worlds. Only he could have changed it. When he lived... when he could pray to Olùdáńdè. His sins are stuck now. Woman, go home. I need to dance round with my other l'Ọba l'Ọba.

YÈYÉ: But what do we do about our son?

AGÚNLÉJÌKÁ: Your son. TURNS TO HIS RETINUE. Call me Ẹlẹ́ṣin. I hear you want to see him too. THE DRUMMERS BEAT ẸLẸ́ṢIN'S CALL TUNE.

CHANTER: ẸLẸ́ṢIN,
　　Ológun Ọbańta
　　Fierce as the Leopard
　　So dance to the drums of Ṣàngó!
　　THE DRUMS CHANGE.
　　Ẹlẹ́ṣin dé
　　Olóòlù dé

AS THEY DANCE, ẸLẸ́ṢIN ENTERS. PERPLEXED. DISTURBED BY THE NOISE.

ẸLẸ́ṢIN: I do not know you. Please. Leave me alone. Why have you called me here?

AGÚNLÉJÌKÁ: Man. This woman wants to see you.

ẸLẸ́ṢIN: A woman. Me? LOOKS ROUND. I don't know anyone here.

YÈYÉ: COMES FORWARD AND HUGS HIM. Démọkẹ́, it is me.

ẸLẸ́ṢIN: I do not know this woman. Who is she?

AGÚNLÉJÌKÁ: A myth who is in search of Ẹlẹ́ṣin.

ẸLẸ́ṢIN: I am not Ẹlẹ́ṣin. I do not know of an Ẹlẹ́ṣin. I am Bádéjọlà. I leave for the world in three weeks' time. I got a new head yesterday. All the things of the past are forgotten now. I am sorry, I cannot help you.

YÈYÉ: I have come to see you about Kábíyèsí's son. You remember our story, don't you? I need help. I did not give birth to him alone. One of you must help me.

ẸLẸ́ṢIN: Son? Kábíyèsí? I say I do not know any of you here. I do not know anything about Kábíyèsí's son. I have a clean head now, no one can force me to see the gory tale of the past. Good night. EXITS.

YÈYÉ: Háà Ẹlẹ́ṣin, don't go. Wait!

AGÚNLÉJÌKÁ: You see? A king is a king, while a man is a man. And only kings can dance forever. Sleep woman, this trip was a wasted one. You gave birth to a bad child, carry him alone.
Drummers!

CHANTER: Wà á jayé Ọba pẹ́
Ọba Agúnléjìká Àjàntálẹ
Àní wà á jayé Ọba pẹ́
Ọba tó bá tójú wa
Tó tún hùwà dáadáa
Á jayé Ọba lọ́run

THE DRUMMERS BEGIN TO DRUM AND SING AS THEY DANCE OUT, LED BY AGÚNLÉJÌKÁ. YÈYÉ IS LEFT ALONE PUZZLED.

YÈYÉ: Men. See how they have cheapened me. See how they have made a failure of my virtue. Gradually I turn into a laughing jackal. Me! But I will show them that the woman is cutlass.

LIGHTS SLOWLY FADE.

WHEN LIGHTS COME ON ARÁBÁMBÍ IS SEEN BOTH HANDS TIED.BETWEEN TWO BOULDERS. HE IS IN PAIN THROUGHOUT THE SCENE.

YÈYÉ: Arábámbí Àjàntálẹ́ Ẹnìtàn Ikúdẹtì ò! Where is my son? There is darkness everywhere, and my eyes find it difficult to pick the figure that I seek. I hear grunts. Where are you son?

IKÚDẸTÌ: LIGHTS FALL BRIGHTER ON HIM. Here, mother. You came. Then indeed a mother is a goddess. Just this morning I prayed for you to come, Ìyá tó bí mi, wá rànmí ṣe ò. Obìnrin tó bí mi, wá rànmí ṣe.

YÈYÉ: I am here son. PAUSE. LOOKS AROUND. So, it is true. Son, you are here?

IKÚDẸTÌ: I am, mother. Between the boulders of sin. My skin stretches and blood flows to my eyes. The boulders were told to tear me apart.

YÈYÉ: You must know how disconcerting it was to hear and see all you did in seven years, Arábámbí. It was like a tale from a dark past. It frightened me. I stayed awake all the way here, my eyes peeled.

IKÚDẸTÌI: I am sorry mother.

YÈYÉ: For what? The disappointments of your acts are littered all over the three worlds. As I transversed the worlds, you stunk.

IKÚDẸTÌ: I am sorry mother. Èṣù, the god I chose to protect me, deserted me. And yet he led me on. Drunk, I danced until I got to the edge of the cliff unaware of the bank of Ìjẹ̀kùn Odò. He nudged me. And I fell until the water filled my lungs.

YÈYÉ: I wept son. But my tears could not wash away your despicable acts. Háà son, you hurt me. The worst king they called you. Some even dared to call you an animal. A beast. A cursed prince they sang.

IKÚDẸTÌ: Mother... even I cannot comprehend. The flush of madness was overwhelming. Power infected me mother. Indeed, I was drunk with madness. I even got enmeshed in my own vomit. It was good while it lasted... but now I know better.

YÈYÉ: It still stinks, son. All the way here it stunk. PAUSE. I offered to give my own life for yours and the elders forbade the thought. Some tried to dissuade me. Motherly madness they called it.

IKÚDẸTÌ: Did you see my grandfather Òjẹ̀?

YÈYÉ: Yes.

IKÚDẸTÌ: What did he say? Death hates me. Èṣù had deserted him too?

YÈYÉ: The man was broken. The messenger of our ancestors had become a ghost himself. I thought he was supposed to embrace me in my fall, but what I met was a shell of an ará ọ̀run.

IKÚDẸTÌ: Pity. I was his king once. And his blood flows in my veins.

YÈYÉ: I reminded him of that, but your blood had turned to gall, his ears were blocked with raw anger. He said that in your gluttony, you swallowed his sense of pity and fatherhood. PAUSE. He says that you must die, crushed by the boulders of sin.

IKÚDẸTÌ: Then, where am I now? If this is not death enough what can one call it? Beg them mother to allow me fall into the pit of hell, roast and really die this time. This agony burns and swallows me in tiny, little bits... a glow of burning pain descends.

YÈYÉ: His backyard, was full of stunted masquerades, some bow legged, some on tethered sticks ebbing magical powers. But one common thing was their tears... like Ẹ̀yọ̀ Àdìmú, they rained curses on runny noses filled with mucous. Curses... hot èpè on your cursed reign. It is a wonder that you still breathe.

IKÚDẸTÌ: Hmm...Breathe? Ìyá mi! I would have been better dead. I hurt mother. Get me out of the clutches of Ikú.

YÈYÉ: Ikú o!
Ikú dóró o!
Mo yíiká ọ̀tún,
Mo yíiká òsì
I sang until my voice cracked. He did not even turn a flip of her eye lids. I have tried...with all the strength I have, I swore, I have. But your deeds outweigh common-sense to her.

IKÚDẸTÌ: I was bad, mother.

YÈYÉ: I know. Even the toads in the river sing it. They told me. They told me even what I did not ask them. Seven years, son. Not one teeny-weeny voice stood for you, no gesture, no matter how feeble, spoke in your favour.

IKÚDẸTÌ: Did you see my maternal uncle, Ògúnbùnmi? I wanted to... the pain rises as a spirit commands it. I promised to buy him a new gun for the village hunters. But issues rose beyond my promise. Did you see him? I swear he could have persuaded Ògún to defend me.

YÈYÉ: He too said so. He was worse than your grandfather Òjẹ̀. After he disowned you, he rained pellet of curses on your cursed reign. Èpè! I ran. chased by the efficacy of his burning tongue... his smelly, rotten mouth of half broken teeth gritting, biting every word between his old shaky lips, until like arrows they aimed at my soul.

IKÚDẸTÌ: But he was my grand uncle. Does that mean a thing anymore?

YÈYÉ: Grand Uncle? CHUCKLES. Did you remember that when you beheaded his son? I say his foul mouth blackened the redness of the once shared blood he shared with you. I say, I ran.

IKÚDẸTÌ: Ran? My own mother? Olorì Kábíyèsí!

YÈYÉ: With my two feet as much sand as they could raise. His bloodshot eyes pieced my weakened heart. My mouth pumped air as I ran.

IKÚDẸTÌ: At the end, what did he say?

YÈYÉ: What could he have said that is different from what the others said? You were a bad king, he screamed. An animal, he bellowed. A brutish beast, he muttered. BEGINS TO CRY. My own son. The only child God gave me. I am finished. PAUSE. But a child is a child. And a mother... a mother. How can I save you from this pain? I asked. What little effort can I make to ease your placid pain which has remained tranquil... unruffled, still... like stagnant water? What?

IKÚDẸTÌ: Nothing.

YÈYÉ: Nothing, they too answered. Just like they said. I was livid. A king dies a useless death, and they said no remedy could be found. Even the Ìwọ̀fà said the matter was beyond their comprehension. Instead they are more interested in enthroning Adéwándé of the Ògúnbádéjọ family. There they even felt you dared the gods. The gods had said you would reign for seven years. But five attempts were made by you to eliminate every male in the Ògúnbádéjọ family. For six weeks, you kidnapped their Olori Ẹbí. Now they have visited your sin on me. I have been asked to pack out of the palace with all your children and wives before the next market day. Why, son? Why did you offend everyone?

IKÚDẸTÌ: They offended me, Màmá mi.

YÈYÉ: I say even the gods, turned their backs on you. The day I went to see the chief priest of the Ṣàngó shrine. It had drizzled in the morning. I went with gifts. I was welcomed well at first. Smiles forcing my cheeks to enlarge. Then came Olúáwo of the Ṣàngó worshippers. As I mentioned your name, thunder and lightning struck. First it struck and burnt the basket of gifts. Then, right in our midst were blasts of black stones. Ṣàngó himself made us a spot to play with. The stones flew until we ran out of the shrine. The next morning, we broke out in smallpox. Ṣàngó had spoken. Son, you hurt the world.

IKÚDẸTÌ: It was power, Màmá. The intoxication knew no boundaries. The world looked small beneath my feet.

YÈYÉ: Indeed, it did. Even the Local Government Chairman has asked for your staff of office back. We hear that as Chairman of the Committee of Ọbas, you embezzled their money. The new Ọba will not be installed until after the village has paid the money back. They threaten to seize your body and stop us from any form of burial.

IKÚDẸTÌ: Did you tell them I was really dead?

YÈYÉ: But they did not doubt us, they only want your body displayed. We were thinking of obeying their law when the Ìwọ̀fà said that the gods have decreed that your body be hung on the Ìrókò tree. Until life drops out of it.

IKÚDẸTÌ: But I know one way out, mother. He told me.

YÈYÉ: He? Who? What did he say?

IKÚDẸTÌ: If only someone who loves me solely will give up his life willingly in my place.

YÈYÉ: But old ways prepared people for this your never-ending death.

IKÚDẸTÌ I know Ọ̀sùgbó Ìlàrí, Olorì Kékeré, and even Ẹlẹ́ṣin were prepared for death. What kind of death! They were forced. That is not the type of love I speak about.

YÈYÉ: I will return and tell them what I saw the followers of Ọba Agúnléjìká did. It is fun and enjoyment for ever. They will come back with me.

IKÚDẸTÌ: No, mother. Willingly, mother.

YÈYÉ: Willingly. Without a tinge of forcefulness or compensation?

IKÚDẸTÌ: With true love.

YÈYÉ: Nobody loves a king, we only fear and respect them.

IKÚDẸTÌ: But my people deceived me. They sang songs of praise to me. Told me that I was infallible. So, I decided to take on death. We played a game of hide and seek. That was why they called me Ikúdẹtì. As death tried to trap me within its fold, I dodged... jumping from tree branch to tree branch. But when death came... I least expected. It appeared like a woman. I dropped my guard... that was when she grabbed me... tied me up and left me in pains to await your visit. For now, Ikú caught me in our game unless we can find someone.

YÈYÉ: Someone? Who can we find? Who will sacrifice his life for a daemon caught between the fangs of death? Who?

IKÚDẸTÌ: One with the spirit of motherly goodliness. A bastion of kindness of heart. There must be someone as pure as you, Ìyá mi.

YÈYÉ: Me?

IKÚDẸTÌ: Yes, you, great mother. You have gone through all the three worlds for me. Please go one step further, mother. Give me your life in exchange! And in atonement for mine, I shall be born again. I shall relive my dotted earlier world... and correct my extremities. This time I swear, Ìyá mi, I shall be more comely. I will be good, I swear! Your love will be more profound, and my reward for your sacrifice will be unprecedented. I promise, mother. For my life, dear mother, give me yours. You have lived... what else do you want? YÈYÉ ỌBA BEGINS TO PACK HER LOAD. Where do you intend to go, mother? I am still trapped between the boulders of death.

YÈYÉ: Home. Where there is a fickle of light. You will not understand, will you? I found that you are all darkness. So, you will not understand light. I must leave for home before it gets too dark and the gates are blocked.

IKÚDẸTÌ: Home, did you say? Without your son?

YÈYÉ: I have accepted that when the feet refuse to learn the dance, we stand aside and watch the ones with nimble feet do it, or jeers will follow. I shall go home and rethink this puzzle of life. Yèyé Ọba, what a jeer-full title this has become. Oh, someone take me out of here.

IKÚDẸTÌ: Motherhood begins to gather new meaning for me. This must be wickedness. Even I, a son can begin to learn to paddle my own life at this late stagehile my erstwhile kind mother watches on, then Èṣù must have his left finger in this, I am finished.

YÈYÉ: Leave Èṣù out of this. Yes, paddle on son. Loneliness and reflection may be your only salvation. Truth itself begins to gather new meanings too, even for me now. Like you, I came to the world alone. You came out of my bowels, alone. We had our lives, mother and son... alone. Now I realize we have to pass on... alone.

IKÚDẸTÌ: You sing an embittered song, mother.

YÈYÉ: The new meanings I have learnt are not of sweet songs any more. When I weaned you, I did my job. Now you are a man, so grow up son. Even in one clove tree, buds differ in the spice they yield.

IKÚDẸTÌ: Mother, your words hurt.

YÈYÉ: I am convinced now that you will never learn. It is finished here. I gave you life, but for now I shall help in taking it. Even Èṣù will find you a worthless acolyte to use.

IKÚDẸTÌ: What do you mean, mother?

YÈYÉ: I am flushed in age. You have lived yours, and I, mine. These two boulders will remain like sharp crooked stones of the great life you once lived. They will always come in your way... even when you are only remembered with scorn. So I will let them be. Here our rivers will part. You in your once over decked up royal ship, now capsized, and I, in a lowly floating canoe... hurting and healing... drifting, flowing away... down the stream... broken and alone. I shall tell Olúáwo to strangle life out of your body tomorrow. Hopefully a new and better king will be installed for Ìjẹ̀kùn Odò. As a mother, I failed with you, let another try.

IKÚDẸTÌ: No mother, please! Mother! Mother! Stay with me! Please stay!

YÈYÉ: IKÚDẸTÌ WATCHES. YÈYÉ STEP FORWARD. Ilé koko ni tagbe. SHE HITS HER LEFT LEG ON THE FLOOR. AND SHARP LIGHTS GO OFF.

SLOW DIRGE OF MUSIC PLAY. AS LIGHTS DIM SLOWLY ON THE FIGURE OF IKÚDẸTÌ.

THE END.

KÚTELÚ

Dramatis Personae

KÚTELÚ
KÁBÍYÈSÍ
OLORÌ
APÈNÀ
MÒMÓ
ÀÀRẸ
IFÁDÈYÍ
ÒTÚN
ÌYÁ MÒPÓ
ÌYÁLÓDE
PRINCE
ÌLÀRÍ

KÚTELÚ

WHEN PLAY OPENS, IT IS A DARK NIGHT.

APÈNÀ AND KÚTELÚ STAND BEFORE THE SHRINE OF ÈṢÙ.

APÈNÀ: Èṣù Láàlú ògiri òkò
Ẹbọra tí ń jẹ́ látọpa.
One with horned head.
I Apènà Ìlú has come.
I am with my son Kútelú, the hunchback of the King.
This was not how he was born.
Yes, I gave him up as Ẹlẹ́ṣin Ọba.
But the king tied his life to him, and now believes that he has conquered all the gods.
And when I mentioned you, he told me to close my rotten mouth.
He asked me who you are, and of what value will the market women price you?
I cried all night.
Let the woman in you reign Láàlú.
Do not forgive him.
Let his soul burn a thousand years.
When I tried to caution him, he slapped me.
To crown it all he sent me with this àdí for you.
And when I tried to caution him, he slapped me again.
POURS THE ÀDÍ ON THE SHRINE.
I beg you Láàlú,
Show him what you can do. His people reject him… and he says what can they do?
I say show him what you can do.
Turn his royal household to the catacomb of hell.
Let doubts and shame be their new toga.
I have given you the message of the king.

I am not your enemy, he is the one.
EMPTIES THE ÀDÍ. Have more of his àdí, and in anger, choke him.
KÚTELÚ: Father, a moment. TURNS TO THE SHRINE. Èṣù, my hunch back tells my tale of bitterness. You know all. Everything has been taken from me. Return them in ten folds. Give me the cunny strength to avenge my shame, and I shall return to glorify you.

SLOWLY LIGHTS FADE.

IT IS A DARK NIGHT. ABỌRẸ̀, ÌYÁLÓDE, AND KÚTELÚ, A HIDEOUS HUNCHBACK STAND. CLOSE TO THEM IS KÁBÍYÈSÍ. IN A HORSE SHOE, THEY STAND, WITH A MORTAR TURNED UPSIDE DOWN AND A BROOM ON TOP OF THE MORTAR'S BOTTOM. ÌLÀRÍ BRINGS OLORÌ ÌWÀTÁYỌ̀, WHOSE FACE IS BLACKENED, SHE WEARS A BLACK WRAPPER, AND COVERS HER HEAD WITH A TORN RAG. ÌLÀRÍ TAKES HER TO THE MORTAR, UPON WHICH SHE STANDS.

ABỌRẸ̀: STEPS FORWARD. KÁBÍYÈSÍ!

KÁBÍYÈSÍ: Continue. The moon moves. What has to be done must be done.

ABỌRẸ̀: STEPS TOWADS THE MORTAR. Olorì Ìwàtáyọ̀, you stand on the highest level of oath taking in our land. The gods of the land are our witnesses here. You know why you are here? ÌWÀTÁYỌ̀ NODS, SOBBING. Do you still want to go on with the oath? ÌWÀTÁYỌ̀ NODS. Kábíyèsí?

KÁBÍYÈSÍ: Do what you have to do Abọrẹ̀. If after the rain has beaten her, she still wants to swear that all day she stayed under the shade, to avoid the dry sunshine, then let what will happen to her, happen. Death is what she has chosen to embrace.

ÌYÁLÓDE: STEPS FORWARD. ON HER KNEES. Kábíyèsí, for the sake of the women of this land which I lead as Ìyálóde, forgive her. We all know her before all the false accusations came. She was your favourite wife, faithful and just to you. She has given us three sons and three daughters in the palace. More than any other wife. And she is the most senior Olorì. We cannot do this to her, Kábíyèsí. Bàbá, this cursed oath will ruin her character or what is left of it, totally.

KÁBÍYÈSÍ: Let her. Kútelú caught her red handed. And he never lies. I say, let her swear. Her claimed innocence smells already. Abọrẹ̀, you waste the time of the gods. I am hungry. Do what you have to do.

ABỌRẸ̀: Olorì Ìwàtáyọ̀, repeat after me. I, Ìwàtáyọ̀, daughter and Olorì of Ìjẹ̀kùn Odò, swear before the gods of the land, Ṣàngó and Ògún, that no man has ever seen my thighs or held the beads of my bottom apart from my husband, Ọba Adéyímiká of Ìjẹ̀kùn Odò. If a man has beheld the glory of the land or touched the flesh of the Olorì Ìwàtáyọ̀, let hot death claim us both. Let the mortar I stand on pound me, let the broom I stand on be used to sweep me out of the land. I so swear. TURNS TO KÁBÍYÈSÍ. It is done Kábíyèsí.

KÁBÍYÈSÍ: Let her come down. Seven days, Olorì, that is all the gods of the land will give you. If you are found guilty and you confess, you will die. If you do not confess, you will still die. You were told. I pleaded with you not to do this, but instead... For seven days, we will not set eyes on each other. May the gods forgive us.

OLORÌ: Whatever happened here tonight shows me how quickly love sheds its skin. The deed is done, and my clock of death begins to tick. See how the cloak of shame sits so well on me. The king has already vomited on me, and the now hushed double edged lashing tongues of the village women stoke me with shame and pain. My blackened face tonight confirms this. I am the supreme adulteress. Me! This false accusation kills my spirits. He believed his hunchback more than me. A mere palacehand. Where do I go now? Where can I go? When my face, darkened by shame, a totem of shame, have made a sibling of gloomy gummy tar? SHE BEGINS TO CRY.

KÁBÍYÈSÍ: I do not believe these crocodile tears will wash even the heart upon which they fall. I am hungry. Abọrẹ̀, prepare for the burial of the Olorì... she has troubled a fearsome god. From this moment on, her shroud newly sewn, death beckons her. In seven days, we shall be here to mourn her. I am hungry.

EXITS. THE OTHERS FOLLOW, LEAVING ABỌRẸ̀ AND ÌYÁLÓDE.

ÌYÁLÓDE: Abọrẹ̀, you failed me. This should never have been allowed to happen.

ABỌRẸ̀: What could I have done? What could anyone do? The Kábíyèsí's temper ran like a whirlwind round the palace. Not a place to force a word in his ears. Once the accusation was brought by his glorified tale bearer, he adorned madness and danced it... unveiling the queen, until she was left naked.

ÌYÁLÓDE: Naked? The queen? What glorified tale bearer did this? Who? Who brought the news? Who accused her?

ABỌRẸ̀: Abuké Ọba. That hunchback who controls the brain of the king was at it again.

ÌYÁLÓDE: He saw a man on top of her, he swore? He saw her thighs revealed to another? Why?

ABỌRẸ̀: So he claims.

ÌYÁLÓDE: Èèwọ̀! Who dared to enter the sacred spot where only gods enter?

ABỌRẸ̀: Another god. Ọba Àdámórí Òkùgbàdà of Ìlosì Ilé. Now safely tucked in with his ancestors, after a moment's pleasure with the queen.

ÌYÁLÓDE: Háà... how come? Where did they meet? He often stammered, and no one could understood him. He looked half dead when I saw him at his Ìwúyè. He could not even call his name to my hearing the day we met. How then could he have convinced our elegant Olorì to sleep with him?

ABỌRÈ: Maybe through the powers of a charm. These men of power will have anything using their powers. When a charmed mouth speaks, a language of love is complete to the ears of the victim. And women often love men for the strangest things. Anyway, when our Kábíyèsí heard about her infidelity, we consulted Ṣàngó, the lover Ọba was found dead, all burnt alive in his own room. An Ọba! That was how we confirmed Kútelú's story.

ÌYÁLÓDE: But why did Kútelú do it? Ṣàngó's pebbles do not know when to stop.

ABỌRÈ: We told him. We warmed Kábíyèsí, but he did not listen to us.

ÌYÁLÓDE: Ṣàngó is a frightening god to dare. Why did Kábíyèsí not leave the Olorì alone? Why did he make her climb the upturned mortar and broom, when he knew the consequence? There will never be trust between them again. Ever! And in seven days, one of them will be dead.

ABỌRÈ: At first, Olorì refused to swear. Then Ìyá Mọ̀pó came, whispered to her. No one heard her. Slowly she rose, led and we followed her to the place the oath was to be administered.

ÌYÁLÓDE: Ìyá Mọ̀pó? How? She was not supposed to be there... it was not her place.

ABỌRẸ̀: She fluttered, and shouted, rolled her fat bulk on the floor, threatening hell if the queen was forced to swear at first, then as if she received a message from the whiff of the air, she rose, and agreed, so we proceeded.

ÌYÁLÓDE: And?

ABỌRẸ̀: Afraid of any confrontation with the gods, we waited for the darkest time of the night, and made her swear the forbidden oath within the walls of the palace. Ìyá Mọ̀pó watching from a safe distance.

ÌYÁLÓDE: Useless me. A lot of water had poured from the broken gourd before I was told. And the sad fact is that even you sound as if you believe she did it.

ABỌRẸ̀: Not me. The walls of the palace speak, you know? Ears everywhere. PAUSE. But what hunts me now is the moving way she cried.

ÌYÁLÓDE: Then you don't know us women. Olódùmarè laced our eyes with tears. Even the tips are filled. If we stare for a second, we can cry a bucket full... with our hearts unshaken.

ABỌRẸ̀: Kábíyèsí already haunts for an addition.

ÌYÁLÓDE: Another one? A third wife? Hm... poor girl. With an heir in the palace, what else does she want?

ABỌRẸ̀: The desires of women come in different mysterious shades. Go home mother, you tried your best, but the truth will prevail in the end. Go home, mother. Release the Olorì from your care... she is now a doomed sacrifice.

ÌYÁLÓDE; I wish I could. But the night is not yet over.

ABỌRẸ̀: My only fear is when the White Administrator hears about what happened here tonight....

ÌYÁLÓDE: Had he heard about it before now?

ABỌRẸ̀: Yes. Adénrelé, the brother of Olorì had reported the matter to him, after Kábíyèsí beat Olorì until she fainted. That day, Kábíyèsí swore that her son, the Sòókò, Prince Ọlágùnsóyè must never be made king when he dies. The whole palace stood still.

ÌYÁLÓDE: Where was I when all these happened? I was not told... not even a whisper in my ears.

ABỌRẸ̀: You were ill and Kábíyèsí forbade us to even whisper a word to you. You needed complete rest... he announced. Remember you had fainted in the market. We were all worried for your life.

ÌYÁLÓDE: Hm... what is the use of the ears that miss good gossip from the palace? And the Whiteman... what did he do?

ABỌRẸ̀: He came with his wife. His face totally red with anger. He left, his right hand twitching with rage.

ÌYÁLÓDE: At whom?

ABỌRẸ̀: Kábíyèsí of course.

ÌYÁLÓDE: Of course.

ABỌRẸ̀: Ọ̀tún, Ìyá Mọ̀pó and myself were there.

ÌYÁLÓDE: Ìyá Mọ̀pó again.

ABỌRẸ̀: Yes. As the Èkejì Ìyálóde, she was there to represent you.

ÌYÁLÓDE: Not me. She represented herself. She never mentioned a word. Not a whisper. I guess she thought I would die, and she would take over everything. The fool wants to be Ìyálóde at all cost.

ABỌRẸ̀: She was there, overdressed as usual. As we ushered the D.O. in, Kábíyèsí came out in his new Guinea brocade. Resplendent. Kútelú, his hunchback larky, followed closely.

ABỌRẸ̀: Nobody knew what the D.O. said to Kábíyèsí, but as Kútelú interpreted, Kábíyèsí's face hardened. I am not a street urchin, Kábíyèsí bellowed. You have no right to come and tell me what do to do with my wife. I am Kábíyèsí, Èkejì Òrìṣà. Being a cousin to the Aláàfin Ọ̀yọ́ and the Ọọ̀ni Ilé-Ifẹ̀, and an in-law to the Tìmì Ẹdẹ, I am a small god myself... Òrìṣà ńlá... ẹbọra ilé. We smelt trouble so we all went on our chests, Kábíyèsí o, we bellowed back. With a blink of the eyelid, he shut us up. His bloodshot eyes widened, I shall not sit here, he bellowed again, and have the D.O. unveil my masquerade. Èèwọ̀! We echoed. You have already eroded my powers with your style of governance, he bellowed again. But not in my house. If you are happy with your skinny wife, I am not happy with mine. I shall marry another wife before the sun sets today. Three stones can never throw away the soup. Three wives will never throw away my happy home. With wild smiles we agreed with him... not quite getting the sense of his statement. Then in one swift move Kábíyèsí walked out of the room.

ÌYÁLÓDE: Ṣọ̀npọ̀nná ò! The... the Whiteman... what did he do?

ABỌRẸ̀: The light of his grace had deemed. He bit his lower lip. Ọ̀tún and I laid flat on our chests, pleading with him. Slowly with what was left of his dignity, he rose. His wife who had started crying through the nose, rose too. Almost stepping on us, they walked out to their waiting car, where Olorì was waiting for them.

ÌYÁLÓDE: Waiting for whom?

ABỌRỆ: The D.O. and his wife. Her clothes torn. Her royal breasts competing to be seen. There and then Kábíyèsí was soaked in trouble... deep trouble. We all agreed that his family madness was ready to creep into his head.

ÌYÁLÓDE: Tonight's dastardly act, manifests it. By this act his madness has grown full blown. Before the sun sets, I must hurry.

ABỌRỆ: To where?

ÌYÁLÓDE: To Bàbá Ifádèyí. All these are not with empty eyes. The hands of evil becloud them all. Kábíyèsí... Olorì and all. I need to know who is beating the drum of madness for Ìjẹ̀kùn Odò that makes all our masquerades led by a sick Kábíyèsí, the now glorified mad Àtokàn, dance upside down. The gods of the land forbid! Not in my time as Ìyálóde. Our mother, the first Ìyálóde, Pègúnrun obìnrin bí ọkùnrin, must not hear of this. She will tear the world apart with her teeth. The evil spirit that looms must be destroyed, I swear! May the spirits of our gods remain with me!

SLOWLY, LIGHTS FADE.

THRONE ROOM. BALÓGUN, APÈNÀ WITH MỌMỌ́ WAIT FOR KÁBÍYÈSÍ.

ỌTÚN: ENTERS. I have spoken with Kábíyèsí. He says that he will be with us shortly. Please Mọmọ́ Ọ̀nà Kakaǹfò, Balógun Ilẹ̀ Yorùbá, bear with us. Your trip was so sudden. The offer to feed your soldiers still stands.

MỌMỌ́: ANGRY. No. Do not feed them. We ate at Ògbómọ̀ṣọ́ on the way here. The message we have is hot, there is no space for food. Once it is delivered, we leave for Ọ̀yọ́. The Aláàfin waits for us. Baálẹ̀ Apòmù expects us. But we cannot go to see him. Our calls are many. My in law, Apènà how are you and my dear sister?

APÈNÀ: We are fine. She will blame me if she hears you came, and I did not force you to come home with me.

MỌMỌ́: Yes. Another day. Not tonight. We have not come to forge relations, but to deliver the dreaded message of the Balógun.

APÈNÀ: Dreaded?

MỌMỌ́: Yes. We do not even have the time to eat or exchange pleasantries. Tell her that about the message she sent, I am working on it. Very soon, she will receive good news. But let her come and see our old mother, she misses her all the time. If she dies, then I will come back and take her to Ìdàhọ̀mì to stay with our big sister.

APÈNÀ; She will come.

BALÓGUN: Kára ó le, if only you could drink a sip of palmwine, we would be less agitated. Just a sip.

MỌMỌ́: I say no! Where is your Kábíyèsí now?

ÒTÚN: Making arrangements for things to take to Ikú Bàbá Yèyé. Please sit.

MỌMỌ́: You sit, if your feet refuses to carry you.

KÁBÍYÈSÍ: ENTERS. Why will the great Mọmọ́ not sit in my palace? What crimes have we committed? Please sit Mọmọ́ Yorùbá.

ALL: Kábíyèsí o!

KÁBÍYÈSÍ: The king greets you all. SITS. Mọmọ́, please sit. I am sorry my chiefs, I brought you all out this late in the night. But when a matter is higher than sleep, the best thing is to speak it. Mọmọ́, the big masquerade of our father the Balógun is here, so night must be defiled.

MỌMỌ́: Chiefs, please sit. Kábíyèsí, Ikú Bàbá Yèyé sends his greetings. I am honoured by your presence, even though late. I shall go straight to the message of the Balógun. He greets you.

KÁBÍYÈSÍ: I greet him too.

MỌMỌ́: Thrice now he has summoned you to Ọ̀yọ́, and you have failed to turn up.

KÁBÍYÈSÍ TRIES TO SPEAK. BUT MỌMỌ́ RAISES HIS HAND TO STOP HIM. We thought that being so close to Apòmù, you would have learnt a lesson from them. Aláàfin is angry. Two, you have been seen severally with the District Officer, whom you have chosen as your new leader. You disrespect the Balógun with this action. Thirdly, for three years now you have made excuses about sending the tributes of Ọ̀yọ́. You sit as king because Balógun allows you to sit. But now you forget yourself. Then first we heard that you had joined the religion of the Whitemen, allowed them to stay in your village and even built a church – all these without the permission of the Balógun. CHUCKLES. That was why we all laughed at the palace when we heard your masquerades fought with the D. O's people, and you sent a message to Balógun to help you. We turned our backs to you like you turned your back to us. How can a son who refuses to call a man his father arrive to seek for assistance in his hour of need? Èèwọ̀!

KÁBÍYÈSÍ: RISES. Mọ̀mọ́...

MỌ̀MỌ́: To this effect... Balógun gives you ten days, starting from tomorrow morning, to begin to clear your things from this world. Abìjà! Abìjà A FIERCE MEAN SOLDIER COMES IN WITH A CALABASH COVERED IN RED. HE GIVES IT TO THE MỌ̀MỌ́, WHO GIVES IT IN TURN TO KÁBÍYÈSÍ. Receive the message of the king. In ten days, fill it with your head. I have given the message of the Balógun. I leave.

KÁBÍYÈSÍ: STILL DUMB FOUNDED, CARRYING THE CALABASH. What just happened? What evil pranks is Èṣù playing with me? At what point of my dance did I step on Ikú's shoes, that now he decides to embrace me. Apènà!

APÈNÀ: Kábíyèsí... it just gives a bad signal, it can still be remedied.

ỌTÚN: Yes Kábíyèsí... ó bà ni, kò bàjẹ́!

KÁBÍYÈSÍ: It is beyond my wildest thoughts.

BALÓGUN: So, what reply do we give the Balógun?

KÁBÍYÈSÍ: What reply do you think we should give him?

BALÓGUN: Ọ̀tún, and I leave for Ọ̀yọ́ tomorrow. We should take all the pleasing things to Ikú Bàbá Yèyé! Then, like good children, we shall plead with him to forgive you and take the calabash back.

KÁBÍYÈSÍ: No. He wants my head. He went too far. Call me Kútelú. We shall do a letter to the D.O. and tell him that the Balógun is envious of his powers and is beginning to instigate junior kings against him. I will present myself as a victim of the loyalty to him.

BALÓGUN: That would have been a good plan if the D.O. liked you, like he does the Tìmì. Kábíyèsí, when a war will consume one, we beg its fangs not to unfold. Let us go to the Balógun.

KÁBÍYÈSÍ: Apènà… what do the gods say?

APÈNÀ: I have not had time to consult them. But they can hear everything. Balógun's plan sounds good. We have our troubles at home. It will give us time to prepare for the Balógun properly. Only the D.O. can stop him.

BALÓGUN: The Mọ̀mọ́ is Apènà's in-law too, we could explore that angle.

Ọ̀TÚN: Yes, but what can the Mọ̀mọ́ do on his own. He carries out the orders of the Balógun. I would have thought of the Ọọ̀ni, but the Ọọ̀ni could not help Baálẹ̀ Apòmù. He will not interfere.

KÁBÍYÈSÍ: You speak the truth Ọ̀tún, but I like Apènà's suggestion. CHUCKLES. All this is turning out to be interesting. Olóhùn iyọ̀ deceives me each time he says I am second to the gods. When indeed I am nothing. I cannot even help myself before the emptiness of a mere calabash.

CHUCKLES AGAIN. To be a king in these times of the white men is like walking the tip of a double-edged sword. But before you go Balógun, wait and give this to the Balógun. HE THROWS THE CALABASH ON THE FLOOR.

ALL: Háà, Kábíyèsí!

KÁBÍYÈSÍ: Take to him the pieces of his damned orders. I shall not die. Not a strand of my hair shall fall from my royal head. Not a strand! SHOCKED, NOT A WORD, THEY ALL FREEZE WATCHING THE CALABASH. JUST THEN THE MÒMÓ ENTERS.

MÒMÓ: I forgot to tell you…HE SEES THE BROKEN CALABASH. Sacrilege!

SLOWLY LIGHTS FADE.

WHEN LIGHTS COME ON, IT REVEALS ÌYÁ MỌPÓ'S ENTERING THE ROOM. OLORÌ BENDS BEFORE A BIG CALABASH BOWL. FOLDED IN IT IS KÁBÍYÈSÍ'S SET OF BEADS.

ÌYÁ MỌPÓ: Are you sure these beads belong to Kábíyèsí?

OLORÌ: Yes Ìyá, I took them from the rack of beads he wears every day. He wore them just yesterday. They still bear his smell and his skin.

ÌYÁ MỌPÓ: And they shall be worn soon after this deed is done?

OLORÌ: Yes Ìyá.

ÌYÁ MỌPÓ: Then they are good. They will carry a piece of him. They will pass through his head, and rest always on his neck and shoulders. They will serve now as the noose that will hang him. ÌYÁ MỌPÓ GESTURES TO OLORÌ TO BEND AS SHE WASHES HER HEAD. When a word is given to a man on the verge of death, it holds. When a woman's spirit is tied to the loins of death, and clutches of death shifts, glides aside, and with the help of fluttering birds, tips the claws of death on the head of the sitting neighbour, no harm is done. Tonight, our daughter, Ìwàtáyọ̀ shifts the claws of the curse to the man who made her swear the sacred oath of shame. Ọba Adéyímiká, by the gods, on your head will it be, shame, madness and death, one by one, all, on your head will they remain. SPITS. So let it be. Rise woman. You are washed clean, Olorì.

OLORÌ: Thank you mother.

ÌYÁ MÒPÓ: Return the cursed beads to where you took them. Let them once again find a doomed space on his neck… let him wear the new cursed ornaments of death.

SHE PACKS THE BEADS, AND WRAPS THEM ON A PIECE OF BLACK CLOTH.

OLORÌ: Thank you mother.

ÌYÁ MÒPÓ: Thank you? What have we done for one of our own that sounds so big? One never thanks oneself, child. Go ahead and commit more atrocities to the near healing sore of the wounded lion. Let him roar and walk majestically to his fall. From now on, misdeeds shall be his shadow. Èṣù blesses you, dearest child, the fluttering birds at the last conclave possesses you. Walk with the pride of the daughter of the land.

OLORÌ: Thank you mother. How do I repay the mothers of earth? What do I have? What do I give?

ÌYÁ MÒPÓ: Hm… what do you give? Did they not tell you?

OLORÌ: No one told me a thing. Not a word. When I hurried to the conclave, I was blinded by fear and the desire to live. Flushed in a pool of tears, they took me and soothed my pains. Reassured me of ease, and the impending victory, I gave my all in the form of trust. No one spoke of giving anything.

ÌYÁ MÒPÓ: All in the form of trust?

OLORÌ: Yes. But not a mention of a specific item. Not a note. Not a whisper.

ÌYÁ MỌPÓ: Then come closer. SHE FEELS HER STOMACH. Good the deed is done. No wonder, even the evening breeze embraces you.

OLORÌ: I do not understand.

ÌYÁ MỌPÓ: A life for a life. Your stomach once filled with the Kábíyèsí's child is empty. They have taken what you promised them.

OLORÌ: My child? When? I swear I did not promise them even a thing. BREAKS DOWN.

ÌYÁ MỌPÓ: They took only a pebble of birth. A nugget of gold. Come closer again. See, you can always have another.

OLORÌ: Another? That was all I had left. Bàbá Ifádélé said so.

ÌYÁ MỌPÓ: Ifádélé? Hm... what does he know? Mere evocative mutterings. The chants of Ifá are limited when the works of Èṣù and the fluttering birds are profoundly spread... darkness multiplies. Anyway, that was all they wanted. They take and give what they want.

OLORÌ: The fluttering muttering birds? And...

ÌYÁ MỌPÓ: Yes... the kind and ever considerate creatures of the world. The only other true gods. Do you still doubt us now?

OLORÌ: No. It is just that I wish I was given a chance to give what they took. PAUSE. IN DEEP THOUGHT. What do I have now? What string do I have to tie the Kábíyèsí to me in this cursed moment of hellish doubts? He has already disowned the child I had for him. A child whose back I was to ride after the Kábíyèsí has gone to sleep with his fathers. Yet I want to punish him. Push him until he stumbles. But now my once filled womb is empty. This gone child was his true seed, all I had left... believe me mother when I say that I am finished. ON HER KNEES. DESPERATE. Help me Ìyá. They will do what you want. You are our mother.

ÌYÁ MÒPÓ: WATCHES HER FOR A WHILE. CHUCKLES. Come closer again. FEELS HER STOMACH AGAIN. Págà! They took everything. It is too late child. The water poured... as well as the calabash. In the yank, they broke it. Nothing can be done. In the absence of delusion, there can never be illusion. With this tragic pull... the intended act of holding the Kábíyèsí on to your apron string is a spent delusion... all that is late now... the egg is broken... all you have now, is an empty shell. CHUCKLES. Evil is at work. The fluttering motherly birds now well fed, spread their wings over you... you are blissfully covered child. At least, you have that left. Go and walk kándú kàndù kándú... like a spoilt child of royalty. Go! Let your dainty feet spatter mud on the faces of your countless enemies. Go child!

OLORÌ: Go? To where mother? When the looming cloak of shame pulls me so much closer.

ÌYÁ MÒPÓ: Not on you child. Èèwọ̀! Not on you. Unless you fail to control your feet, nothing can touch you now. Yes remember, you and the beads abhor each other now. Kábíyèsí must not touch you when he wears them. If you see them on his neck... death could embrace one.

OLORÌ: May the gods forbid. Tickle me further mother. You say nothing can hurt me mother?

ÌYÁ MÒPÓ: Nothing, child.

OLORÌ: There is one with the hunchback who whispered to the ears of the king my awful deed. I shall like to bite his padded hunch. The fools... the sacrifice of the land... but kind thoughts overwhelm me.

ÌYÁ MỌPÓ: It can be done. But for now, let it be. His blood is boiled in the sadness of the earth. Only Kábíyèsí can cause his death. Their lives are entwined. But it can be done if you insist.

OLORÌ: Again, you promise me, and now even I begin to flutter with joy.

ÌYÁ MỌPÓ: Slowly child. Hot soup is better enjoyed when cool. Slowly. The dust of your reversed oath must settle first. CHUCKLES. Very soon wickedness which sounds so sour to your tender palate now will become honey to your lips as your teeth begin to gather the strands of sweetened tender flesh. Indeed, patience has virtue.

OLORÌ: So Sùúrùlérè?

ÌYÁ MỌPÓ: I swear it does. THEY BOTH LAUGH.

SLOWLY THE LIGHTS FADE.

THE THRONE ROOM. THE CHIEFS ARGUE. KÁBÍYÈSÍ IS ANGRY. KÚTELÚ LISTENS ATTENTIVELY.

KÁBÍYÈSÍ: How dare he threaten me with removal from the throne of my fathers? Who is he?

ỌTÚN: The District Officer, Kábíyèsí. He represents the all-powerful woman king of England.

KÁBÍYÈSÍ: All powerful woman king of England my foot. The D.O. dares me. Did he know how many gods picked me? Does he know how Ifá announced my kingship when my pebbles filled the royal cup more than that of six other princes? I say does he? Does he know what I ate and what I swallowed in the sacred Ìpẹ̀bí enclave. Does this D.O. know what Irúnmọlẹ̀ and which Èbọra know me by first name? Oh, Abọrẹ̀ what is this? Have my powers eroded so soon? I pronounced death on his head, and yet he lives long enough to sign a stupid letter removing me from the throne my people gave me. How can this happen?

ABỌRẸ̀: Orí òyìnbó ni ò gbàbọ̀dè. I have no name for his spirit. We could not call his spirit to death. Being an albino also nullified the potency of our charms. We appeared in his room, but we just could not call his soul, and drag it from him. Olúáwo, please say something.

OLÚÁWO: Yes Kábíyèsí, the names of his father and mother eluded us also. To our gods, he does not exist.

KÁBÍYÈSÍ: I am finished then. I have sent a message to the Balógun and the Tìmì. They will know what to do.

ỌTÚN: They will do nothing, Kábíyèsí. Ikú BàbáYèyé knows how well to make his move. He has learnt how to dine with the devil and survive. Remember he is ọmọ Ikú, ọmọ òfò.

The skill to meander the rough road of life is in his pouch of existence.

KÁBÍYÈSÍ: And the Tìmì?

ỌTÚN: The side apron of the Balógun. He is the Òṣùgbó which the Balógun uses to adorn his powers. Nothing will happen, Kábíyèsí. No one will come to help you.

BALÓGUN; You know me for speaking the truth Kábíyèsí. I am the war general of Ìjẹ̀kùn Odò. Give me the red flag. Let us declare war on the white man and his stupid soldiers who wear short knickers and speak strange language to move their bulk which they have stolen our food to maintain themselves. ON ONE KNEE. Grant me this order to drive the finger of death in to their hearts. The Whiteman's spirit that cannot be killed at night will embrace death at noon.

KÁBÍYÈSÍ: Balógun, your voice makes me jump. But Èṣù's fingers are long. I feel his hand in all these. How could the D.O's visit turn to a death trap. Maybe I was too angry. Maybe I should have been more understanding. After all, he was speaking against my action of beating the queen and making her take the sacred oath of death.

ỌTÚN: Then the issue of marrying the second wife after being baptized in his church, which you razed to the ground.

KÁBÍYÈSÍ: Yes. That one too.

BALÓGUN: Kábíyèsí... aṣọ kò bá Ọmọ́yẹ mọ́, Ọmọ́yẹ ti rìnhòhò wọjà. The whole village believe that she has gone mad. She roamed into the village square naked, no piece of cloth can cover this matter now, please grant me the order of war.

KÚTELÚ: What war, Kábíyèsí? The D.O. and his men carry guns. They stand from afar and shoot down their enemies. Even his white colourless spirit eludes the potent charms of our fathers.

KÁBÍYÈSÍ: What do you want to say Kútelú?

KÚTELÚ: Send me, Kábíyèsí. Let me be the emissary of peace.

BALÓGUN: You?

KÚTELÚ: Yes, me.

KÁBÍYÈSÍ: Then come closer and whisper your plan my dear Kútelú. KÚTELÚ COMES CLOSER TO THE KING. HIS MOUTH CLOSE TO HIS LEFT EAR. Silent whisper... do not let the fiery blood of the bystanders soil the kindness of your words. Talk strange king fellow. KÚTELÚ WHISPERS HIS PLANS INTO KÁBÍYÈSÍ'S EAR. FOR A MOMENT, KÁBÍYÈSÍ DOES NOT SAY A WORD. THE PEOPLE, INCLUDING KÚTELÚ, ARE APRREHENSIVE. THEN SLOWLY HE BREAKS INTO A SMILE. Ìlàrí Qba where are you? Ìlàrí! THE OTHERS ECHO HIS NAME.

All: Ìlàrí! A SCRAGGY OLD MAN RUNS IN.

ÌLÀRÍ: I am here my lord. HE PROSTRATES.

KÁBÍYÈSÍ: Run to the room where I keep the beads of the chiefs. Bring a rich set. Then also bring a set of the rich sányán, by the left of the big iron box. Hurry.

KÚTELÚ: Do you like my plan, Kábíyèsí?

KÁBÍYÈSÍ: I like it. But you shall not go as a mere hunchback of the king. You shall go as the Bóbajíròrò of Ìjẹkùn Odò. All subsequent Abuké Qba who follow in your good steps and do well in oiling the ears of the Ọba with good and kind words of wisdom shall bear this title. The letter of the D.O. cannot change my word which is law.

THEY ALL PROSTRATE: Kábíyèsí!

KÁBÍYÈSÍ: You shall go with the sonorous timbre of palace music. Dressed resplendently. Take two female slaves of your choice and go and see the Whiteman. Tell him what you have said and let us see if he will carry you on Whiteman's horse which I envy so much or drag your body in a smelly tumbrel of worn out horses. Go 'Bọ́bajíròrò. Ìlàrí go with him.

KÚTELÚ: I swear I will not fail you Kábíyèsí.

KÁBÍYÈSÍ: You dare not. The Abọrẹ̀ awaits your neck with the sword of Ògún, if you fail. Go!

THEY LEAVE HAPPY.

ỌTÚN: STEPS FORWARD. But Kábíyèsí, was that wise?

KÁBÍYÈSÍ: Did I ask for advice from any one? Yours is to advise. Mine is to listen and make my decision. Away with all of you. Let us await the magic Kútelú wants to perform. Even he worships Ṣàngó with me. He may just get a smile from the tempestuous god. Where is Olóhùn iyọ̀?

ỌTÚN: He followed Kútelú.

KÁBÍYÈSÍ: BREAKS INTO A LAUGH. Let him… his voice can sooth even the veins of a mad fool like the D.O. Call the remnants of the musicians left behind… I need to hear the call of a king. The Whiteman's letter bites edges of my very heart.

AMIDST MUSIC AND NOISE, SLOWLY LIGHTS FADE.

IFÁDÈYÍ'S HOUSE. ÌYÁLÓDE SITS ON THE MAT WITH ABỌRẸ̀. IFÁDÈYÍ SITS WITH THEM.

IFÁDÈYÍ: Ṣàngó, Olúkòso threw a stone of doubt. He got great friends Gbọ̀nkà and Tìmì to fight. They fought and they fought until Gbọ̀nkà killed Tìmì. Now seized by his new power, Gbọ̀nkà turned on Ṣàngó. He shamed Ṣàngó. In anger, Ṣàngó turned on his people. He killed and burnt his own people. Then the people turned their backs on him. Ṣàngó fled with his wife Ọya. Half way to nowhere, Ọya decided to return home. Alone, Ṣàngó hung himself. Then the people took pity on him and said he did not hang. They made him a god, but the story tells it all. Did Gbọ̀nkà forgive Ṣàngó? Did Ṣàngó forgive Gbọ̀nkà? Did he even forgive his people of Ọ̀yọ́... and did Ṣàngó's wives forgive Ọya who decided to return home? Did Ṣàngó forgive himself?

ÌYÁLÓDE: I do not understand Bàbá.

IFÁDÈYÍ: Then look as you listen Ìyálóde. Will Ṣàngó ever forgive his people? Will the people ever forgive Ṣàngó after all the cries have subsided, and the dead bodies have been buried? Will they?

ÌYÁLÓDE: No Bàbá.

IFÁDÈYÍ: It is therefore easier to listen to a plea than to accept it. That is why our people say I heard does not mean I have accepted. Do you understand now?

ÌYÁLÓDE: PAUSE. In the matter of Olorì. No.

IFÁDÈYÍ: LAUGHS LOUDLY. Then open your eyes and take a peep at the darkness of the heart of Olorì. She will never forgive Kábíyèsí. Infact as I speak, Kábíyèsí carries the burden of her curse. But the shadow of shame still looms and follows her. Her cursed thighs remain the pith of her ill luck. No medicine can wash her clean. Not even the fluttering birds, nor the gods can help her now. She is too long gone into the bush. No one. It is a curse inherited by her ancestors. Ifá has spoken.

ÌYÁLÓDE: Then the matter of the Balógun! Bàbá, the village is tense.

IFÁDÈYÍ: Before heavy rains fall, the whirlwind welcomes it. Death descends, either way a soul must ascend. Ifá says it shall be well in the end. The wondering doves will return home. Go, mother. What will happen will happen.

ÌYÁLÓDE: The doves…

IFÁDÈYÍ: Go home mother. The night will come when it is time to. The village will be at peace once again. Once the sacrifices have been made.

LIGHTS SLOWLY FADE.

THE KING'S INNER CHAMBER. APÈNÀ IS ALONE, CONSULTING THE ADÍFÁLÀ.

APÈNÀ: Báwo l'Ọba ṣe ń jíjó ẹ̀tẹ́?
Fàkìà, fakia, l'Ọba ń jíjó ẹ̀tẹ́.
Kí l'Ọba ṣe tó fi ń jíjó ẹ̀tẹ́?
Ìwà Fàkìà, fakia, ló ń m'Ọba jíjó ẹ̀tẹ́.

KÁBÍYÈSÍ RUSHS IN.

KÁBÍYÈSÍ: I kept you waiting?

APÈNÀ: Not too long. But I had time to double check the statement of Ifádèyí on what is going on in the palace.

KÁBÍYÈSÍ: Tell me what I should hear. Especially the white stranger who says he will dethrone me.

APÈNÀ: He cannot.

KÁBÍYÈSÍ; I have sent Kútelú to see him. He attended secondary school. He speaks his language better than most of us. PAUSE. Will he come back with good news?

APÈNÀ: CHECKS THE ADÍFÁLÀ. He will. But not too long from now darkness shall engulf him. Does he know?

KÁBÍYÈSÍ: Know?

APÈNÀ: That he is the Abọ́bakú. We have also hidden some charms in his hunch. He is a sacrifice to you. Does he know this?

KÁBÍYÈSÍ: No. He thinks I am just his benefactor. He likes the palace. I trust him. In his eyes, I see sincerity. I think he is a good man.

APÈNÀ: But be careful. His hunch back does not make him less of a man, especially when he knows that he was not born with it. He carries your life in that pouch.

KÁBÍYÈSÍ: Leave that alone. He is trapped in his pouch. Let us talk about more serious things. Why has nothing happened to Olorì Ìwàtáyọ̀? She prances about with an arrogance even to the gods. The oath had no effect on her. Today is the fourth day, there is no sign of impending death on her fore head. Why?

APÈNÀ: Kábíyèsí… have you forgiven her? Only you can reverse the oath.

KÁBÍYÈSÍ: Never. I have turned my back on her forever.

APÈNÀ: CHECKS THE ADÍFÁLÀ. Háà… this is it. KÁBÍYÈSÍ. She has turned it on you. And now we must turn it on the head of the hunchback Kútelú. He is our sacrifice.

KÁBÍYÈSÍ: Kútelú kẹ?

APÈNÀ: Another will be found. That was why I said that you should give him the red beads and the rich sányán dress we worked on.

KÁBÍYÈSÍ: I did as you requested. He wears them as we speak. PAUSE. But Kútelú…

APÈNÀ: What about him Kábíyèsí?

KÁBÍYÈSÍ: I want to send gifts to his parents. He has served us well. Do you know where I can find them?

APÈNÀ: No Kábíyèsí. We found him. Oro caught him in the night. He has not said a word about them. But besides, no parent will take him, or even acknowledge him, when they see what we have done with their child. He is now a distorted animal, far from who we brought to you as Abọ̀bakú.

KÁBÍYÈSÍ: I gave him too much load to carry, did I?

APÈNÀ: Yes. And it is irreversible. It is best to let him be, until he dies peacefully. I hope he has not offended the king?

KÁBÍYÈSÍ: Offend? No. PAUSE. What about me? Am I safe?

APÈNÀ: Nothing will touch you Kábíyèsí. But an animal of yours will be missing. The fluttering birds stand with the Olorì, so we can only touch their chick or its nest with caution.

KÁBÍYÈSÍ: Caution? How about the Balógun?

APÈNÀ: His fingers will not touch you. His anger blows hot and cold. PAUSE. I wish you had not broken the calabash.

KÁBÍYÈSÍ: I had to. A whiff of madness. A touched ego. Now my head is on the block.

APÈNÀ: Nothing will touch you, Kábíyèsí.

KÁBÍYÈSÍ: Yes, nothing will touch me. I mean take me.

APÈNÀ: Nothing Kábíyèsí. Just one more very important issue in all these.

KÁBÍYÈSÍ: What is it? THE SOUND OF MUSIC IS HEARD. Wait! Who dares to play the royal gbẹ̀du drums of the Ọba in my palace when I am not there. Who? THE ÌLÀRÍ RUNS IN.

ÌLÀRÍ: Kútelú is back with great news Kábíyèsí. The palace is agog.

KÁBÍYÈSÍ: RISES. Apènà I must leave. HE LEAVES APÈNÀ IN A HURRY.

APÈNÀ: Háà Kábíyèsí wait. How do I tell him that even he dances too close to the shrine of Èṣù and Ikú. How? When his spirits out run his body. PAUSE.

Báwo l'Ọba ṣe ń jíjó ẹ̀tẹ́?

Fàkìà, fakia, l'Ọba ń jíjó ẹ̀tẹ́.

Kí l'Ọba ṣe tó fi ń jíjó ẹ̀tẹ́?

Ìwà Fàkìà, fakia, ló ń m'Ọba jíjó ẹ̀tẹ́.

SLOWLY, LIGHTS FADE.

THE THRONE ROOM. THE CHIEFS DANCE HAPPY. KÚTELÚ DANCES WILDLY. KÁBÍYÈSÍ ENTERS, SEES THEM DANCING AND JOINS.

AFTER A WHILE, THE DRUMMERS COME TO A STOP WITH THE GREETING BEAT OF THE KÁBÍYÈSÍ. THEY ALL PROSTRATE TO GREET HIM.

KÁBÍYÈSÍ: We have danced without knowing the meaning of the beats. Kútelú why are we happy?

KÚTELÚ: GOES BEFORE KÁBÍYÈSÍ. PROSTRATES. HOLDING A LETTER. Kábíyèsí, we went there, we saw the D.O. I spoke with him, and he watched us for a while, then gave us the letter, retracting his earlier decision. You can be king until our ancestors send for you.

KÁBÍYÈSÍ: COLLECTS THE LETTER. OPENS IT. STARES AT THE LETTER FOR A WHILE. What does it say? Òsì who normally reads my letters is not here.

ỌTÚN: Kábíyèsí, he is still very ill.

KÁBÍYÈSÍ: Send someone to pay my respects to him. Now the D.O.'s letter.

APÈNÀ ENTERS.

KÚTELÚ: READS SILENTLY. He greets you.

KÁBÍYÈSÍ: I greet him too.

KÚTELÚ: He is sorry he offended you at your last meeting.

KÁBÍYÈSÍ: Then the Whiteman has some sense.

KÚTELÚ: He is sorry, he poked nose into your personal matter with Olorì.

KÁBÍYÈSÍ: I forgive him.

KÚTELÚ: He says he hopes to improve relations with you.

KÁBÍYÈSÍ: What kind of relations? I know how wise he can be. He will invite you to his house at night and invite his policemen to arrest you for theft. What relations o jàre Kútelú?

KÚTELÚ: He has released the three men in custody who razed down the Church.

KÁBÍYÈSÍ: Good.

KÚTELÚ: He has released the two masquerades also.

KÁBÍYÈSÍ: I too release him from the list of the names of my kingdom. Did he mention the issue of my second and intending third wives?

KÚTELÚ: READS. He dares not. He pleads for peace and harmony.

KÁBÍYÈSÍ: This is where I am getting a bit worried. The D.O. is too kind here. Why?

ÒTÚN: Me too Kábíyèsí. He did this to the Baálẹ̀ of Òrùlé. He cleverly sued for peace, allowed the night trade to continue, and sent his men to arrest the Ọba. It was a pitiful sight. They put the Àkàrà-oògùn of Òrùlé in chains. Just because two young maidens were missing in his palace.

ABỌRẸ̀: I guess no one told him that the palace is a market place where even the king can go missing.

KÁBÍYÈSÍ: Fools. Now that he has left us alone. I remind the kingmakers in this room that upon my death, my son

Ọlágùnsóyè, should not be allowed to climb the seat of my fathers.

APÈNÀ: Then who will be Kábíyèsí? Ọlágùnsóyè is your only child. When he was born, it was him we took to the shrine of the gods to bless. Ṣàngó named him king. Ọ̀rúnmìlà agreed. And when he was three, when you could carry a child for the first time as custom demands, it was him you carried after the ètùtù had been performed at the river banks of Yèyé Ọ̀ṣun. Now, what do we tell the gods?

KÁBÍYÈSÍ: Tell them what you want. I did not ask for advice. It is an order.

BALÓGUN: Àṣẹ sì ti gùn ún, Kábíyèsí. Who should we make king, Kábíyèsí?

KÁBÍYÈSÍ: Adérójú... the son of my sister. Apènà, you shall exchange their destinies. Tell the gods I commanded it.

APÈNÀ: Ikú Bàbá Yèyé ò. Even the gods will understand.

BALÓGUN: But Kábíyèsí, Adérójú is the son of a woman. The lineage of women does not count in matters of ascension to the throne.

KÁBÍYÈSÍ: This time it will, in fact, it must. I say I do not need to be advised. It is an order.

ALL. Kábíyèsí.

KÁBÍYÈSÍ RISES. AND THE OTHERS LEAVE THE ROOM EXCEPT APÈNÀ AND A BAFFLED KÚTELÚ.

KÚTELÚ: Father, you heard him?

APÈNÀ: With both ears.

KÚTELÚ: But why?

APÈNÀ: He who the gods want to kill they first run mad. Patience son.

KÚTELÚ: I did not offend him. I have given him all. Including my life. The only favour I expected of him… was my son Ọlágùnsóyè becoming king of Ìjẹ̀kùn Odò. Now, he decides to deny me. I did not offend him. It was Olorì Ìwátáyọ̀ who offended him. I agreed to all this because of my son. So, the agony of my hunch amounts to nothing? Ogun will judge. ON HIS KNEES. Father, by the gods I beg you.

APÈNÀ: Why beg me? I am your father.

KÚTELÚ: Is it true that the Balógun wants his head?

APÈNÀ: Yes, but it will be resolved. I have spoken to the Mọmọ́, he will placate the Balógun's spirits. The arm of death is far away from your necks. Live and enjoy son.

KÚTELÚ: I am grateful. And Olorì? I want judgment.

APÈNÀ. PONDERS FOR A WHILE. Oh my son, then you don't know me. Èṣù onílé oríta looms already. When a load cannot be placed up or down, we still find a place to put it. I may have to lose something, but your son, my grandchild shall be king after his mother's husband. KÚTELÚ PROSTRATES. Get up, son. One cannot thank himself. Get up and hug your father. My left eye twitches. This happens when I am about to lose something. Do what I asked you to do with Olorì and all will be well. Her mouth opens too wildly. With her hot body, she could reveal the secret of the body that was buried in the dead of the night.

KÚTELÚ: Already she scratches the wet earth, and the stretched hand of the stiff corpse will soon be revealed. Something must be done to keep her quiet.

APÈNÀ: Just let her hug you. A woman one has slept with once always wonders about what is left in the man. She will fall for the trap. Also dare her strength. She believes the fluttering birds cover her. But what she forgets is that where one medicine stops is where another starts. That is why all medicine men start with ìjúbà. Go and do what I asked you to do. Hurry, go and bring your woman home.

KÚTELÚ: PROSTRATES AGAIN. I thank you father, but I beg you father, nothing must happen to my son.

APÈNÀ: Not your son. Heavens forbid, not my grandchild. Just go! HE WATCHES KÚTELÚ LEAVES. But a son will dance with the spirits soon. Hm… either way, a son's corpse walks in the shadow of death soon. And a father's heart will hurt. Now, cold with impending loneliness, let these bright lights go off.

SLOWLY LIGHTS FADE.

THE KING'S INNER CHAMBER. THE KING LIES ON HIS BED. WHEN LIGHTS COME ON. ÌYÁ MỌ̀PÓ STANDS BY HIS BED.

KÁBÍYÈSÍ: I can smell you from afar. Your fluttering feathers pick so much when you fly, and the smell is pungent.

ÌYÁ MỌ̀PÓ: Abuse me Kábíyèsí. It is the privilege of the king.

KÁBÍYÈSÍ: Why have you come?

ÌYÁ MỌ̀PÓ: To tell you how we are angry with you. You treated us with disdain when you made Olorì to swear the sacred oath of shame. I begged you not to makr her.

KÁBÍYÈSÍ: And I begged you to let me. The shame I had to endure was beyond the rich folds of the king. Now she has three more days to live before her death.

ÌYÁ MỌ̀PÓ: CHUCKLES. What if she does not die?

KÁBÍYÈSÍ: You will see that I am right.

ÌYÁ MỌ̀PÓ: What if the platter of her feet continues to step on the hard-baked earth?

KÁBÍYÈSÍ: A big shame to Ṣàngó. And that will never happen.

ÌYÁ MỌ̀PÓ: Then you have not asked wise Apènà what Ṣàngó can do and cannot do. Even his wife left him at the crossroads of shame. He is a god whose shame was covered up by his people, who loved him. Ọba kòso they say, but he did in the darkness of his heavy heart.

KÁBÍYÈSÍ: It is late, mother, let me sleep.

ÌYÁ MỌPÓ: I will let you. But I have a message from the mothers. Do not touch Ọlágùnsóyè, the son of Olorì. He must be king.

KÁBÍYÈSÍ: He is not my son; I will give him what I want out of my properties at the moment of death. I do not want his wayward mother in the palace of my ancestors after my death. She must never be queen mother. Adérójú is the king I want after me.

ÌYÁ MỌPÓ: No.

KÁBÍYÈSÍ: But I am king. I have powers even over the fluttering birds. It must be done.

ÌYÁ MỌPÓ: Yes. You bring your meat, we cook it and share it to eat. Together. That is what we told you when we visited you in the sacred room of Ìpẹ̀bí. Together. But now without wings you want to lord our powers over us. Ẹ̀sọ̀ pẹ̀lẹ́ Kábíyèsí. But if that is what you want… the fluttering birds can consider.

KÁBÍYÈSÍ: That is what I want.

ÌYÁ MỌPÓ: Why do you want that? What has she done that was not agreed upon?

KÁBÍYÈSÍ: Her actions. She shamed me.

ÌYÁ MỌPÓ: What actions? You knew what kind of a woman she was when we brought her to you as wife. You had given us your manhood to be king, we all agreed Kábíyèsí Adéníran Adéyímiká, that she could have a lover and give you a son for the throne. I knew it. As your fat neck began to spread in folds, you forgot everything. You started to talk of shame when you were the figure of shame in the first place. That was why I begged you not to allow her to swear at the shrine of Ṣàngó. You only dragged outside an old hidden matter.

KÁBÍYÈSÍ: But she slept with other men after. Feelings give birth to relationships. And when I see her, I see a used baby Ṣìgìdì which all the children in the neighbourhood play with. I hate her.

ÌYÁ MỌPÓ: Another man. Awósànyà Awóyẹmí, a once handsome man, whom you turned into a despicable figure to make your powers stronger than ours. He slept once with your wife as we agreed upon. She had a son for you as we agreed upon. Once. And now you treat her like a house rat.

KÁBÍYÈSÍ: Another has touched her.

ÌYÁ MỌPÓ: In her room, with your permission Kábíyèsí! It was her sacrifice for your honour KÁBÍYÈSÍ CHUCKLES But now, it is so easy to forget. I must remind you that she is not made of wood. Her veins run with blood, you know? But your ego swims with the flowing flood. And now agreed thoughts are washed away.

KÁBÍYÈSÍ: What do you want now?

ÌYÁ MỌPÓ: A life.

KÁBÍYÈSÍ: Whose life now?

ÌYÁ MỌPÓ. Kútelú.

KÁBÍYÈSÍ: He holds the key of my life. I cannot release him now. I must prepare another.

ÌYÁ MỌPÓ: Why?

KÁBÍYÈSÍ: It is all very complicated. All I can say is that I need you to have faith in me. Apènà must be called. Please support me when I say the son of Olorì and that the distorted palace fool Kútelú should not climb the throne of my fathers. It is forbidden for an impostor to climb the throne. He will die the minute he sits.

ÌYÁ MÒPÓ: There you go again, singing songs of honour when all is lost. We have decided. Olorì has paid a price, and we are happy with her. Leave the throne to the ancestors to choose who sits on it. But Kútelú must surely die.

KÁBÍYÈSÍ: I agree. Give me two days. How about Olorì?

ÌYÁ MÒPÓ: We have no need for her anymore. The spirit of her harlotry hunts her. We have left her to her fate… she will be consumed by the darkness of her fate. But she must die a queen… a request from the fluttering birds.

KÁBÍYÈSÍ: I agree. That is shameful enough. Then you can have Kútelú.

ÌYÁ MÒPÓ: Good. Do you know his father?

KÁBÍYÈSÍ: No. He wandered here, led in by Apènà and Òtún. We needed a carrier… an Abòbakú… two days before my ascension to the throne. Our knots were tied, and he walked in… he has not left since. But now I want him out.

ÌYÁ MÒPÓ: It will be easy to find out. Even the wind talks to us. It is done then.

KÁBÍYÈSÍ: I will like to know too. Just thank his parents for giving me such a willing son. He has served me well. If only he has not touched my wife.

ÌYÁ MỌPÓ: Then you would have been a fool of a king. The villagers would have asked to see your child. He too saved your shame. But why does it without question amazes even the fluttering Birds.

KÁBÍYÈSÍ: He is a willing servant. In gratitude, I gave him a title... he even speaks the Whiteman's language.

ÌYÁ MỌPÓ: A willing fool more likely. We too want to know who gives his or her son up for sacrifice and backs him.

KÁBÍYÈSÍ: And me? You heard what the Balógun wants from me.

ÌYÁ MỌPÓ: We heard. We even heard of the visit of the Mọmọ.

KÁBÍYÈSÍ: He came with the Balógun's calabash. He wants my head.

ÌYÁ MỌPÓ: Why? What have you done?

KÁBÍYÈSÍ: I did not send the Ìsákọ́lẹ̀. We had a bad season. Then he wanted me to send soldiers to fight Ìbàdàn. Balógun Ògúnmọ́lá would have killed them all with one wave of his sword. But my greatest sin is that the Balógun feels I have given the respects due to him to the D.O. But even he respects the D.O. PAUSE. What do you think?

ÌYÁ MỌPÓ: You are the King of Ìjẹ̀kùn Odò... nothing can touch you.

KÁBÍYÈSÍ: I will sleep better tonight. My head will stay better on my neck.

ÌYÁ MỌPÓ: The gods of the land cover you, except your time is up, and no star is set to fall. But the gods forbid that such a mishap should take place. The night draws towards the morning clouds. I must leave.

KANIYESI: With that settled, when do we meet again?

ÌYÁ MỌPÓ: When the Vultures turn up to lick the bones. PAUSE. One more thing.

KÁBÍYÈSÍ: What?

ÌYÁ MỌPÓ: Olorì shall come to you tonight. For the last time, honour her. The fluttering birds demand it.

KÁBÍYÈSÍ: Demand? Why?

ÌYÁ MỌPÓ: No, request... if that will sound more gently to your ears.

KÁBÍYÈSÍ: Request. The request of the birds is an order of the gods.

ÌYÁ MỌPÓ: Honour her... I plead with you.

KÁBÍYÈSÍ: Honour her? Never! I take another wife soon.

ÌYÁ MỌPÓ: Until then. But why not keep the secret of your spent spirits within the folds of your wrapper. Why take another wife who will complicate your tale? We have spoken Kábíyèsí.

KÁBÍYÈSÍ: And I have heard you.

ÌYÁ MỌPÓ: Before I go, the wife of the late Òsì will come before you, treat her gently.

KÁBÍYÈSÍ: Let her come. We shall listen with care. May the gods guide us right. His death was a painful one. But you know me. I shall not be partial. If she has done right, then she has no need to fear.

ÌYÁ MỌPÓ: Treat her with care... she sits next in line to me. Her shame is our shame. You are our King, rule us well.

KÁBÍYÈSÍ: It is done. May the gods guide us. Now hurry home, before the morning dew wets your wings.

SLOWLY LIGHTS FADE.

APÈNÀ'S HOUSE. HE SITS ON A WOODEN RESTING CHAIR. ÌLÀRÍ ENTERS WITH YOUNG PRINCE.

ÌLÀRÍ: Bàbá, may the gods awaken you with wisdom.

APÈNÀ: Ìlàrí, I hope all is well at the palace?

ÌLÀRÍ: All is well. Kábíyèsí sent us to you. He wants the young Prince Ọlágùnsóyè prepared.

APÈNÀ: And so will he be. REMEMBERS. RISES. Before I forget. He also wanted me to prepare his sister's son.

ÌLÀRÍ: Yes. I shall bring him once you have finished with our young prince here.

APÈNÀ: Wait for me. HE HURRIES IN. SOON AFTER, HE EMERGES. Young prince, go in. EXIT PRINCE INTO THE HOUSE. Here. Give this to him. Tell him to drink it with ọkà bàbà pap in the middle of the night. And here. GIVES HIM A LITTLE BAG. Some money to keep your lips sealed.

ÌLÀRÍ: PROSTRATES. I thank you, Bàbá. May the gods remain with you. When do I come back for him?

APÈNÀ: In three days' time, when the moon is ripe enough to show the hidden inner shadows of the world's masked darkened hearts.

ÌLÀRÍ: Hm?

APÈNÀ: Three days' time, Ìlàrí. EXIT ÌLÀRÍ. So he sent him did he? I should wash away the head of one, my own flesh and blood and enrich the other. Am I a fool? Where is it heard that a woman throws away her beans just to enrich the land of her neighbour? My bean is my bean, and their land is theirs'.

PRINCE: ENTERS. Bàbá Apènà, why has my father sent me to you?

APÈNÀ: Er… to teach you how best to be a king. And prepare for the task ahead. And to learn the secrets of blurred images from the past and brighter ones from the future. Rules of closed thoughts… do you understand?

PRINCE: No.

APÈNÀ: How to speak in the language of man and gods…

PRINCE: Like…

APÈNÀ: What to see… what to eat… how to take decisions that make men cry or laugh and still keep a dead panned face of cold emotions. Do you understand now?

PRINCE: No.

APÈNÀ: Then sit down. It is difficult to understand words of wisdom standing. The feet won't let you think.

PRINCE: I see you live alone. Don't you have a family?

APÈNÀ: I had a wife once. She died while giving birth to my son in the farm. I buried her there, took the son, and gave him to my distant sister to bring up.

PRINCE: I am sorry. Where is your son now?

APÈNÀ: Dead, he died a painful death trying to help a wild buffalo escape the hunters trap. A hunter shot him in the back, thinking he was a thief.

PRINCE: Pity. A sad story.

APÈNÀ: Not so sad. He too left a son, whom I am yet to meet. He lives in a village not too far from here. But one day soon, I shall bring him home. And tell him who I am to him. But first, I must prepare you for the difficulties ahead.

PRINCE: Difficulties ahead. Is it true Bàbá, that the Balógun wants my father's head?

APÈNÀ: Not a thing to worry about. It can be resolved. I shall see to it. But in matters of royalties, heads come and go. No matter how strongly built. Even the stiff strong ones like those of buffalos.

PRINCE: Buffalos. I had a dream last night about buffalos... sad too. And it will be good to start with it. Since you know so much, I will like to tell you my dream. Should I?

APÈNÀ: Yes. CHUCKLES. It is good to know that princes dream.

PRINCE: Why?

APÈNÀ: I thought you had everything. Yours is to wish, and it is done.

PRINCE: We dream. My dream is always about losing everything I have. I love the palace. I have everything like you say. I will hate to lose the power of having everything I have now. Do you think I will?

APÈNÀ: No. May the gods never let you. Tell me about your dream.

PRINCE: Two buffalos chased after me. One wild, ferocious and ready to kill. Its horns curved and ready to pierce. The other fat and wild, with folds that looked like a hump in its back. With red bloodshot eyes, they chased me. And with a breathless lip, I ran, praying... looking for a high tree to climb. As we all ran, the dust followed... impeding suffocating death of dust blocking my nostrils. Then I saw it.

APÈNÀ: What? What did you see, son?

PRINCE: A tree. I ran up it like a monkey, and with the bang on two sides of the tree, it shook until I could feel the trunk pull. Then a fight followed. The huge wild buffalo too angry to think. With a little flip, the smaller buffalo pierced the throat of the bigger one and left it wounded, until it started to bleed profusely. A long breath and a drag of what sounded like raw pain, it fell. From nowhere can an old man with a spear. He took the very tired buffalo and pieced it with his spear. As the two buffalos died slowly, the old man beckoned me to climb down. Too tired to say a word, I obeyed, still breathing heavily... my heart racing. That was when I woke up.

APÈNÀ: The stupidity of dreams makes us foolish most times.

PRINCE: I don't understand. It was so real. What does it mean, Bàbá?

PRINCE: Nothing. Sleep again tonight. Another dream will come. Then you can tell me that one. This appears simple enough. Hm... an important visitor approaches; go into the room. There is food for you there. Soon we shall see what your dream was about. Do not fret, son. The wonders of the world are overwhelming. Sometimes, they spill into the other world of dreams. Hurry, go in. Not a sound.

EXIT PRINCE INTO THE HOUSE.

ÌYÁ MỌPÓ: ENTERS. The morning sun showed where you are. Apènà, why did you not tell me. You did not dig the ground deep enough to hide it.

NA: What an odd way to greet one in the morning. I do not understand a word of what you said.

ÌYÁ MỌPÓ: I shall not beat about the bush then. We know that Prince Ọlágùnsóyè resides here with you.

APÈNÀ: Oh, that is the mountain edge from which you saw what you say you saw. He is here. On the orders of Kábíyèsí. And as it is with custom, I am to prepare him.

ÌYÁ MỌPÓ: For what? Is Kábíyèsí dying soon? Why the haste to prepare a prince who does not suffer from an ailment?

APÈNÀ: I do not know. The king commanded, so we carry it out.

ÌYÁ MỌPÓ: I want to know something from you. Since apart from preparing princes for life or death, you also keep secrets.

APÈNÀ: what do you want to know?

ÌYÁ MỌPÓ: I want to know about Kútelú. Who gave him life? What is the name of his father?

APÈNÀ: I do not know. But you should know. The fluttering birds know everything.

ÌYÁ MỌPÓ: So we thought. But his life is well hidden. Even beyond the darkness of our sight. We see shadows of blurred images. His mother is dead because we see her dried up bones. But his father appears as burning smoke, covered by the red cloth of Ṣàngó, and possessed of the deadly wise wit of Èṣù. You say you don't know him?

APÈNÀ: No mother.

ÌYÁ MỌ̀PÓ: CHUCKLES. He must be a powerful medicine man, don't you think?

APÈNÀ: CHUCKLES. If you say so.

ÌYÁ MỌ̀PÓ: We know so. We want Kútelú.

APÈNÀ: Kútelú? Why? His life is tied to that of the king.

ÌYÁ MỌ̀PÓ: He has a secret he threatens to reveal. He also wants to kill a member of the conclave of birds. Will he get my message, old wise one?

APÈNÀ; I will tell him when and if I see him. But he is the beloved of Kábíyèsí now. He even just gave him a big title.

ÌYÁ MỌ̀PÓ: Title? For how long. We also hear that Kábíyèsí sits at the edge of death. We hear that the Balógun sent him a gift... a calabash which is now broken. All this rush... all this anger... all this search for power... Ọmọ Ikú... Ọmọ òfò. He insulted the Balógun, he must pay for it.

APÈNÀ: With his head?

ÌYÁ MỌ̀PÓ: With his life if possible. But he never listens to the fluttering birds. Anyway, if you see Kútelú, whisper into his ears that two little darts will be shot at his hump. A loss to a father will be much don't you think?

APÈNÀ; Yes... I suppose. But either way, he is doomed... death embraces him completely.

ÌYÁ MỌPÓ: We have spoken then. SHE BEGINS TO WALK AWAY.

APÈNÀ; Wait! What about his father? What do I tell him?

ÌYÁ MỌPÓ: GIVES A WILD LAUGH. Nothing.

EXITS ÌYÁ MỌPÓ.

APÈNÀ: She knows. They all know. But first, the wind must first blow before the dust settles. Háà... Kútelú hurry... too many musicians will spoil the dance. Hurrry son... hurry. Èṣù Láàlú, steady his hand, I beg you.

MỌMỌ́: ENTERS FROM THE HOUSE. I heard it all.

APÈNÀ: I know. MỌMỌ́ KNEELS BEFORE APÈNÀ Why? What is this for?

MỌMỌ́: Thank you for bringing joy to the house once again.

APÈNÀ: I don't understand.

MỌMỌ́: You know. The prince our grandson's return home.

APÈNÀ: Panu de! Not a word! Not a whisper! No one knows, except us.

MỌMỌ́: I am sorry. PAUSE. Maybe that was why he asked what I was to you?

APÈNÀ: And what did you say?

MỌMỌ́: Your second wife. He told me your first wife died during the birth of your son. Begins to cry. Lies. Too many lies. If only you had not tried to push your son, we would be one big family. You were already Apènà, what else did we want?

APÈNÀ: I am sorry.

MỌMỌ: You are not. You don't understand the love of a woman for her son. The pith of my womb cries for him. I want my son back. My own grandson thinks I am a cheap woman who stays with the Apènà of a village he was born to rule over. Me? His grandmother, a second wife. Too many lies, my husband.

APÈNÀ: I know. I told him it will be alright. We will tell him the truth at the right time. For now, the lies will have to remain.

MỌMỌ: I don't even remember what to say anymore. All I feel is pain. The king gave our son a title and I could dress and walk with pride. All he did was nod to me from his horse. I hear he will soon pick a wife, and I won't have a say. What kind of life is this? SHE BEGINS TO CRY.

APÈNÀ: There you go again. All tears and no moment of joy. Indeed, I must make plans for you to go and see your sick mother in Ògbómọ̀ṣọ́.

MỌMỌ: When?

APÈNÀ: Soon… When the coast line is clear and the boats can sail safely. When the chickens hatch and the chicks survive. Very soon my dearest Adérónkẹ́ Ìbàdíàrán, ọmọge ìdílé Mọ̀mọ́ ọ̀nà Kakañfò. ìdílé Àgbára. ìdílé Balógun Yorùbá. ọmọ Kotonú, ilé ìdí àgbọn.

MỌMỌ: Let me be. It was you who pushed your son to become Abọ́bakú… then Kábíyèsí turned him into a monster. My own child. My breasts and womb will judge you both.

APÈNÀ: They will judge Kábíyèsí. Like a father, I wished him well. The rule said that only foreigners could become

Abóbakú. We already had Àjàsá who was our first child who was to become Àpènà after me. So we made Kútelú the Abóbakú.

MỌ̀MỌ́: Kútelú is not my son. That monster is not my son.

APÈNÀ: Gbẹ́nu ẹ dákẹ́. Neither is he my son. Be firm woman, our feet are already in the stream, how can we now complain of cold? Be strong.

MỌ̀MỌ́: I want my grandson to know me. I want to be the grandmother to a king who knows me. You are the Àpènà… the voice of the gods. Let them for once speak for us.

APÈNÀ: They will. Èṣù has given his word to fight for us. Ṣàngó will see us through this battle. Be strong, Mọ̀mọ́.

MỌ̀MỌ́: How soon?

APÈNÀ: Soon. The soup boils. Soon your tears will stop. The world will be as you want it.

SLOWLY LIGHTS FADE.

KÚTELÚ'S HOUSE. KÚTELÚ WAITS ANXIOUSLY.

KÚTELÚ: Why is love so strange? The ferocious energy with which it evokes the heart when the mood is cool is the same savage rage with which it destroys. Why? Even if the whirlwind of death blows tonight, I am ready. Olorì Ìwàtáyọ̀ breaks my heart. She rubs me with mud and announces my filth to the world. When she came to me, I was the chosen one, blessed and adored. But now she pushes me to the noose. Our son, my only child, disowns me because he does not know who I am. I Kútelú saved the face of the king so his wife could have a child. And then I became the Abọ́bakú chosen to honour him till death. The only succour, I now forfeit. Then death must reign. If the rat will not have the food on the trap, then let it be and remain for a child to play with. Come and embrace me Olorì. Wherever you are, drop what takes your fancy and come and embrace death. It is the only soothing balm for now. Come!

OLORÌ ENTERS.

OLORÌ: Kútelú.

KÚTELÚ: You came.

OLORÌ: You asked me to. I heard your voice from afar. Why have you sent for me?

KÚTELÚ: I was shocked to find you in the arms of the D.O. It was as if he wanted me to see both of you. I mean, asking his men to bring me to his private official office where I saw you laid out as a dish for an Abẹ́lẹ́jayán. You played your part well. I hear his wife never goes there. That was when I knew that someone wanted me to see something. That was when I linked the dots, and I came out sour.

OLORÌ: And you did see something?

KÚTELÚ: I did.

OLORÌ: I am happy. She is always down with fever. She grows weak each day. She might return home soon, and the D.O. shall be all mine. I see envy in your eyes.

KÚTELÚ: Envy? Why Olorì?

OLORÌ: Why Kútelú? Thanks to you, Kábíyèsí disowned me. For that I shall never forgive you. You the father of my son took me to the market and sold me cheaply. I was left unattended. I needed protection... a form of power to stay in the palace. If the Whiteman is on my side, then who can dare touch me. Did you think his letter and threat to remove the Kábíyèsí came from the gods? I saw you dancing that you had persuaded the Whiteman to change his mind about dethroning Kábíyèsí. In your wildest dreams, how did you achieve that? You spoke with him for only a moment, and his letter which I dictated my desires was full. CHUCKLES. Abọ̀bajíròrò. What advice can a hunchback possibly give to a king? I heard Kábíyèsí gave you a title you did not even deserve. Did you think all that was your doing? Fool.

KÚTELÚ: Whose doing was it then? You denied me your love after our son was born.

OLORÌ: My son. I denied you in order to save him. Eyes and noses were coming too close to us. So I decided that the only way to hurt you was to leave you, and save our son. When Kábíyèsí laced you up and tied his life to yours, I knew that it was over. If you touched me, he would know. So, I chose to reveal all to you... make you see me with the D.O. You had become too bitter to keep a secret. I did not need to reveal my secret to the Kábíyèsí.

KÚTELÚ: Your secret? What secret?

OLORÌ: I want my son to be king after his father.

KÚTELÚ: I am his father.

OLORÌ; No one knows but you. Kábíyèsí believes he is the father. And that is alright by me.

KÚTELÚ: He knows for now. He has even pronounced that he should not be king when he joins his forefathers. It is not alright by me. But my lips are sealed for now. I have not told the Kábíyèsí that I saw you in the arms of the Whiteman.

OLORÌ: That is why I came. If you have not told him, then you want something more precious in return. What do you want Kútelú, hunchback of the king, Abọ̀bajíròrò of Ìjẹ̀kùn Odò.

KÚTELÚ: You. CHUCKLES. I saw you spread out on the bed of the Whiteman, an albino… and I wanted you for one last time.

OLORÌ: Me?

KÚTELÚ: Yes. I was pained. How have you survived even with the oath of death?

OLORÌ: Swimming the two rivers of life.

KÚTELÚ: CHUCKLES AGAIN. You really gather us as fools.

OLORÌ: Yes. I am a woman. Into my harem of despicable souls, fools gather. I despise you.

KÚTELÚ: Then add me to your husband's list of death? See what your dear husband turned me to. I am now the scorned lover. Should I let him live? Me, the last born son of the Apẹ̀nà of Ìjẹ̀kùn Odò?

OLORÌ: No.

KÚTELÚ: Good. I gave him my life to serve and carry his personal problems and will die when he dies. But I never knew I had to carry his life along. I am now his hunchback. Is a moment's hatred for him wrong?

OLORÌ: No.

KÚTELÚ: When I walk in the town, the jeers of the people pinch me. The little children have a song for me.

OLORÌ: So I heard. But you decided to climb on my back to the ears of the king. Wicked soul. At least you succeeded, you got him to hate me. But no one can be used to bring about my downfall. Èèwọ̀! It is you Kútelú who covers him with a cushion of pain. I shall destroy him… both of you, if I have to. You see how the feeling of hatred is of equal measure?

KÚTELÚ: Forgiveness eludes me too. Fresh wounds often open too quickly. They become festered when not properly cared for. The wound you put in my heart festers each day. Don't you know me?

OLORÌ: Who are you, if l may ask?

KÚTELÚ: I am Kútelú, the tender clove of the bitter kola… I have the sting of a bee, and the fullness of my mouth is filled with the bitterness of gall. Olorì, tonight you shall rise with your mouth filled with the dregs of pond water. My heart bleeds.

OLORÌ: Sting of a bee? Do you know what I am? Undressed of worn out mortar. Do you know what I have to do? I say, who are you? What are you? What do you amount to? You caused my shame, stripped me with your loose lips. Are you a wizard, or a distorted crazed wild spirit? Speak to me.

KÚTELÚ: I speak of anger. I seek revenge. You broke me.

OLORÌ: Broke you did you say? I am what I am because of what I was built to be by Olódùmarè. My parents died one after the other as I grew. I never knew the possessive love, the type you display. When I asked you to have me, I wanted a child. Kábíyèsí cannot get a woman pregnant. To buy life, he sold everything. And when I got what I wanted from you, it was over, but now you are like a little child who has lost his bean cake.

KÚTELÚ: I still feel a constantly swelling anger.

OLORÌ: Anger? To whom? For whom? Kútelú, your real shame has arrived. Prepare to sit on it. Fluttering mothers, your child calls for help. Determined, the man I love wants my life.

KÚTELÚ: Call them, they too will flutter into a pot of shame. I am kolanut.

OLORÌ: It is matters that do not concern obì àbàtà that kills it. That brings about its down fall. Your down fall draws nearer than you think.

KÚTELÚ: Then come and get me. Spread your wings and embrace me.

OLORÌ: Kútelú leave me alone. If you think you are clever at biting, the bumble bees are cleverer. Alápààǹdẹ̀dẹ̀ built the two worlds of heaven and earth. Fire burns you today.

KÚTELÚ: Your stupid goat has wandered into the fire today. The snail tasted salt and it died, today you have tasted salt, so your end has arrived Olorì.

OLORÌ: Èèwọ̀! When Ṣàngó roars from above, all males and females run kíjokíjo. The black pebbles of Ṣàngó will fall on you. I say fall to a shameful end. We promised at the beginning of the world that we will not kill the person who knows our names. You do not know our names, you will die today.

KÚTELÚ: Shut up. The needle outside belongs to the fire that will consume it. The goat outside is a broken calabash. Pànkàrà outside is empty akèrègbè. The leaves in the fire belong to the fire. The wood in the fire become ashes. ARMS STRETCHED. Come closer to the death of a bird, I say come closer. Embittered jeers fill me with gall. I shall never forgive Kábíyèsí either, that is the twin that links us together. SLOWLY OLORÌ GOES CLOSER INTO HIS ARMS UNTIL THEY HUG.

OLORÌ: SCREAMS. Something touches me. Like the cold scratch of death, it touches me. Háà... I am finished. SHE BEGINS TO FALL, SLOWLY INTO THE ARMS OF KÚTELÚ. SCARED KÚTELÚ LAYS HER ON THE THE CHAIR, HE REMOVES HIS AGBÁDÁ, AND REVEALS THE BEADS. The beads... truly, I am finished. SHE DIES.

KÚTELÚ: What do I do now? A darkened effigy embraced me, just when I thought I saw a ray of light shine down my disjointed dark brown hole. Am I the fool? The manacle of life further cuffs me... and I rot, I stand. OIori, I am finished too. Slowly the noose tightens round my distorted beaded neck and dry gangrene sets in. Wait for me... before Kábíyèsí finds me in the dark forest. What do I do now?

APÈNÀ: ENTERS. What have you done?

KÚTELÚ: The way you said it, that is the way it turned out to be, father. She came, we saw, now she lies dead. What do I do? I did not intend to kill her. Just as your lips had said it, but death was never mentioned. What do I do now?

APÈNÀ: Nothing. I shall handle it all. You go, hurry to the palace. Tell Kábíyèsí nothing of this, until I come before his presence.

KÚTELÚ: Yes. HE HURRIES OUT.

APÈNÀ: LOOKS AT OLORÌ. You fool... you, the promiscuous effigy of foolery... see how she lies still as a stoned image carved in shame. You turned my son into a henpecked lover. You stooped always too low. Now I must reach the eager ears of the Kábíyèsí and blame this on the oath of Ṣàngó. It is fulfilled. She died exactly on the seventh day and the sun still shines. Èṣù's anger over Kábíyèsí's insulting message still boils. LOOKS AROUND. Where are the men I asked to come? TWO PALACE messengers ENTER. Take her to the shrine... wrap her gently, she was once a queen, remember? Not a soul will see you... not even your darkened shadows must whisper a tale of what you carry. Now hurry!

SLWOLY LIGHTS FADE.

THE THRONE ROOM. KÁBÍYÈSÍ AND THE CHIEFS ARE SEATED. A WOMAN KNEELS BEFORE HIM. WHEN SCENE OPENS, APÈNÀ WALKS IN. HE PROSTRATES.

APÈNÀ: Kábíyèsí.

KÁBÍYÈSÍ: Is it done?

APÈNÀ: Yes Kábíyèsí. HE LOOKS AROUND. I thought Kútelú will be here by now.

KÁBÍYÈSÍ: But I am sure he will come. You know this woman?

APÈNÀ: Yes, Kábíyèsí. She is the third wife of the late Òsì.

KÁBÍYÈSÍ: Thank you. We have not even completed the burial rites of Òsì, and the third wife of Òsì comes to complain about the inheritance of her husband's properties. This world is going upside down.

APÈNÀ: She had six children for Òsì. May be she felt the number should increase her lot.

ÒTÚN: Which lot Kábíyèsí? I know how many times I went to his house to settle quarrels between him and this woman, or this woman and the other wives.

KÁBÍYÈSÍ: How many wives did he have in all?

APÈNÀ: Four. The first one had a son, who is the headmaster in Ìsẹ́yìn. The second wife had two sons who live in Lagos. She had six. And the fourth wife had a girl, who works with the white men in the city as a Clerk.

KÁBÍYÈSÍ: Olórí ẹbí. What did your brother leave for his ten children?

OLÓRÍ ẸBÍ: He provided for each of them. He gave them land and houses. He was a man of wealth. He even gave us the extended family properties too.

KÁBÍYÈSÍ: Then this woman?

OLÓRÍ ẸBÍ: A thief. Our son left the house where he lived and was buried to his first son. With the hope that when the son becomes the Òsì, he would live there as his palace. But Ìyàwó says she must stay in the house with him. She also wants the cocoa farm by the river side.

KÁBÍYÈSÍ: Did he leave a house for her?

OLÓRÍ ẸBÍ: He built her one, and made the family swear not to collect it from her after his death. Then he gave her another house to move into immediately after his death.

KÁBÍYÈSÍ: A very wise move for a man who had plenty. Òsì will surely meet Olódùmarè where he will be fed with plenty too.

OLÓRÍ ẸBÍ: Indeed, he planned for his death. But this wicked woman wants to tarnish his good memories. Now the children are not on speaking terms when they are the envy of the whole village.

KÁBÍYÈSÍ: Woman, are you a daughter or a wife of the late Òsì?

WOMAN: Wife, Kábíyèsí. But I was more than a wife. I served him until after death.

KÁBÍYÈSÍ: I do not understand.

WOMAN: Thank you, Kábíyèsí. He died alone in the room. No one was there. I had gone to bring him food. When I entered the room, I found him gone. His mouth ajar, his hands and legs everywhere. I became a man and a wife. I removed my scarf and tied his jaw!

ỌTÚN: Ṣọnpọnná ò!

WOMAN: Bent his hand, dragged them together. Tore strips from my new wrapper and tied his legs and hands together, so that he looked decent for his burial.

KÁBÍYÈSÍ: Apènà, what does she say?

APÈNÀ: Sacrilege Kábíyèsí. No woman touches the body of a high chief of Ìjẹ̀kùn Odò in death. Were you not told the day you married him woman?

WOMAN: They said so. But my love for him and the honour of my six children made me do it.

APÈNÀ; That was why we buried him without much of the proper ritual, she had defiled the body.

KÁBÍYÈSÍ: Woman...

WOMAN: Forgive me, Kábíyèsí.

KÁBÍYÈSÍ: You did all that? Who the heck are you to have touched his body, and then shed crocodile tears? Woman, you banter over properties with his children. You cause disharmony amongst them. I heard you swore that until your death, your children must not speak with the other children. Did you say that?

WOMAN: Kábíyèsí...

KÁBÍYÈSÍ: Did you say that?

WOMAN: I did. But he forgot me in death. He should have asked me what to give to who stood by him. But instead, he took all his properties and denied my children their rights.

OLÓRÍ ẸBÍ: Kábíyèsí... he gave even his daughters properties. Even those married. A great favour which is not the practice and privilege extended to daughters.

WOMAN: Kábíyèsí... I will die first before losing any more property to the children. We must redistribute the properties. I know what they are; I shall divide them myself. Only death can stop me. I know those who stand for me.

KÁBÍYÈSÍ: Hear her. She threatens the throne. I am king even over those who stand for you. Are you a god? Are you worshipped? I am the doer without questions. Èkejì Òrìṣà. We can help you achieve death. Apènà can cut off your head as we speak in the shrine of Ògún... and divide it to all your six children. Fool.

WOMAN: No, Kábíyèsí. I plead...

KÁBÍYÈSÍ: Háà. Now she pleads. Greedy fool.

ỌTÚN: This woman is indeed very greedy, Kábíyèsí. Her late husband was my cousin. We know what kind of marriage she had with him. We also know how many lovers she had. Even when Òsì was ill, she smuggled in lovers to the house through the back door. We all saw her, but we knew a day like this will come. She would kill her husband, and she would be brought to judgment.

KÁBÍYÈSÍ: You mean that Òsì had such a wound and he covered it all up. Apènà, let her swear on the upturned mortar tonight. I can accept all forms of misbehaviour from women, but not promiscuity. Death awaits you. Could you have tried this with a husband before the Whiteman's religion came? Òsì should have put mágùn on you, and you and your lovers will all be dead by now. THEY ALL KNEEL AND PROSTRATE TO BEG. ÌLÀRÍ ENTERS. Then go, all of you. Not one more word from you on this matter. Òsì was a great man, please let him rest in peace. THEY ALL LEAVE. THE CHIEFS STAY BEHIND. Ìlàrí, what now?

ÌLÀRÍ: Kábíyèsí, Kútelú has passed on to the big bush.

KÁBÍYÈSÍ: Apènà, speak with this fool. What message is this?

APÈNÀ: What did you say?

ÌLÀRÍ: I was going to bring the slaves from the farm when two women ran to me screaming and crying that Kútelú had been wounded and bleeding in the bush. I followed them there and behold it was true. Two soldiers of the Whitemen were said to have had an argument with him and shot him from behind. Two pierced holes in his hump.

KÁBÍYÈSÍ: An argument?

ÌLÀRÍ: Yes Kábíyèsí.

APÈNÀ: Kábíyèsí, a word inside. Hurry!

KÁBÍYÈSÍ: Please let me finish, Apènà. TO ÌLÀRÍ. That cannot be true. The D.O. sent all his policemen to Bádore to quell the people fighting over the position of Baálẹ̀. Balógun followed them there with ten of our men. I don't think the D.O. would have two soldiers to spare just to kill Kútelú. I smell a rat.

ÒTÚN: Let the rat die, Kábíyèsí. Follow Apènà into the room. Kútelú was your Abọ́bakú. Now he has died before you. There are sacrifices to be made. Rise Kábíyèsí.

KÁBÍYÈSÍ: Suddenly I feel weak all over. My limbs run cold.

APÈNÀ: Hurry. Go home, all of you. Wait for Kábíyèsí's call. There are rites to be performed. THEY TAKE KÁBÍYÈSÍ IN. THE LIGHTS FADE FOR A WHILE. APÈNÀ AND ÒTÚN RE-ENTER.

ÒTÚN: So, he left? It was so sudden. Too soon.

APÈNÀ: Yes. Fàkìyà fakiya he treaded the earth, Fàkìyà fakiya, and he fell. I warned him. Now see how he ended.

ÒTÚN: You could have saved him if you wanted to. I have seen you save worse patients. It seemed as if you were digging the grave even before he breathed his last. Apènà you took too long to try.

APÈNÀ: I was overwhelmed. My son Kútelú had died too, remember? I was not settled. My mind was confused. PAUSE. A common man is like a sleeping lion. Kábíyèsí woke me up, so I tore him apart.

ÒTÚN: You?

APÈNÀ: He killed my son you know. Distorted a child I gave him to serve the land, then he turned him into a pitiable sight. Abuké Ọba, the Hunchback of Ìjẹkùn Odò. He would mock him with cheap clothes. He promised he would love him, that we his parents will be rich... but all he gave us was scorn... jeers and ridicule. We gave him Àdìsá Ọmọlèrè... but when he used him, I could not recognize what he called Kútelú. He inflated my son with his life, so to stop him, we burst Kútelú's hunch in order to take him. And now death has embraced him. All will be well now from tonight.

ÒTÚN: We must tell the Olorì. The poor woman will be relieved now.

APÈNÀ: CHUCKLES. Relieved? That mistake of a woman? She too waits at the gate of the heavens to receive Kábíyèsí.

ÒTÚN: So they all died? Ṣàngó Olúkòso! Olójú orógbó. Seven days. Just as Ṣàngó said she would… seven days. All is avenged.

APÈNÀ: Yes. PAUSE. Ọ̀tún.

ÒTÚN: Yes.

APÈNÀ: One thing eludes me in all these happenings.

ÒTÚN: What?

APÈNÀ: The two soldiers who shot Kútelú at the back. Who sent them? Was it the D.O? Or the Aláàfin?

ÒTÚN: What does it matter now? He died. They all died.

APÈNÀ: Yes, they all did. Seven days. Just in time to herald Ṣàngó's supremacy. ÌLÀRÍ COMES IN. Hà, Ìlàrí Ọba, tell the drummers to announce the death of Kábíyèsí. There will be Orò for three nights. The markets will be closed. Take Prince Ọlágùnsóyè to the inner chamber. We must begin to prepare him. Ìjẹkùn Odò will cry, mourn and laugh again. Ayé ń lọ, à ń tọ̀ ọ́. Another leaf of our lives is plucked, and Èṣù remains accomplished. I must hurry home to my wife. I must tell her to stop her tears. She too has become something in the village. There is no need anymore. The Balógun can have his calabash filled. We shall take Prince

Ọlágùnsóyè to see him with the Mọmọ́. The inner turmoil is over. Once again, we can be at peace.

ÒTÚN: So much to do... há hà... the drummers have started with the sad message of Kábíyèsí's death. Before I forget, as agreed, my daughter Moróuntódùn marries the new King?

APÈNÀ: Yes. As always, you have my word.

AS THE DRUMMERS BEAT THE DIRGE OF THE ỌBA, ÌYÁLÓDE HURRIES IN.

ÌYÁLÓDE: Òtún, is this true?

APÈNÀ: Where have you been?

ÌYÁLÓDE: I went to perform all the sacrifices Ifádèyí asked me to, to appease Èṣù. I guess Láàlú was too angry. His evil spirit loomed everywhere I went. Ifádèyí asked me to hurry, but there were too many things to do. I must have been too late. As I returned, three times I hit my left foot. The sound of the sad drums welcomed me. Is it true?

APÈNÀ: It is true. All is late now. Kábíyèsí sleeps. Èṣù has done his worse again.

FINAL LIGHTS SLOWLY FADE.

ÒṢUN

Dramatis Personae.

ÒTÚN
APÈNÀ
ÌLÀRÍ ÀJÀSÁ
OBA ÒGÌDÁN
IKÚSANRÍ
ÌYÁ ODÒ
ÌYÁ ÒSUN
BÀBÁ IFÁDÉLÉ
IYEMOJA
AJÉ
KÓRÌ
ÒSÚNTÓMI
IFÁDÈYÍ
LEADER
DANCERS, DRUMMERS AND MUSICIANS

ỌṢUN.

WHEN DIM LIGHTS COME ON, SLOW DRUMS BEAT. KÁBÍYÈSÍ ÒGÌDÁN IS SEATED ON THE MORTAR TURNED UPSIDE DOWN. HE TIES A RED WRAPPER ROUND HIS WAIST. IKÚSANRÍ, A MEDICINE MAN, STANDS OVER ỌBA ÒGÌDÁN AND CUTS INCISIONS ON ÒGÌDÁN'S HEAD WITH A SMALL SACRED KNIFE. ÌLÀRÍ ÀJÀSÁ AN ELDERLY MAN LOOKS ON, HOLDING A CALABASH.

IKÚSANRÍ: Be strong, we are almost there. Two hundred and ninety seven. CUTS. Two hundred and ninety eight. CUTS. Two hundred and ninety nine. CUTS. Three hundred. It is all over Kábíyèsí. Now tie his head with the red wrapper. ÌLÀRÍ TIES KÁBÍYÈSÍ'S HEAD WITH A SMALLER RED WRAPPER. It is done. You now have a covenant with death. You cannot die any more. You have altered your own destiny. O ti ré ikú dànù.

ÒGÌDÁN: I am grateful Bàbá Ikúsanrí. I was meant to die three weeks ago, but here I am, dizzy once in a while, but still alive. This amazes me. I have emerged victorious.

IKÚSANRÍ: It is my god Àjàngbádìlú that we have to thank. And of course, the son of Ajagunṣèlú who serves you as Olórí Ìlàrí.

ÒGÌDÁN: I thank him too. When Ìlàrí mentioned you, I did not believe it was true, and that it could be done. Ten babaláwo told me it could not be done. We even went as far as Ilé Ifẹ̀. That I had spent my time on earth just three years after ascending the throne of my fathers was to be unheard of. What have I done? I kept asking myself. Who did I offend? I started to put my house in order. My five Olorì, all young women. My little children. Ìjẹ̀kùn Odò, my ancestral home.

Then Ìlàrí came to me and said that it could be done through you. When you sent the message to me that it could be done, life had a new meaning. Once again, I thank you.

IKÚSANRÍ: We thank the mighty spirits of my small village Ajagunṣèlú and our son Ìlàrí Àjàsá. His father was a slave here, taken at the battle which your father Ọba Arógunmásàá fought against my village over a woman.

ÒGÌDÁN: A woman.

IKÚSANRÍ: Yes. Our king then would not let him have his wife, and in anger he set his soldiers upon Ajagunṣèlú. He swore to wipe the village out. He spared my village only after Tìmì Ẹdẹ and Àtàọjà Òṣogbo pleaded with him. The war left our village broken and our people, scattered. Now I have brothers and sisters everywhere. That is why when all this is done, I beg you Kábíyèsí, free our son Ọmọba Àjàsá. Let him come home to die and be buried there. Let him bring the remains of his parents to us and bury them with their people.

ÒGÌDÁN: Do you know where your parents are buried here?

ÌLÀRÍ: Yes, my lord. In the servant space of this palace of Ìjẹ̀kùn Odò. My sister Òṣúnbùnmi is also buried here.

ÒGÌDÁN: She too served here?

ÌLÀRÍ: Yes, Kábíyèsí. I am the only survivor from my immediate family from that war. Kábíyèsí Arógunmásàá killed them all.

ÒGÌDÁN: I remember the young girl now. My father desired her. She refused, but the elders found her dead in the morning. She had committed suicide. A painful one. They found her womb torn out of her stomach. Her hands all bloody. That was what the elders said.

ÌLÀRÍ: But...that was not how it happened. He wanted her against her will. She refused. But he forced himself on her all the same.

IKÚSANRÍ: Àjàsá pa ẹnu rẹ mọ́! Họ́wù!

ÒGÌDÁN: No. Let him. His mind is heavy with bitterness. Let him empty it. Pour it all out. Go on Ìlàrí.

ÌLÀRÍ: GOES ON HIS KNEES. No Kábíyèsí, please forgive me.

IKÚSANRÍ: Enough, CHUCKLES. See how tears already gather at the tips of my eyelids. But what has a man not seen that he will cry blood? Let it be, Kábíyèsí. Old stories are often coated until the truth becomes blurred. But one day, it will emerge. Let it be Kábíyèsí. We have had no king since the death of his father, sixty years ago. If you will oblige us of their bones, we shall be eternally grateful. So that we can give them befitting burials and then crown our prince. My people will be eternally grateful.

ÒGÌDÁN: Speak no more. It is done. I never knew Ìlàrí Àjàsá was a prince. He can even go with you today.

ÌLÀRÍ: No, Kábíyèsí. I swore with my life to serve you. I shall return when all this is over, and you are settled on the throne of your fathers. Only then will I return to the throne of my own fathers.

IKÚSANRÍ: Spoken like a true son of Ajagunṣèlú.

ÒGÌDÁN: I shall release you from your oath. And he shall have his freedom when all this is done. It will be well with us.

IKÚSANRÍ: Àṣẹ! I must thank you Kábíyèsí. May the gods continue to bless you a thousand folds. It shall be well with you.

ÒGÌDÁN: No, it is me who should thank you. If you had not forgiven me for my father's deeds, who will I have to play with today? I say who? I would have been here clutching the folds of my bed sheets, waiting patiently for the cold hands of death.

IKÚSANRÍ: Èèwọ̀! That will never happen. You are a good man. When I saw the gifts you sent… a big fat cow from Mòro, a hundred tubers of yams from Ọ̀wọ̀, rich palm oil from the palm trees of Òndó, and rich aṣọ òkè from Ṣakí, I knew Kábíyèsí was a generous man, and generously will I help you. I never leave my village… not for any man. My master never lets me. But when I showed him your gifts, he asked me to stay with you for as long as I want. Kábíyèsí Ògìdán, you shall live longer than your fathers.

BOTH KÁBÍYÈSÍ AND ÌLÀRÍ ÀJÀSÁ: Àṣẹ!

IKÚSANRÍ: There is just a little part left to complete the ritual of life.

ÒGÌDÁN: What part? Say it and it shall be done.

IKÚSANRÍ: Just the small part of two little doves. The blood and life are needed to take from them and add to yours.

ÒGÌDÁN: Two little white doves?

IKÚSANRÍ: Yes.

ÒGÌDÁN: TURNS TO ÌLÀRÍ. Àjàsá, go to the shrine of Ọbàtálá and bring ten white unblemished doves for him. This is the time they usually hatch their squabs.

IKÚSANRÍ: LETS OUT A WILD LAUGH. Ten doves? Kábíyèsí, you make me laugh. If it was that easy, I would have brought twenty myself. I did not mean that type of doves.

ÒGÌDÁN: Then I misunderstand you. What type of doves do you need Bàbá?

IKÚSANRÍ: Er... er... I must come closer for a whisper. Do not worry, Esu's cloak will blur the sight of those who will peep. Nothing will be able to touch you. You would have conquered life itself. Ẹ́ẹ gbó, Ẹ́ẹ tọ́ Kábíyèsí.

ÒGÌDÁN: Àṣẹ! The very desire of my heart Baba. So what kind of doves do you need?

IKÚSANRÍ: This is a simple task really.

HE MOVES CLOSER TO ỌBA ÒGÌDÁN AND WHISPERS INTO HIS EAR.

ÒGÌDÁN: Háà Èèwọ̀!

SLOWLY LIGHTS FADE.

WHEN LIGHTS COME ON, APÈNÀ IS ON THE WOODEN "ÀGBÀ N TARA" CHAIR, SLEEPING. ỌTÚN WALKS IN AGITATED AND ANGRY. HE STANDS OVER APÈNÀ FOR A WHILE.

ỌTÚN: He sleeps. The whole of Ìjẹ̀kùn Odò burns. But here he lies, at the last stop to hell, slurping his saliva, snoring like the worn-out bellows of a tired bronze smith. Sleeping like an unconcerned over pampered fat foolish child, while the impending turbulence in the village festers. Apènà!

APÈNÀ: STIRS IN HIS SLEEP. Hmmm. Who calls me?

ỌTÚN: Me. Agúnléjìká, the Ọtún Oba of Ìjẹ̀kùn Odò. Wake up and speak with me. You sent for me. Here I am. I have come.

APÈNÀ: BEGINS TO AWAKEN. My childhood friend and in-law. You delayed. I did not come to your house alone. I had a feeling you saw us, but you refused to meet with us. Did your wife not tell you that I came with the Kábíyèsí?

ỌTÚN: You came with Ọba Ògìdán?

APÈNÀ: Yes. He was the one who covered his face with a brown wrapper.

ỌTÚN: CHUCKLES. Ha! And I thought he was an old woman. That worsened your case. I had hidden between the folds of the sheets of my wife's bed, thinking of coming out, but when I heard his muffled voice, I was mummified... frozen. Slowly, I rolled down and crawled under the bed. Why did you come? He had sworn never to set eyes on me until his death. So what was he looking for in broad day light, covered like an old woman? He wants to end my life himself now does he?

APÈNÀ: No. Would I join him in such a dastardly act? May the gods forbid. No!

ÒTÚN: No? Then why did he come to my house? He had announced publicly that once the Ọdún Odò was done, he would place the beaded necklace of my family on his favourite larky Ọtẹ́dọlá... the deceitful Ṣàmù. That clumsy snake of a man. I say what did he want from me?

APÈNÀ: The Alálẹ̀ sent us.

ÒTÚN: The ancestors? Why?

APÈNÀ: This was why he disguised himself. HE SITS UP. You know, Ọtún Agúnléjìká, that seven days to the festival of Òrìṣà Odò, the Ọba does not step out of the palace. But when Ifágbàyí consulted Ifá, he said Èṣù demanded that we forgot the past happenings and let peace be restored to the land, or Yèyé Odò will not accept the sacrifices which the Arugbá will carry to the Ijẹ̀kùn river on the day of the celebrations.

ÒTÚN: Well I heard that Ṣàmù stood in for me. He came and asked me if he could, and I taught him everything. Step by step for three days. I taught him well.

APÈNÀ: And he performed well, enjoying the euphoria of being the second to the Kábíyèsí... except for the one time when he walked in front of Kábíyèsí, who almost stepped on Ṣàmù's agbádá. Imagine Kábíyèsí falling in the midst of the crowd on the way to pay his respects to Ọ̀sun Ṣ̀ẹngẹ̀ṣẹ́ of Yèyé Ijẹ̀kùn. He was about to fall when we held on to him... both sides. He too looked dizzy. His legs heavy. Sweat seething from his now red eyes.

ÒTÚN: Èèwọ̀! Foolish man that Ṣàmù has turned out to be. What would people have said? I told him not to walk in front of the King. They even say that I wanted to shame the king… a ploy to spoil the whole festival. The gods forbid!

APÈNÀ: Our ancestors were awake and with us. That was what averted his fall. Quickly, Ṣàmù and I closed in on him and held him up close on each side. Ṣàmù was strong. Kábíyèsí staggered for a while until he took control of himself. WORRIED. But… each time Kábíyèsí appeared weaker and weaker… as if power was draining out of him. But after the calabash had floated away, we quietly took him to the palace. He just stared at us, most of the time his mind was wondering, as if it was somewhere else.

ÒTÚN: IN A LOUD BITTER WHISPER. May be between the thighs of an innocent maiden. You know him and his lecherous ways with women.

APÈNÀ: Ọtún! That is yesterday's story. He swore to change after we caught him with Aṣípa's young daughter. We forced him to marry her.

ÒTÚN: Yes. But she became his tenth wife… and yet she was only a child. How can one man be so insatiable with women?

APÈNÀ: Leave him alone. Let him enjoy the life of opulence of the king. How is my sister?

ÒTÚN: She lives, still in raw pain though. Bitter pain lingers. Every time she runs to the river, calling Ọṣun to avenge her pain. Two nights ago, possessed, she danced half naked, except for her white wrapper and beaded hair, as she ran to the river, her two servants running after her. There she sang as if in a battle ground:

Ìbà, ìbà
ìbà ni mojú,
Ládékojú mo júbà rẹ,
Ládékojú mo ríbà rẹ,
Ìbà rẹ,
Ọdún kò ní báwa jà,
Àwa náà ò ní pọdún jẹ,
Àkàlàmàgbò é è é pọdún jẹ,
Àwa náà ò ní pọdún jẹ,
Àkàlàmàgbò é è é pọdún jẹ.

In one swift twirl, she jumped up and fell into the water. I held myself as the two young girls rushed to carry her, as she shook violently.

APÈNÀ: Bídèmí was not like this before your daughter's death.

ỌTÚN: She was usually calm like the Ọṣun water itself... then all this came and turned our lives upside down. My daughter went into that palace to play with her friend. No one was in the palace except the servants and Kábíyèsí. Then my daughter was found raped, naked in the bush, seven days after entering the palace. I still say Kábíyèsí's hands are not clean.

APÈNÀ: And I believe that it may have been the neighbouring village of Ayédé. The servants said so. I mean what would Kábíyèsí want with a fourteen-year-old child?

ỌTÚN: My fourteen-year-old child. The same question we asked. We consulted many Ifá Priests... none of them mentioned the people of Ayédé. They all said we should look within. I tell you, the kòkòrò that eats the vegetable leaves is Kábíyèsí. My daughter's blood smells in the hands of a fragile man whose life is slowly ebbing out. Ọba Ògìdán must confess. If he does not, with my bare hands, I will kill him, without a flinch.

APÈNÀ: Calm down Ọ̀tún… the walls have ears. Mind what you say. Did you catch him? Did anyone see him? Did he carry the body alone from the palace to the crossroad of the bush near the Ijẹ̀kùn river in broad day light? They all swore.

Ọ̀TÚN: Who swore? The messengers of the palace who are prepared to lie and die for him? I say they all lied.

APÈNÀ: Before Ṣàngó?

Ọ̀TÚN: Even before Olódùmarè, they will lie for him. He has an uncanny grip on their tongues. They will rather die than utter a whisper of truth.

APÈNÀ: Háà! Ọ̀tún. We took them to the shrine of Ṣàngó. If they had lied, all they had were three days, which ended yesterday. Even him, the great King would have been long dead, if they had lied. But as we speak, he lives… they all live. Leave the matter alone, Ọ̀tún. Ṣàngó does not rest… his hot splinters of fire stones await the heart of the enemy and liar. He is always quick to anger. He will solve it at his own time.

Ọ̀TÚN: Ṣàngó's time takes too long for a grieving father, so I have turned my weeping face to another. Ọṣúntáyọ̀ was the sweetness of my heart. The only child I had. She was the replacement of Ìyá Ológì, my late dear mother. She was a comforting presence when she was born, and someone snuffed her innocent life with a puff, just like that. Some animal wasted her young life. ANGRY. May all the gods and deities of the land, Ṣàngó, Ògún, Ọ̀ṣun, Pègúrun, waste him too. I include you Èṣù láàlú ògiriòkò.

APÈNÀ: Is that why you have refused to listen to the drums of the pleas l make? I hear even the women, led by Ìyálóde, came to your house and you did not listen to them. You did not even open the door of your house to them. Why?

ÒTÚN: They came to jeer.

APÈNÀ: Why would they feel any form of pity for me? These same women had come to me to say that my daughter should carry the calabash of the people to the river of Ìjẹ̀kùn Odò. They said that Ifá had picked her. I refused. My daughter had been admitted to a good secondary school in Ìbàdàn. That night, I resolved to send her to Ìbàdàn to stay with my sister there before her school started. I did not want any form of distraction for her. But see what became of her now?

APÈNÀ: Ọ̀tún, you should have let her. She would still have gone to school. And served and be protected by Ọ̀ṣun Ṣèngèṣé.

ÒTÚN: Her mother was a Christian and did not want her near the river. Now see what happened. She was found in the bush by the river as if she drowned. If the river killed her, did the river strangle her too? Everything was done with so much audacity. APÈNÀ DOES NOT ANSWER. Say something, Apènà. At least she was also your niece too.

APÈNÀ: What pains loom so much in the soul of a man that he forgets everything?

ÒTÚN: Forget everything? I don't understand. Do you know the extent of the pain that comes with the loss of a child? We all pray that our children bury us. Not us bury them. CLOSE TO TEARS. What I buried was a used spent carcass of my once lively child. That killed a part of me. But I know it must be Kábíyèsí.

APÈNÀ: How?

ỌTÚN: The first time they met, she complained about Kábíyèsí's gaze. I remember she could not sleep that night. That was when we decided to send her to Ìbàdàn to stay with my sister. From that moment she felt unsafe.

APÈNÀ: But she was close to Kábíyèsí's daughter as a friend.

ỌTÚN: Friend? A foolish mistake on my part. I should have known better. See how it has all ended. See. But it is alright. The gods will judge.

APÈNÀ: I am sorry. I understand. Be a man, Ọtún. But I cannot believe that Kábíyèsí would have a hand in the death of a child he is supposed to protect. The Alálẹ̀ will not forgive him.

ỌTÚN: Even the womb of motherhood will not forgive him. My wife just stares like a fool… stupefied. Her pain comes cold… it seeps… drop by drop until it soaks the soul with bitterness… undiluted gall flows, it dulls the senses, Apènà. Sometimes, I still call out to her. Or go into her room searching for her. But all that is gone now. All is gone. ANGRY. IN A SAD WHISPER. They will all die, Apènà. One by one, I swear!

APÈNÀ: Let this be, Ọtún.

ỌTÚN: Why? My dear wife has become a living mummy. She covers everything… all wrapped up, except for her eyes. Even she does not see me as a man anymore. I am just a failed casing who could not guarantee the safety of her only child. These few days, when she looks at me, all I see is in her eyes is pity for my manhood. Me, Ọtún Agúnléjìká! Me!

APÈNÀ: Ọtún. Sit down and be a man. I shall come myself to see my sister. But seriously, I am worried, Ọtún. Very worried. Danger looms. A black bird perches on my roof and screeches each time; evil is about to take place in the village. For three days now it has always perched, cry for an hour and leave, flying away into the darkness of the night. I asked Ifá and I got no answer.

ÒTÚN: Where? Here in Ìjẹkùn Odò?

APÈNÀ: Everywhere. The air is stale. Dry and cold. Evil looms. And my dream has shown me that the world may turn upside down soon. Three mothers of the night sit by a cooking pot, with rich sányán and the crown as ingredients in their boiling pot, cooking all through the dream. Then I hear gentle grunts of pain.

ÒTÚN: Grunts of pain? Cooking what? Who? Talk to me Apènà!

APÈNÀ: I always wake up when their cooking is almost done and a boiled human finger wearing a golden ring, is about to be raised. At first, I thought it was the anxiety of the coming celebrations. Knowing how angry you were, I was also afraid of your anger and boasts at the palace before Kábíyèsí, I become really scared for you. But, even now, as we speak, the dream lingers... same dream. Same three women... cooking. I am still afraid, Òtún.

ÒTÚN: Afraid? For whom? A big fat lie! Lie! Nothing can touch you and the Kábíyèsí now. When the sacred calabash has carried the ills and secrets of last year, my daughter's murder washed away with the streaming whirling, bubbling clean water... life drifting as the water flowed... all is washed away. Òrìṣà Odò Òṣun did not even sympathize with me, even after I gave up Islam to worship her. I remain blacklisted by the Lèmọmù. She did not even accept my supplications. She left as a once proud eagle, broken, wingless and limping. Me? Every night, I hear her acolytes chanting her praise songs. Then I see her in all her glory, swimming in great joy... leaving me... my mouth agape like that of a demented fool. So don't fool me any further Apènà... all was buried yesterday in that cursed calabash which the Arugbá dutifully left in the river to drift away.

APÈNÀ: Fool you? I say I too remain worried.

ÒTÚN: Lie! You lie again! From afar I watched the proceedings. The procession to the river was full. Even the masquerade danced well. I saw the contingent from Òṣogbo were more than last year. Those from other villages danced to their hearts' content, drunk in the sacred water of the river. It was beautiful. Caught in space of possessed suffocation, I too snapped my fingers, but now... I forget in what direction.

APÈNÀ: Then you must have followed us and seen it all... but...

ÒTÚN: Seen it all? I don't understand. I saw enough to know that it went well. It was like watching a dance one has always partook in, from afar, for the first time. I would have been with Kábíyèsí, and the Arugbá always reaches the river before the king. But this time, I saw her stand before the river waiting patiently for the Kábíyèsí's arrival. The villagers swarm around her. The red cloth... the sacred Òṣùgbó, covering the calabash, kept refracting between the sun and the water. She was a sight to behold. It was so colourful. For one brief second, I thought I saw Òṣun's hands stretch to receive the offerings. So don't deceive me now.

APÈNÀ: You must have seen it all then?

ÒTÚN: Seen what all?

APÈNÀ: Everything was tense. The unsettled spirits. The fluttering, and flustering wavering souls. Everything. Did you see it?

ỌTÚN: HESITATES. No! Was there anything that I was supposed to see beyond the colours of the festival? Kábíyèsí must remember that when evil seeds and deeds are planted, doubts are sown. I shall never trust him with anything in my life again. My daughter, a whole human being, got missing in his palace. I know what I know. I saw everything my eyes wanted to see at the celebrations. Was there something in particular you wanted me to see?

APÈNÀ: No. If you did not see it... then you did not see it. I want it all to end.

ỌTÚN: End? No. Once the fragile egg is broken, that is it. The shell, the yolk and the white of it are thrown away. The once valuable egg becomes a thing of waste. Do you understand me?

APÈNÀ: WATCHES ỌTÚN STEP ASIDE, READY TO LEAVE. I do not want you to ever to regret this action. Even Olódùmarè is begged and he listens. As Ọtún of Ìjẹkùn Odò, by the name of all the ancestors of the land I, Dòsùmú Agbabíàká, the Apènà, plead with you, the Awo beg you, let peace reign. Forgive Kábíyèsí.

ỌTÚN: I knew it would come to this. What do I tell them at home? How do I break the news of this forced reconciliation to my wife? Each night, I hear my daughter's cries. I hear her call out to me. Asking for vengeance. My wife's eyes have become swollen, empty of tears. Apènà, I am resolved. Let Kábíyèsí continue to live. We have had others worse than him. Ọba Ikúdẹtì lived, and his awful deeds made him neither dead nor alive for two years before he was strangled to death by the kingmakers. His rotted body was shovelled into a shallow grave. No rites of privilege were ever accorded him. This pompous one's fall will be worse, I swear!

APÈNÀ: I say let it go. If we do not forget the ills of friends, who will be left for us to play with? Hm? Awo, jèbùrẹ́. ÌLÀRÍ, AN ELDERLY PALACE SERVANT ENTERS. A YOUNGER SERVANT FOLLOWS WITH THE ỌBA'S STAFF OF OFFICE. Háà! The palace is here. What message do you have for me?

ÌLÀRÍ: The message is for both of you, Bàbá Apènà.

ỌTÚN: For us? Are you sure?

ÌLÀRÍ: Yes. Kábíyèsí wants to see both of you this evening for the celebration of thanks for the just concluded festival of Yèyé in Ìjẹ̀kùn Odò land. Òrìṣà Odò Ọ̀ṣun was gracious... we need to celebrate her together as one family, says Kábíyèsí.

ỌTÚN: I shall not...

APÈNÀ: We shall be there. Tell him that we shall be there. Ọtún and I, as one family.

ÌLÀRÍ: MOVES FORWARD. HE BRINGS OUT A WRAPPED BUNDLE. ON HIS KNEES, HE STRECTHES HIS HANDS WITH THE BUNDLE TO ỌTÚN. Kábíyèsí says you forgot this in the palace the last time you left in anger. He asks me to return it to you, the rightful owner. ỌTÚN DOES NOT MOVE. HE JUST STARES AT HIM.

APÈNÀ: Ọtún... your message awaits you. Collect the bundle from Olorì Ìlàrí. The palace waits. Collect the message and we shall talk. Please, do not keep the old man stooping for too long. SLOWLY, ỌTÚN COLLECTS THE WRAPPED BUNDLE.

ÌLÀRÍ: Kábíyèsí wants you to forget the fights of yesterday. It was the work of the Èṣù.

ỌTÚN: Èṣù kẹ? Which one?

ÌLÀRÍ: IGNORES HIM. He restores you to the position of your fathers. He needs you in the palace. He wants you to come this evening. ỌTÚN STILL DOES NOT COLLECT THE BUNDLE. NOW VERY ANGRY.

APÈNÀ: By the gods, Ọtún, go on, take it from him.

ỌTÚN: UNSURE, BUT SLOWLY HE COLLECTS AND UNWRAPS THE BUNDLE. My beads. But Apènà, is this safe?

APÈNÀ: Págà! You ask the wrong question. When is it not safe for a child to walk in his father's room? Ìjẹkùn Odò belongs to you Ọtún... gbà!

ỌTÚN: I know, but I want to be careful. I have been careful to this point, and the gods have seen me through. With one wrong step... one careless over confident move... I could trip.

APÈNÀ: Trip kẹ? Does a child get frightened of the masquerade he saw his father wear? Even when both he and the followers call the masquerade, baba, he knows who he refers to. Have no fear, your father returned your beads. Harbour no fear.

ÌLÀRÍ: Awo, Olùgbẹ́bẹ̀, ẹ jèbùrẹ́.

ỌTÚN: I cannot...

APÈNÀ: Let it go. Tell Kábíyèsí that I was there when he collected it. All is well.

ỌTÚN: Apènà, you assume too much.

APÈNÀ: Let me. After all, it is human to make mistakes. Sit and have a drink with me.

ỌTÚN: No… I must hurry home.

APÈNÀ: Hurry? Oh yes… there must be so much to say. But in the end, let it be good news that we will hear. And you may go into your inner room and ask yourself this same question of doubt. No man lies to himself, except he is a fool, and you are not one Ọtún. Indeed, hurry home. EXIT ỌTÚN. TURNS TO ÌLÀRÍ. Return to the palace Ìlàrí. Tell Kábíyèsí, that all is well. AS THEY TURN TO GO, LIGHTS SLOWLY FADE.

ÈṢÙ'S SHRINE. SÀÙRÁ STOOPS BEFORE THE SHRINE.

SÀÙRÁ: My father Láàlú, the Òrìṣà Odò Ọ̀ṣun festival has come and gone. Plenty was our gathering. Láàlú o, you refused me touching the gifts from the palace, why? When you behave this way, I know my master has not finished with the matter. They gather dust, and some dry up due to the evening cold. Láàlú I feel uneasiness all over. Cold hot wind blows, as if... as if my master is yet to unfold and spread discontentment in the land. What does my master want? HE PRETENDS TO LISTEN AS IF HE IS BEING SPOKEN TO. I hear you master. Háà. When? Soon. Let havoc be their lot then. He who steps on your club must feel its impact on his head. Yours is not to change the actions of the universe, it is not to change destinies, but to nudge time... speed up the actions of men until Olódùmarè's will is fulfilled... in your desired pattern. ENTER Ọ̀TÚN. Master, I hear footsteps. Who?

Ọ̀TÚN: STANDS AT THE DOOR WAY. It is me. Ọ̀tún Agúnléjìká.

SÀÙRÁ: Ọ̀tún come in. The doorway is your passage. Where footpaths meet... the quiet but deadly crossroads is my master's place. My master awaits your presence. Ọ̀TÚN ENTERS THE ROOM. GIVES A BAG TO SÀÙRÁ. Háà, more gifts! You make more offerings to Bara, Bara will bless you, you make offerings to Láàlú, Láàlú will compensate you. May Èṣù bless you. Have you started to feel my master's hand on the matter you brought?

Ọ̀TÚN: Yes. Today, Kábíyèsí returned my beads.

SÀÙRÁ: LAUGHS WILDLY. Láàlú o. You favour no one empty handed. You have not even started, and Ọ̀tún has gains to show. CHUCKLES. The entrapment of the cocoon begins. Ensnared, there is no place to hide. You invited my master, now his blessings are upon you. Now beyond your imagination... even beyond your desires, you shall reap. CHUCKLES. Did you give the mothers of the night their gifts?

ÒTÚN: Yes.

SÀÙRÁ: Hm? LISTENS AS IF BEING SPOKEN TO. BREAKS INTO ANOTHER LAUGH. Even your daughter's spirit is restless. She wants all revealed. That is you what you want also, isn't it?

ÒTÚN: Yes.

SÀÙRÁ: Then go home. The drummers begin to gather drums. Òşun heaves, her anger festers. Everything is set. My master manifests, now human beings will dance to the rhythm of my master's tickles. Is there anything more you want?

ÒTÚN: Justice.

SÀÙRÁ: Justice you will get in ten folds. Beyond your wildest imagination. Èşù over satisfies the crier.

ÒTÚN: Er... one more thing, great one. Kábíyèsí has asked me to come for a celebration this evening. Should I go?

SÀÙRÁ: Go. The dance begins. But first send some gifts to Òrúnmìlà and Ògún. Take white doves, seven in number, to the shrine of Òrúnmìlà, then all you will utter shall be wise and thoughtful. And a small white and black dog to Ògún. This will fold his hands and my master's path shall be cleared. The ways of the gods appear blurred to men. But to each one, its own... my master at the centre... he connects the spirits of the divine folks... all individual, and yet all whole. Did you send Òşun her gifts?

ÒTÚN: Yes, seven sweet things that man eats, and a bottle of hot drink.

SÀÙRÁ: Then sweetness shall be yours too. But your wife owes her gifts also.

ÒTÚN: My wife? No.

SÀÙRÁ: My master never lies. She owes her a promised set of gifts which she is yet to redeem. Òṣun does not react kindly to non-keepers of oaths. Háà, see my master, as he hurries to Ajegunṣèlú.

ÒTÚN: Àjẹ́gunselu kẹ̀? Why?

SÀÙRÁ: There is a wild spirit of death he must appease. All will be well. You will see.

ÒTÚN: Àṣẹ Baba.

SÀÙRÁ: Hurry home.

ÒTÚN: Yes.

SÀÙRÁ: And as for your wife's nightmares, tell her that it won't be long again before she will embrace a peaceful sleep. In fact, Òṣun Ṣẹ̀ngẹ̀ṣẹ́ has promised to reward her with another, but she will visit her. That will be after all these have been laid to rest... you will see. On the day you come to bid us a farewell for a while, the good news will come with you.

ÒTÚN: Good news. But my wife is old. Her womb...

SÀÙRÁ: Leave that to Òrìṣà Odò Òṣun.

ÒTÚN: HAPPY, BRINGS OUT MONEY FROM HIS POCKET. This is for you Baba Sàùrá. Already, I begin to feel the sweetness of vengeance at the tip of my lips.

SÀÙRÁ: For me? I am just a messenger. But if you insist. I am grateful. COLLECTS THE MONEY. It is for little pecks of this nature, that have made me stay with my master all this while. He is an Òrìṣà who knows how to pamper and yet bite, he knows how to laugh with man and yet leave one crying alone. He understands man more than he understands himself. That is why he is always invited to every feast. Man's casing is his home. Man's desires never end, so does my master's work. Now hurry home, before heavy rains descend.

AS ỌTÚN TURNS TO LEAVE, SLOW LIGHTS BEGIN TO FADE.

INNER CHAMBER OF THE KING'S ROOM. ỌBA ÒGÌDÁN IS SEATED ON THE BED, IKÚSANRÍ IS ON THE FLOOR.

IKÚSANRÍ: You did it Kábíyèsí. The earth will bow before you now. All is complete.

ÒGÌDÁN: The joy I feel is that it all went well, and not a soul suspected... not even my shadow.

IKÚSANRÍ: You are a spirit, father. When you stare at nothing, you see nothing. I told you, your destiny could be changed. See how easy the Alálẹ̀ have made it. No one will know.

ÒGÌDÁN: Remember, our elders say that secrets can only be kept for a while.

IKÚSANRÍ: Not this one. This is kept and buried forever. Not even a flinch... a whisper or a thought in your direction, ever. You are more than an ordinary man now. You took on the gods and won.

ÒGÌDÁN: The very way it happened amazed even me. I was like a brazen wind... flowing unperturbed. So how many more years do I have now?

IKÚSANRÍ: Thirty years. For a man who was to die on the eight day of the eight month, ten days ago to be precise, to be granted thirty more years is a privilege of the gods. You seized your head from the clutches of Ọbàtálá and changed your àyànmọ́.

ÒGÌDÁN: Yes. PONDERS. But was it worth it?

IKÚSANRÍI: Yes. RISES. If such questions begin to arise, then it is time to for me to leave. Moments of regret must never be part of your royal thoughts. I shall leave now. My village, Ajagunṣèlú is far from here and the rains must not catch me outside my forest. Besides, darkness will soon unfold, deaths will follow, but once again, remain unperturbed. Even that foul air will blow pass.

ÒGÌDÁN: Should I worry then?

IKÚSANRÍ: I say not a wondering thought... not a flicker of ponder. Do you doubt me master?

ÒGÌDÁN: No!. The gods forbid. CHUCKLES. Why? The feast... the celebrations is this evening. I was only wondering if you will not stop to see me thank my people.

IKÚSANRÍ: Not for me. I must leave before lips begin to whisper. The hearts of men are deep. Do not forget to offer the white dove every seven months.

ÒGÌDÁN: White doves?

IKÚSANRÍ: CHUCKLES. Kábíyèsí, again, you make me laugh. The real ones this time.

ÒGÌDÁN: Yes, yes, I will not forget, now go. Through the back door. Ìlàrí will take you there. CLAPS HIS HANDS. ÌLÀRÍ APPEARS. Take him and his gifts out of the palace through the secret passage. All must be well, friend.

IKÚSANRÍ: All will be well. As a matter of fact, all is well. The spirit of the people of Ajagunṣèlú are with you. Failure shall not form part of our discussion. Ever!

ÌLÀRÍ: Àṣẹ.

IKÚSANRÍ: Our son, when shall he return?

ÒGÌDÁN: Soon... once all this is scrapped into a stony crypt, until even those who dug the grave forget its location. Soon.

For now, I need him to continue to fan the embers of the festering fire that may burn within.

IKÚSANRÍ: Kábíyèsí Ògìdán, remember your promise. My master is too steeped in the embrace of Ikú àlàmúntù... he lacks the finesse of Èṣù Láàlú.

SLOW LIGHTS FADE.

THRONE ROOM. ALL THE CHIEFS ARE GATHERED. THERE IS DRUMMING, WHILE THE CHIEFS BANTER. ÒTÚN ENTERS, FULLY DRESSED, WITH BEADS AND ALL. THEN ENTERS THE KING'S MUSICIANS. ỌBA ÒGÌDÁN ENTERS WITH A RETINUE OF CHIEFS DANCING. AND THEY ALL PROSTRATE TO GREET HIM.

CHANTER: Tó, tó, tó
    Ògìdán ọmọ Arógunmásá
    Jùrù dédé, jùrù dédé
    Yíò jẹ gbèsè kún gbèsè ni
    Aláàárù tó pe Ọba léjọ́
    Yíò jẹ gbèsè kún gbèsè ni
    Tó tó tó.
    Tó tó tó.
    Ìwọ la rí bá wí
    Ìwọ tó o gbàlẹ̀kẹ̀ oyè
    Tó ò bẹ́rí wọn,
    Ìwọ la rí bá wí
    Tó tó tó.
    Tó tó tó
    Ẹ ṣí filà fádé

ÒTÚN REMOVES HIS CAP AND DANCES BEHIND ÒGÌDÁN.

    Ìwọ tó ò ṣí filà fádé iyà lo ó jẹ
    Àní ẹ ṣífilà fádé.
    Tó tó tó tó.
    Tó tó tó
    Ọba Ògìdán, àkọ́bí Arógunmásàá
    Baba rẹ ló nilẹ̀
    Ìwọ máa rìn, máa rìn máa yan
    Baba rẹ ló nilẹ̀.
    Tó tó tó

Ọba tó
Ẹrù Ọba ni mo bà
Ẹrù Ọba ni mo bà
Ọba tó, Ọba tó
Ẹrù Ọba ni mo bà
Ògìdán ń jayé Baba rẹ́
À ló ń jayé Baba rẹ́.
Ẹni tó ní o má jayé
Ikú ní ó paá láyé Baba rẹ.
Tó tó tó
Òrìṣà ló bá òrìṣà
Òrìṣà ló bá òrìṣà
Tó tó tó

ÒGÌDÁN DANCES TOWARDS ỌTÚN. HE STOPS BEFORE ỌTÚN, WHO PROSTRATES. ÒGÌDÁN GREETS ỌTÚN WITH HIS HORSE TAIL AND BECKONS HIM TO RISE. HAPPY, HE DANCES TO THE THRONE AND SITS.

ÒGÌDÁN: I welcome you all. I ask who says we have no reason to celebrate and thank our ancestors for the success of our Ọdún Yèyé? I thank them. Then I must thank the Àtàọjà Òṣogbo who has kept faith with us and continued to support us in our celebrations of Òrìṣà Odò Ọ̀sun. His delegation this year were not leftovers of the bigger Ọ̀sun festival in Òṣogbo, but original fatherly contributions. The Ọ̀sun river runs into our river here in Ìjẹ̀kùn Odò, and so we are bound by the promise to continue to worship and venerate our mother Ládékojú, Òrìṣà Odò Ọ̀sun by the first Àtàọjà, Ọba Gbádéwọlú Láaróyè of Òṣogbo. All of us that this year's celebrations met on earth, we thank the gods of our fathers, our ancestors and those whom we live together with. I see that Ọ̀tún has returned to our fold. Ọ̀TÚN PROSTRATES. We forgive your wrong accusations of the crown. My late father Ọba Àjàká used to say that the elder is an incinerator... a huge rubbish bin... all sorts are poured. The chiefs have spoken, and I must listen. I see you all complete and healthy, I am happy. HE RISES. As we were complete this year that is how we will be complete next year. Our lives will not end with this New Year.

ALL: Àṣẹ!

ÒGÌDÁN: As we go about our work, death will not kill us.

ALL: Àṣẹ!

ÒGÌDÁN: Ẹ̀gbà will not deny us of our goodness.
ALL: Àṣẹ!
ÒGÌDÁN: Yèyé a bojú kugun
　Oṣè múrèré níyì
　Èrèré bí ilé jégé
　Ọdún kò jọ bí èsín,
　Àkàlàmàgbò ó kọ̀ kì ń pọdún jẹ
　Èmi ò ní pọdún jẹ
　Ọdún ò ní pamí jẹ
　Àkàlàmàgbò ó kọ̀ kì ń pọdún jẹ
　Ẹ̀yin kò ní pọdún jẹ
　Ọdún kò ní pa yín jẹ
　Àkàlàmàgbò ó kọ̀ kì ń pọdún jẹ

MUSIC START AS DANCERS DANCE IN.

LEADER: Ládékojú, Ṣẹ̀ngẹ̀ṣẹ́,
　Mo kóre Òrìṣà odò fún Ọ̀sun
　WOMEN: Oore Yèyé Òrìṣà odò o
　Omi ò
　Ọta ò
　Ẹdan ò
　Ẹri ò ò
　Àgbá ò

Oore Yèyé Òrìṣà Odò o

LEADER: Àgò onílé, ṣé ká wọlé?
Àgó àlejò ṣé ká máa bọ?
Kábíyèsí Ọba Ògìdán Arógunmásàá,
Ìwọ ló pè ìyá wa,
Òrìṣà odò Ọṣun,
Ṣé kí wọ́n wọlé?
Ìyá ń bọ̀ o

WOMEN: Àgò lọnà o

LEADER: Ọṣun mà ń bọ̀ o

WOMEN: Àgò lọnà o

LEADER: Oore Òrìṣà odò mà ń bọ̀ o

LEADER: Àgò lọnà o

ÌYÁ ODÒ ENTERS WITH A RETINUE OF ỌṢUN WORSHIPPERS IN WHITE WRAPPERS. CRYING. ÒGÌDÁN REMAINS CALM. MUSIC STOPS. THERE IS CONFUSION. ÌYÁ ODÒ RUSHES TO ỌBA ÒGÌDÁN, WITH HER FOLLOWERS, THEY KNEEL.

ÒGÌDÁN: Ìyá Odò you came late. We were wondering why you had not arrived. They said you went to the river, but the sky gathers. We were afraid that the rains will hold you up. It appears your supplications have been heard. Òrìṣà Odò Ọṣun is ready to pour showers of blessings on Ìjẹ̀kùn Odò. Ọṣun must be happy with us.

ÌYÁ ODÒ: Òrìṣà Odò Ọṣun is not happy Kábíyèsí. Hell is set to unfold.

ÒGÌDÁN: Hell? What happened?

ÌYÁ ODÒ: I had a sleepless night. Not a wink. Òrìṣà Odò Ọ̀ṣun and Iyemọja were turning and turning round and round until the once peaceful river became a turning whirlwind, with me caught in the middle. So, I woke up the women and we ran to the riverside. There was turbulence everywhere. Before taking another step, we must consider the consequences around it... I ran to Ṣàmù who said that Ṣàngó and Ọ̀ṣun were up in arms against the enemies of Ìjẹ̀kùn Odò. There were sacrifices to be made to appease Òrìṣà Odò Ọ̀ṣun. We had no time, so we got to work. First to the market... then the shrines...

ÒGÌDÁN: We are all awo here. We know the secret of knowledge. To the point Ìyá Odò... just tell us what happened after.

ÌYÁ ODÒ: When we got back to the river bank, the rains had started... and with it came the roar of Ṣàngó. First, Ṣàngó struck the sacred tree where Kábíyèsí stands to offer prayers. The tree was split into two, burning.

ÒGÌDÁN: In the rain? The tree caught fire in the rain?

ÌYÁ ODÒ: Yes.

ÒGÌDÁN: Incredible!

ÌYÁ ODÒ: The very word from our lips. This confirmed that Òrìṣà Odò Ọ̀ṣun was not happy with us.

ÒGÌDÁN: What happened then?

ÌYÁ ODÒ: Then it happened.

ÒGÌDÁN: What happened?

ÌYÁ ODÒ: The water rose, and with arms stretched from the river. It picked up Ṣàmù and dragged him down the river.

WOMEN SING.

Lílé: Òrìṣà Odò o
Ẹbọrạ tí ń gbé nínú omi
Ìwọ ni mò ń ké sí
Omi ò lápá,
Omi gbégi
Omi ò lẹ́sẹ̀,
Omi gbé èèyàn lọ o
Ìṣòro ayé mi ò
Ègbè: Omi gbe lọ
Lílé: Ìdàmú ayé mi ò
Ègbè: Omi gbe lọ.

ÒGÌDÁN: Quiet, women. Ṣàmù pulled down in the river? What did the Àwórì do?

ÌYÁ ODÒ: Some jumped in. The others, stupefied, just had everything open... mouth, eyes and all. PAUSE. The strange thing is that it appeared he was pushed by some unseen hands.

ÒGÌDÁN: You colour your words again. To the point old woman... to the point.

ÌYÁ ODÒ: That was when we saw it.

ÒGÌDÁN: Saw what?

ÌYÁ ODÒ: From afar... floating... the calabash.

ÒGÌDÁN: Calabash? Which calabash?

ÌYÁ ODÒ: Igba Ọ̀ṣun which the Arugbá had taken to the river the day before. The calabash which contained the woes of Ìjẹkùn Odò was returned. A curse! Èèwọ̀! The cursed calabash which the Arugbá had taken to the river came back. Òrìṣà Odò Ọ̀ṣun must loath us now! We are doomed. We are doomed, Kábíyèsí.

ÒGÌDÁN: Where is Ìyá Ọ̀ṣun? Did you call her?

ÌYÁ ODÒ: On her way back to Òṣogbo. She left after the morning prayers. She had gone to see the Arugbá... she prayed for her and left for home before the rains could gather.

ÌYÁ Ọ̀ṢUN: I am here. I know traitors blow like the wind, but there is one in this palace, with feet firmly rooted and his or her heart firmly transfixed. I returned as the evil air became more foul. A big tree fell and blogged the only passage to Òṣogbo, and I heard cries and wailings of the people of Ìjẹkùn Odò. So I returned. Now I am back. What has happened? What news do I take to the Àtàọjà? What do I say happened here, that Òrìṣà Odò Ọ̀ṣun could not be consoled by Iyemọja weeping all day, accompanied by the angry roars of Ṣàngó? Ọba Ògìdán Arógunmásá, what is happening here?

ÒGÌDÁN: The very question we are trying to answer. You entered just in time. I was worried for your safety. I hear the rain is much.

ÌYÁ Ọ̀ṢUN: Much is little great King. Houses breaking up into mashed clay muds. Puddles where roads and markets once stood. Ọ̀ṣun is angry.

ÒGÌDÁN: Why?

ÌYÁ ỌṢUN: Something has gone grievously wrong. Some managed to destroy the sacredness of Òrìṣà Odò Ọṣun by been deceitful. Now, mishaps will know no bounds.

ÌYÁ ODÒ: Ọṣun has returned the calabash.

ÌYÁ ỌṢUN: Òrìṣà Odò oò! Why?

ÌYÁ ODÒ: Ọṣun holds Ṣàmù captive underneath the belly of the river.

ÌYÁ ỌṢUN. Ọṣun… what have the people of Ìjẹ̀kùn Odò done to you? This has never happened in the fifty years that I have worshipped Òrìṣà Odò. What do all these mishaps mean? Answer, Òrìṣà Odò.

ỌṢÚNTÓMI, AN ELDERLY WOMAN, RUNS IN WITH TWO OTHRR WOMEN.THEY KNEEL.

ÒGÌDÁN: What now?

ỌṢÚNTÓMI: Trouble, Kábíyèsí. But first the ears of the mothers must hear this.

RUNS FIRST TO ÌYÁ ODÒ WHO WALKS TO ÌYÁ ỌṢUN WITH HER. ỌṢÚNTÓMI WHISPERS TO THEM.

ÌYÁ ỌṢUN: Èèwọ̀! Er… my mouth remains too heavy to say this. Since I am a visitor, I will prefer Ìyá Odò to speak Kábíyèsí. Ìyá, speak.

ÒGÌDÁN: Our ears are all yours.

ÌYÁ ODÒ: Kábíyèsí, the Arugbá has fainted. She bleeds from everywhere. As if she has been defiled. She fights for her life as we speak.

ÒGÌDÁN: RISES IN ANGER. Apènà what night is this turning out to be. Devastation everywhere. Non stopping rains. Ṣàmù is held captive under the river. And now the Arugbá who carried the countless worries of the land of Ìjẹ̀kùn Odò to the goddess faints. What disaster is this? I am sure someone is plotting my downfall. Baba Ifádèyí speak.

IFÁDÈYÍ: STEPS FORWARD. Speak my lord?

ÒGÌDÁN: Yes. I know that the Arugbá must come from the royal house. But how was this one chosen?

MULTI-MEDIA. A BIG WIDE SCREEN SHOWS IFÁ PRIEST CONSULTING THE ỌPẸ̀LẸ̀.

IFÁDÈYÍ: Ifá chose a girl that would bring peace and progress to the land, a virgin as pure as a dove... so we announced her.

ÒGÌDÁN: How?

MULTI-MEDIA. SCREEN SHOWS THE SELECTION PROCESS AS SHE SPEAKS.

ÌYÁ ODÒ: As always, ten girls volunteered. Ifá found none of them fit to carry the calabash. Then we checked again and Ọ̀tún's daughter was picked by Ifá. But when she refused to accept Òṣun's calling, we tried again and Òṣúnfúnkẹ́ was chosen. We went to her in her school. At first, she cried. But when she saw we had convinced her father who was a Muslim and her mother who was a Christian, she followed us to the palace. It was in the palace that she agreed. She saw all the beautiful things she had always desired. Her mother told us of her immediate needs. We bought everything and more. PAUSE. But one night, while we were preparing her for the task ahead, she saw...

ÒGÌDÁN: Yes? She saw...

ÌYÁ ODÒ: Her body floating on the river. The sacred calabash placed on her stiff stomach, her mouth open, slowly pouring... open, streaming, blood.

ÒGÌDÁN: Háà! Ìyá Odò, you drift again. Stick to the facts of the questions I ask you. Not a young girl's nightmare.

SCREEN SHOWS ACTION AS SHE SPEAKS.

ÌYÁ ODÒ: I am sorry my lord. Then we as custom demands, we brought her to you for the royal prayers of acceptance and strength for the task she was about to embark upon... the next morning. PAUSE. That day she...

ÒGÌDÁN: Oh, not again. Yes? That day... continue. Did I not pray for her?

ÌYÁ ODÒ: You did Kábíyèsí. But she told me later in a frightened whisper... that she was afraid of... your gaze.

ÒGÌDÁN: My gaze? How?

ÒTÚN: Yes, how Ìyá Odò? We all know that Kábíyèsí's famous stern gaze can frighten a young child that way. Even the elders are shaken by his gaze... first, it deadens the feet and slowly a cold line of sweat runs down the spine. I am sure we all here know that gaze... àbí?

ALL: Yes.

ÌYÁ ODÒ: Only this time... the effect of the gaze was different. It was lustful.

ALL: Háà, Ìyá Odò.

ÌYÁ ODÒ: I swear I do not lie! She felt stripped by Kábíyèsí's gaze.

ÒGÌDÁN: Do you hear? Now she wants to pour all her failures on my poor head. What stupid gaze of mine strips a girl who is already unsettled by the task ahead? What have I done? What kind of woman is this? Old mother of Ìjẹkùn Odò, answer what we ask only. This world is a cruel, cruel place. Even kings are now footmats for people to step on.

APÈNÀ: Woman, please face the path you intend to follow. Do not digress or make conclusions on your own. Kábíyèsí's integrity is in question here.

ÒGÌDÁN: Thank you. Mother, please continue.

MULTI-MEDIA. SCREEN SHOWS ACTION.

ÌYÁ ODÒ: On the morning of the day of the celebrations, we met her seated on her bed... crying. We pleaded with her. She wanted to say some things which she muttered in fear. As we could not comprehend what she was trying to say, we took it for fear. We covered her head with aṣọ òkè cloth and took her to meet the waiting crowd. Then we took her to the room of power where we prepared her finally for the sacred walk to the river.

APÈNÀ: What happened in the power room?

MULTI-MEDIA. SCREEN SHOWS ACTION AS SHE SPEAKS.

ÌYÁ ODÒ: In the room was the already packed calabash. We took her first to Iyemọja asking for protection. We begged her to convince her sister Ọ̀ṣun to accept and bless our offerings, then we went before Ìyá Olóde, whom we fondly refer to as Kórì, the mother of abundant blessings, and finally Ajé, the òrìṣà of wealth and plenty. After that we carried the Igbá, took the Arugbá out, and before the eyes of all, covered by the women of Ọṣun, we placed the calabash on her head. But then...

ÒGÌDÁN: There she goes again.

ỌTÚN: What happened mother?

MULTI-MEDIA. SCREEN SHOWS ACTION AS SHE SPEAKS.

ÌYÁ ODÒ: Her feet wobbled a little. She was not supposed to feel the pain. But on her face was raw pain. I became worried and called the attention of Ìyá Ọṣun to it.

ÌYÁ ỌṢUN: I moved to her and she reassured me that she would carry it. But something more worrisome had taken place. The two kolanuts placed in her mouth to stop her from talking had on their own crumbled... she could not even remember how they were dissolved in her mouth. I became worried. I inquired if there was an old Arugbá who could help carry the calabash if she could not continue. Ìyá Odò reassured me that nothing would happen. But both of us moved closer, having also asked an older Arugbá to stand close to her should she feel dizzy.

ÌYÁ ODÒ: She cried all the way from the palace to the river.

APÈNÀ: Why?

ÌYÁ ODÒ: I don't know. Stream of tears flowed. So, I started to pray to Òrìṣà Odò Ọṣun save her. Do not shame your people, I kept saying. But when Kábíyèsí arrived, she almost stumbled again... it was as if there was a struggle. Òrìṣà Odò Ọṣun wanted to enter her, but could not go in. She was never possessed. It was all due to the shared power that she carried the sacred calabash. Then I knew that the purity of the Arugbá had been compromised. ALL SCREAM.

ÌYÁ ỌṢUN: Ẹ̀rọ̀ Òrìṣà Odò o!

ALL: Òrìṣà Odò o!

ÌYÁ ODÒ: Once she dropped the calabash, we rushed her to the palace where she fainted. After a lot of care, she woke up feeling better. And we thought all was well. But…

RUNS IN TWO WOMEN DRESSED IN WHITE.

WOMAN: Kábíyèsí! The Arugbá Ìjẹ̀kùn Odò is dead!

ÒGÌDÁN: JUMPS UP. How? Where? Who gave her the grace to die?

WOMAN: We don't know. She just laid there, foaming in the mouth, while her life ebbed out. We just watched as sweat like water flowed all over… helpless, we could not raise a finger.

ÒGÌDÁN: Did she say a word.

WOMAN: Not even a faint sound… but in pained whisper of dying breath, she just laid there until her feeble light dwindled until the light of her life, in a fickle… puffed out into a white small smoke like a burnt out imperfect wick in bad palm oil. Ọṣun took our royal carrier. Where do we go from here?

SLOW LIGHTS FADE.

THE SHRINE OF ÈṢÙ. ỌTÚN SITS WITH SÀÙRÁ. WHEN LIGHTS COME ON, IT REVEALS AN EXCITED ỌTÚN, SÀÙRÁ LISTENS ATTENTIVELY.

ỌTÚN: Once Kábíyèsí received the news, we all froze. In anger, he sent us all home, asking Ìyá Odò and our visitor from Òṣogbo to go and find out why the Arugbá died.

SÀÙRÁ: Like a common chicken.

ỌTÚN: Yes. I could smell my vengeance... In fact, I smelt it... before me it stood. I raised my eyes... searching everywhere for Èṣù, wanting him to plunge a sword or bang Kábíyèsí's stubborn head with his dreaded club. But once again, Ọba Ògìdán triumphed. That is why I have come to find out if my offerings were not enough. Is there more for me to do to claim my justice?

SÀÙRÁ: CHUCKLES. Nothing.

ỌTÚN: Then why do I feel this way? Why have the gods turned their backs on me? I have given them all you asked me to give. Why?

SÀÙRÁ: Man, be patient. My master is not an impulsive fool. Decisions rushed often become decisions regretted. Give Èṣù more space to roam. Your matter is more complicated than it looks.

ỌTÚN: Then ask him how long I still have to wait. How long?

SÀÙRÁ: Wait... she speaks.

ỌTÚN: She? No wonder... like a woman, she dawdles. Banter with life. She toys with my pain, and instead plunges deep the sword into my heart. HE RISES.

SÀÙRÁ: PLACES A FINGER ON HIS LIPS. IGNORES ÒTÚN AND LISTEN'S ATTENTIVELY. Listen a message from my Mistress. Repeat after me.

SÀÙRÁ: Adíá fún Odùladé...

VISITORS: Adíá fún Odùladé...

SÀÙRÁ: Ọ̀rọ̀ kan tó dunni dódò ikùn...

VISITORS: Ọ̀rọ̀ kan tó dunni dódò ikùn...

SÀÙRÁ: Ó ní Ajé ó sọ ayé òun di tAdédigba...

VISITORS: Ó ní Ajé ó sọ ayé òun di tAdédigba...

SÀÙRÁ: L'òhun para rẹ̀ tí ò bá digba...

VISITORS: L'òhun para rẹ̀ tí ò bá digba...

SÀÙRÁ: A bIfá wó...

VISITORS: A bIfá wó...

SÀÙRÁ: Ifá fọhùn...

VISITORS: Ifá fọhùn...

SÀÙRÁ: Ó ní kí làá fi ń worò nílé Ifẹ̀?...

VISITORS: Ó ní kí làá fi ń worò nílé Ifẹ̀?...

SÀÙRÁ: Sùúrù, sùúrù làá fi ń worò nílé Ifẹ̀...

VISITORS: Sùúrù, sùúrù làá fi ń worò nílé Ifẹ̀.

SÀÙRÁ: Did you get the message now?

Ọ̀TÚN: Patience?

SÀÙRÁ: Yes, patience. My master says only patience can find the needle at the bottom of the river. There are too many tangled knots to be untied. Go home and ask your wife to take food to her father's grave. She should ask the family's masquerade to come out in two days' time. She and you must dance round the village with the masquerade and in front to the river bank.

ỌTÚN: My father in law? He died a long time ago. What has he to do with this?

SÀÙRÁ: Did he ever collect the pride price on your wife from you?

ỌTÚN: I offered him the money and gifts and he refused to touch them.

SÀÙRÁ: Angry... and because you had impregnated his daughter before marrying her. He committed suicide.

ỌTÚN: Suicide? They said he died after a fall from the palm tree. He was a palm wine Tapster.

SÀÙRÁ: Yes, Ọdẹ́dìran from Ìpetumodù. I say go and do what I sent you. This will reduce the burden of your pain. She has spoken.

ỌTÚN: Now I am all confused. How does this matter affect the death my daughter?

ỌTÚN: Baba, she speaks again?

SÀÙRÁ: My master is shapely shapeless. This why we say to him: A lè ga, lè kúrú. A lè kúrú, lè ga, the magician with the cloak and shape of many brightness and sizes. Láàlú ògiri òkò, Ẹbọra tí ń jẹ́ látọpa. He takes the shape and turns the sides that concerns a matter to it. That is why he lives at the crossroads, to see who is coming from the paths where four paths meet. Today, and for you, my master Èṣù has taken the shape of a woman too. Háà! Too many women have their fingers in your matter. Send more gifts to the mothers of the night one more time. There is a cloak they must pull from the face of the killer of your daughter, and then all will be revealed. Hurry. Leave for Ìpetumodù tonight... the restless angry spirit of your father in law waits. Just a few more steps to get to the stream. Patience. Nothing stays hidden for too long.

ÒTÚN: Sùúrù...patience.

SLOWLY, LIGHTS FADE.

THE BEDROOM OF ÒGÌDÁN. APÈNÀ CUTS HIS BACK WITH SMALL MARKS. ÌLÀRÍ LOOKS ON.

ÒGÌDÁN: This is utterly painful. This was why I asked you to come with Ọ̀tún. His hands are usually gentle in matters of this nature. Where is he?

APÈNÀ: Ìpetumodù. He had to leave suddenly. There is a death in the house of his father's friend. He will be back tomorrow morning.

ÒGÌDÁN: Ìpetumodù. That is your ancestral home, is it not?

APÈNÀ: Yes... that was why my sister, his wife, went with him. They will be back in the morning. Now, that completes the incisions. Nothing can touch you now.

IYEMỌJA: FROM BACK STAGE. You lie. Apènà! THE LIGHTS GO OFF. WHEN LIGHTS RETURN, THREE ELDERLY WOMEN DRESSED IN RED AND BLACK OSUGBO SURROUND ÒGÌDÁN. ÌLÀRÍ AND APÈNÀ TURN THEIR BACKS TO THEM. ÌLÀRÍ AND APÈNÀ REMAIN FROZEN THROUGHOUT THE SCENE.

KÓRÌ: Our ears are full Kábíyèsí Ọba Ògìdán Arógunmásàá.

ÒGÌDÁN: Mine too.

IYEMỌJA: You are King of Ìjẹ̀kùn Odò. Ọ̀ṣun weeps, angry. Iyemọja consoles her. Why did you send a broken spirit to carry the sacred calabash to the riverside for Ọ̀ṣun?

ÒGÌDÁN: I did not know... I and my chiefs are still trying to find out the truth.

IYEMỌJA: The truth? You don't know?

APÈNÀ: I swear èyin Ìyá wa, Kábíyèsí does not know.

KÓRÌ: Shut your stinking mouth, Apènà. We kept you at the gate of life to look after our son... a simple task, but you failed us. See how now our poor son out of fear lacerates his poor royal flesh. Henceforth, speak only when Ìyá Mòpó speaks with you. You forget yourself. You parade yourself as a great protector, but here you are empty with a limp of a wounded deer. Answer Ìyá Mòpó, Kábíyèsí. She awaits your answer.

ÒGÌDÁN: I swear, I do not know.

KÓRÌ: In that case we shall....

ÒGÌDÁN: Why? Wait a while mother. Keep me company. I need to speak with you.

AJÉ: Speak with us, but you waited until we came to you. We, Ògìdán?

KÓRÌ: Easily you forgot your promise at the beginning. Now you flutter gàlègàlè like the king birds that we are. Are you one of us now?

ÒGÌDÁN: Forgive me mothers. I remember that night very well. As you there placed your hands on my head, you said, O ti di Ọba. Ọba tó ba lérí ohun gbogbo. That same night, you blessed me.

IYEMỌJA: ALL THREE LAUGH. We did not bless you alone, we prepared you for war. Remember that I said that what will kill a king lives within him. Come closer... let us show you how far you have damaged the spirit of power we gave you. Sick child, I say come to me, Kábíyèsí, come.

APÈNÀ: No, Kábíyèsí, don't move, not one step. No! They will take everything. No, Kábíyèsí.

TRANSFIXED, AS IF IN A TRANCE, ÒGÌDÁN MOVES CLOSER TO HER. THE OTHER TWO WOMEN MOVE CLOSER UNTIL ÒGÌDÁN IS TRAPPED WITHIN THE THREE OF THEM.

IYEMOJA: Kneel Ògìdán. ÒGÌDÁN KNEELS.

APÈNÀ: Mothers, please. He is only a child.

IYEMOJA: A child who bites his mother's nipple and laughs is no longer a child. This one has grown big fat teeth, so this time, he will chew stones. He shall be laced with a big fat òpá, as a grown up.

KÓRÌ: You need to hear the gods complain. Òṣun weeps. For days, we could not agree. Òṣun wept like a child until the river swelled. And we were blamed for the ills of a fool.

IYEMOJA: Three of us were supposed to protect her. But the damned fool used a charm that covered our eyes and defiled her in a haze of false smoke. His soul is damned... all the gods are agreed on this.

ÒGÌDÁN: Mothers, I am innocent.

AJÉ: Are you? Was it not your watch to protect her also? You did not even come to us who made your kingdom. Instead, you turned to those set to slaughter him. Fool.

IYEMOJA: Women, we banter. We have a task at hand.

SLOWLY THEY RAISE THEIR HANDS ABOVE HIS HEAD.

APÈNÀ: No, Kábíyèsí, no!

ÌLÀRÍ: SLOWLY FALLS ON HIS KNEES. HIS BACK STILL TURNED. Mothers, I beg you, spare my master.

KÓRÌ: Who speaks? Who dares speak when the spirits are here?

AJÉ: I say, who is he? How come he can break the freeze of the dreaded presence? Who gave him eyes that pierce the screen of the spirits? Who are you?

KÓRÌ: He is the son of the bereaved. Son of the weeping bones. SHE MOVES CLOSER TO ÌLÀRÍ. He bears the mark of an initiate. Even the mothers of the night know him. But henceforth, fold your tongue, clap it between your teeth. Not one word.

IYEMOJA: Then keep quiet, son. You are the reason for whom we cry. The chief mourner at this funeral of rites... which prepares the people of Ìjẹkùn Odò for the bath of tears. Clap your teeth until we are gone, if you love yourself.

ÒGÌDÁN: Mothers, a moment please. My village is set to crumble... but how can I appease the river goddess? How can sanity be restored again?

AJÉ: What?

IYEMOJA: Sister, please, the child speaks. Like a failed magician, he tries his trick of deceit on his mothers.

AJÉ: You want to appease the river goddess, do you? Then you must find the culprit who defiled her river and the sacred carrier. Call the Àwòrò and your chiefs all dressed in white; dance and sing for Ọṣun, whom you angered. Amuse her with pleasantries. And she might just smile on your people again. Mothers, we came for a purpose. HER HANDS RAISED SHE MOVES CLOSER TO ÒGÌDÁN.

ÒGÌDÁN: Mothers, what is this for?

KÓRÌ: To reaffirm our stand with you. To strengthen you broken arm. THE THREE WOMEN GIVE A SHRILL LAUGH. KÓRÌ RETURNS TO THE CIRCLE. THEY PLACE THEIR HANDS ON ÒGÌDÁN'S HEAD. You came an empty shell, we filled you up with the power to protect our daughter, the Arugbá, but you allowed her to be defiled.

AJÉ: Hà! Ọba Ògìdán Arógunmásá, today wealth shall no longer be yours. Sickness replaces health. All good things are gone from you, until you find the culprit.

IYEMỌJA: Àṣẹ ti gùn ún.

KÓRÌ: From this moment, we remove you... you are nothing to us. Until the land of Ìjẹkùn Odò is cleansed with the blood of the culprit, your land shall know no peace. Mothers, we must leave. Our task here is done. Henceforth, you shall remain an empty shell.

IYEMỌJA & AJÉ: Àṣẹ!

SHARP LIGHTS GO OFF. WHEN IT COMES ON AGAIN, IT SHOWS ÌLÀRÍ CROUCHED, SEATED, ASLEEP BY THE FOOT OF THE BED. ÒGÌDÁN IS ON HIS BED SLEEPING. HE AWAKENS, FRIGHTENED. HE RUNS TO THE CORNER OF THE ROOM AND BRINGS DOWN A HANGING CHARM.

ÒGÌDÁN: By the charms of all the gods of all the land protect. Kings before me do not sleep. Nothing can penetrate a stone... tonight... now, nothing will touch me. Èèwọ̀! PAUSE. CALMER. Thank the gods it was a dream. CALLS OUT. Ìlàrí! Ìlàrí! Where is the fool who is supposed to keep watch over me?

ÌLÀRÍ: STARTLED. I am here master. Do you want a drink of cold water?

ÒGÌDÁN: No. Did you see them? Or hear people talking? They even called you the son of weeping bones. Where is Apènà?

ÌLÀRÍ: No one else is here. PAUSE. Weeping bones. Me? May the gods forbid.

ÒGÌDÁN: They know you well. You say you heard nothing?

ÌLÀRÍ: Not a word Kábíyèsí… not even a whisper. Like a log, I slept, but 1 think 1 heard voices from afar. Voices faintly echoed through.

ÒGÌDÁN: Good, then you heard something. Which part did you hear?

ÌLÀRÍ: I heard nothing. Only my whispering snore.

ÒGÌDÁN: Then you heard some things.

ÌLÀRÍ: No, my lord. Is there something I should know? Let things be, Kábíyèsí. No need chasing figments. A worried mind races. It remains only a mile wide and perhaps an inch deep into illnesses of the heart. It must have been a nightmare… a very bad one. Let it be.

ÒGÌDÁN: But they were here.

ÌLÀRÍ: Who, Kábíyèsí?

ÒGÌDÁN: The ones whose voices you faintly heard from afar. The mothers of the land. They insinuated that I know the one who defiled the Arugbá.

ÌLÀRÍ: Do you, Kábíyèsí?

ÒGÌDÁN: No. I swear!

ÌLÀRÍ: Is that the truth, Kábíyèsí?

ÒGÌDÁN: Believe me. Even though it is said that truths have many shapes. This one is fixed. I swear I do not know.

ÌLÀRÍ: Mothers of the land? PAUSE. I thought they were supposed to be on your side?

ÒGÌDÁN: Not any more. They stripped me. Removed everything from my tongue, limbs, stomach and even my eyes which burn a man alive just by a steady stern gaze. I am finished. Call Apènà too.

ÌLÀRÍ: Where, Kábíyèsí?

ÒGÌDÁN: Here. All six of us. HE SEES THE CALABASH ON THE TABLE. GOES TO IT AND PICKS IT UP. Now it is empty. It was there too... with water from the river, sacred herbs and my blood. From it came the power of the charms which Apènà used while lacerating my back. With power. Now all that is gone... stripped.

ÌLÀRÍ: Your back?

ÒGÌDÁN: Yes. HE RAISES HIS DRESS. See... are fresh cuttings there?

ÌLÀRÍ: STEPS CLOSER LOOKING CLOSELY AT ÒGÌDÁN'S BACK. Háà... I see them... but one by one, they disappear!

ÒGÌDÁN: It is true then. They came. Run your hand on my back. ÌLÀRÍ RUNS HIS HAND. Hm... not a whimper of pain... not a feel. Nothing is there now. All is finished.

ÌLÀRÍ: It must have been a bad dream then. Turn to your right side when you sleep again. Bad dreams are eliminated in that pose. You are the king, nothing can touch you, Kábíyèsí. The night mothers will not let it.

ÒGÌDÁN: CHUCKLES. The night mothers. Those ones are yet to arrive. JUMPS UP. I must do what they asked of me. In the morning send for Ikúsanrí. I need to see him again; the potency of his charms begins to dwindle. I still felt a pang of fear when the mother came to see me.

ÌLÀRÍ: How can? I thought he said you had conquered fear and even death.

ÒGÌDÁN: His very words. You would have seen me shake a like a thin reed in a windy forest. All the charms failed me. Tell him to come quickly... their visit has left me vulnerable. Even now as I speak, my heart races.

ÌLÀRÍ: Yes, Kábíyèsí. But er... Kábíyèsí...

ÒGÌDÁN: Yes?

ÌLÀRÍ: Balógun came with Apènà while you slept. The body of Ṣàmù was found washed to the river bank. His stomach was swollen, his mouth filled with rotten fish.

ÒGÌDÁN: Èèwọ̀! A bad àrokò from the goddess of the river. Ṣàmù! DEJECTED. IN A WHISPER. We shall bury him in the morning.

ÌLÀRÍ: Yes, Kábíyèsí. Now sleep.

ÒGÌDÁN: AS HE RETURNS TO HIS BED. Summon every one... invite the acolytes of Ọ̀ṣun... everyone dressed in white. Tell them to bring their bands and instruments... Food too. We need to worship... while we try to unveil the meaning of this shrouded secret... finding an end to this unending impending darkness. Go to your room and sleep now. Since you hear nothing when I need you to.

SLOWLY, LIGHTS GO OFF.

THE THRONE ROOM. WHEN LIGHTS COME ON, ONLY APÈNÀ AND A FEW SOLDIERS ARE ON STAGE. ỌTÚN ENTERS.

APÈNÀ: I went to your house and I was told that you were here. They gave me your message. We are all to wear white dresses, why? What is going on? The Ọṣun festival is over.

ỌTÚN: No one knows. Kábíyèsí sent word round in the morning. Gather here at the palace in white dresses, so I am here in white dress as commanded. How was your trip to Ìpetumodù?

ỌTÚN: It went very well. All the rites were performed.

It had nothing to do with the dowry. Bídèmí was supposed to have honoured her pledge to Ọṣun before our daughter attainted the age of ten. She forgot and now we have paid for it dearly. Ọṣun never forgets a promise.

APÈNÀ: But even then, no one had the right to kill her. No one. But I am happy you went home. Did Ìyá Agbọmọlà hug her?

ỌTÚN: She did. She told us that Ọṣun would give us a child soon. My wife's spirits improved on the way home. One word to a dozen.

APÈNÀ: Then you have work to do. Not a moment's rest until my sister is heavy with child.

ỌTÚN: I pray Ọṣun answers our prayers. So what is happening now? I hear Kábíyèsí's mood changes by the minute. The rains are still heavy... destruction everywhere. Have they found Ṣàmù?

APÈNÀ: Yes. His body floated to the river bank. Àràbà led a group of elders to bury him in the early hours this morning.

ỌTÚN: What was the rush for? Ṣàmù was not a small child. Why did they bury him so quickly?

APÈNÀ: IN A WHISPERING VOICE. His eyes were plucked out. The whole place was smelling of rotten fish. They could not wait for the normal ritual... he would find more grace under the earth. So he was hurriedly buried.

ENTER ÒGÌDÁN AND SOME OTHER CHIEFS, ALL DRESSED IN WHITE. ÌLÀRÍ FOLLOWS. APÈNÀ AND ỌTÚN PROSTRATE.

ÒGÌDÁN: Háà... I am happy you came early. Let us settle down. Ìlàrí, call the women in.

THE WOMEN LED BY ÌYÁ ODÒ AND ÌYÁ ỌṢUN DANCE IN.

    Lílé: Ẹ kóre Òrìṣà Odò o
    Ègbè: Ẹ kóre Òrìṣà Odò Ọṣun
    Lílé: Ẹ kóre Òrìṣà Odò o
    Ègbè: Ẹ kóre Òrìṣà Odò Ọṣun
    Lílé: Ṣe bíwọ lò ní o
    Ègbè: Ṣe bíwọ lò ní n wá
    Lílé: Ṣe bíwọ lò ní o
    Ègbè: Ṣe bíwọ lò ní n wá
    Lílé: Ẹ máṣe yèyé Òrìṣà Odò
    Ègbè: Ẹ máṣe yèyé Òrìṣà Odò Ọṣun
    Lílé: Ẹ máṣe yèyé Òrìṣà Odò
    Ègbè: Ẹ máṣe yèyé Òrìṣà Odò Ọṣun
    Lílé: Òrìṣà Odò o
    Ègbè: Òrìṣà Odò o
    Lílé: Èrù rẹ ń bàmí Eléjiwọ̀rọ̀
    Ègbè: Òrìṣà Odò o
        Òrìṣà Odò o
        Èrù rẹ ń bàmí Eléjiwọ̀rọ̀

All: Oore Òrìṣà Odò ò
   Omi ò
   Ọta ò
   Ẹdan ò
   Ẹri ò ò
   Àgbá ò
   Oore Òrìṣà Odò Ọṣun.

ÒGÌDÁN: STEPS FORWARD. My people and great worshippers of Òrìṣà Odò Ọṣun, I thank you for coming. Today will be a long night, because after the dances in the palace, we shall proceed to the river bank of Ìjẹkùn Odò. Our mother weeps. She is angry with us. The mother of the land has asked us to do this in her honour. We all know what happened to our Arugbá. This morning we buried her; still in mourning, we buried our beloved Ṣàmù too. Yes, the land is not at rest... peace and plenty begins to elude us. Why? Someone has touched the tail of Ẹbọra inú omi, the giant mermaid who resides under the water. Ìyá Ọṣun, please come and call our mother.

ÌYÁ ỌṢUN: Oore Òrìṣà Odò ò
   Omi ò
   Ọta ò
   Ẹdan ò
   Ẹri ò ò
   Àgbá ò
   Oore Òrìṣà Odò Ọṣun.

THE WOMEN RAISE ANOTHER SONG AND DANCE. ÒGÌDÁN AND THE CHIEFS JOIN.

ÒGÌDÁN: Now to the river bank. To the Ọṣun shrine. HE RAISES A SONG.

ÌYÁ ODÒ: Not one step, Ọba Ògìdán. ALL FREEZE. The river rejects your supplication even before it is given. Away! Away from here. Ọṣun herself approaches.

IN A SLOW MUSIC, AN ARUGBÁ CARRYING THE SACRED CALABASH COVERED WITH RED AṢỌ ÒKÈ DANCES IN. TWO ELDERLY WOMEN DANCE BY HER SIDE. A YOUNG ARUGBÁ WITH HER HEAD COVERED WITH THE SAME ASO OKE AS THE ARUGBA, WEEPING, FOLLOWS. THE STATUES OF IYEMỌJA, KÓRÌ AND AJÉ ARE CARRIED BY THREE DIFFERENT GIRLS DRESSED IN WHITE. AND AN ELDERLY COUPLE FOLLOW. EVERYBODY ON STAGE KNEEL, EXCEPT ÒGÌDÁN.

ALL: Oore Òrìṣà Odò ò
 Omi ò
 Ọta ò
 Ẹdan ò
 Ẹri ò ò
 Àgbá ò
 Oore Òrìṣà Odò Ọṣun.

ỌṢUN: Ògìdán, I have come.

ÒGÌDÁN: Who are you? We have no Arugbá. We buried our own this morning and now it is nightfall. Who are you who dares to carry a calabash to my palace when custom demands the calabash is carried out of the palace to the river side? I say, who are you?

ÌYÁ ỌṢUN: POSSESSED, STEPS FORWARD.
 Can't you recognize, Ọṣun ṣẹngẹṣẹ́?
 Can't you see the marks of Ládékojú?
 Amawomárò welcome. Mother welcome.
 Confused, we did not know which steps to take.
 Indeed, what does our mother want?

ÒṢUN: Good question. Three maidens of mine have been defiled here. One was forced to kill herself. The others were forced to die. My brother Èṣù has revealed the culprit to me. But the kolanut will chew better in the fouled mouth. Ọba Ògìdán, do you know who I seek? Give the person to me and I shall depart.

ÒGÌDÁN: I thought you already had the man? When Ṣàmù died, I thought all was over.

ÒṢUN: Ṣàmù was a foolish stooge. It was he who lured Ọtún's daughter to the spot of death. It was he who carried Ọtún's daughter to Èṣù's abode at the crossroad in the forest. He was dead before he slipped and fell into the river... pushed by hands of another. You know the truth now. Tell me who defiled my Arugbá?

ÒGÌDÁN: I swear I don't know. That is the truth.

ÒṢUN: CHUCKLES. The truth. Such a simple word which needs so many layers of lies to hide.

APÈNÀ: Please, Òrìṣà Odò, if you know who did this, name him... take him away... let him or her join Ṣàmù, and let peace be restored to the land. Or better still, since the late Arugbá was from the royal family, we could replace her with two new virgins... from the royal family.

ÒGÌDÁN: Yes. From my blood. I could... er.... even give up two of my own daughters to appease you, Òrìṣà Odò.

ỌTÚN: We could even worship you and Èṣù all year long. At least now I know that contrary to the belief and gossips, my daughter was not a loose girl. Someone lured her to where she was killed. The same person carried her body to the bush. I wish Ṣàmù had not died, I would have blackened his face and made the youths sing around him as they lead him round the village in shame. HE KNEELS AND BOWS. I shall worship you, Òrìṣà Odò, for the rest of my life.

SLOW SONG BEGINS THE ACOLYTES DANCE ROUND HER. SLOWLY SHE BEGINS TO GET POSSESSED. SHE TURNS INTO ỌṢÚNTÓMI THE LATE ARUGBÁ. ÌYÁ ODÒ STEPS FORWARD.

ÌYÁ ỌṢUN: Abiyamọ tó ń retí igbe,
  Ládékojú Ọṣun ṣẹ̀ngẹ̀ṣẹ̀
  Olóòyà iyùn
  Oníbú owó lóde Ìjẹ̀kùn Odò
  Ìyá mi oníbú Ajé
  Ọmọ a jí bẹ wàjí ò

BREAKS INTO A SONG.

  Lílé: Alágbo, alágbo
  Ègbè: Alágbo àwẹ̀yè.
  Lílé: Ọmọ Ládékojú o
  Ègbè: Alágbo àwẹ̀yè
  Lílé: Bámi tọ́mọ̀ mi
  Ègbè: Alágbo àwẹ̀ yè
  Lílé: Bámi wọmọ̀ mi láwòyè o
  Ègbè: Alágbo àwẹ̀yè.
  Ọṣun Ṣẹ̀ngẹ̀ṣẹ́, cure these inflictions on your daughters. Do not let any harm come to them.

ÌYÁ ODÒ: Ọṣúntómi... I see her in you. You have come to tell the story which they so desperately want to distort and hide. Who defiled the Arugbá? Speak... the truth is not too far now.

ỌṢUN: He! The crooked man with the crown. The epitome of evil. Ọba Ògìdán Arógunmásá.

THE CHIEFS AND ACOLYTES ARE ANGRY. ÒGÌDÁN SAYS NOTHING. SLOWLY, THE ARUGBÁ MOVES CLOSER TO HIM.

ỌṢUN: Ìlàrí, from my head lift the message of the gods for your king. SLOWLY ÌLÀRÍ MOVES TO ỌṢUN. ÌYÁ ODÒ AND ÌYÁ ỌṢUN LIFT THE WHITE CLOTH COVERING THE SMALL CALABASH BOWL FROM THE BIGGER CALABASH. ÌLÀRÍ PICKS IT UP. A life for lives, Kábíyèsí Ògìdán Arógunmásá. This completes the curse of Ọṣúnbùnmi of the village of Ajagunṣèlú whom your father Ọba Arógunmásá, defiled. Out of sheer lust, he attacked the village and almost burnt all of them to death. He brought the king, his wife and their son and daughter to Ijekun Yèyé. He enslaved them. One night, he forced himself on the young daughter who was the Arugbá of her village. She committed suicide, but before she did, she cursed that any child from the house of Arógunmásá will only rule for two years. You learnt of the curse and ran to find remedies. This is why we are here today. The white calabash must be filled… drips of blood like the ones you took from my virgins must flow. An eye for eyes forced to close. Apènà, you know what to do. After, let his head be taken to the shrine of Ògún. Then all will be well. I have spoken.

ÒGÌDÁN: My people, pity me not…. aware and with open eyes I walked into this. I thought I could change my destiny… multiply my years… but see how my foolishness has shortened me. Pity. Apènà… Ìlàrí, you heard her. Ọtún… you will have your revenge tonight. Èṣù Láàlú, I hear you chuckle. Ṣàmù did me in at your crossroad. SLOWLY, A SLOW DIRGE BEGINS, APÈNÀ, ÌLÀRÍ AND ÒGÌDÁN GO INTO THE INNER ROOM.

ÒṢUN: This is done. Let us return sisters. This soiled land must be cleansed.

AMIDST SONGS AND DANCES FOR ÒṢUN, SLOW LIGHTS FADE.

DIM ROOM, IKÚSANRÍ'S INNER ROOM. HE SITS BEFORE THE ÒPÈLÈ ALONE.

IKÚSANRÍ: Gbogbo Ọlá omi tí ń bẹ nílé ayé
Kò le è tó t'òkun
Gbogbo Yèyé tí ó ṣe l'ókè
Iyì wọn kò tó tọ̀sà
Adíá fún Ọbàtálá Òsèrègbó
Ní'jọ́ tí yíò jẹ Alaba-láṣẹ
Tí gbogbo Irúnmọlẹ̀ ní wọn yóò
Gba ọkan nínú oríkì rẹ
Tí Ọrúnmìlà yẹhùn
Tí Ẹlẹ́gbárá tèlé e!
With the combined help of all three of them, all issues are resolved. Hà, Ọbàtálá...the great molder of human casing. The porter. Ọrúnmìlà, the accountant of human frailties. ÌLÀRÍ ENTERS. WATCHES IKÚSANRÍ AS HE SPEAKS. SLOWLY HE STOOPS. The adviser of uncontrolled stupid tempers, the foolish self-acclaimed wise men and you great Èṣù Ẹlẹ́gbárá, the arbiter of selfishness, the knotted idiocy of man's unplanned ambitions. I thank you all for this resolution. Ìlú Ajagunṣèlú will sleep again. Your functions were all well served here. Three stones of life that will throw man's destiny away if he listens to their guidance. I greet you all. HE LOOKS AT ÌLÀRÍ. You have come.

ÌLÀRÍ: We have. The bones of my father are laid back to rest. I could feel the other kings sigh as we buried his head. The rituals are completed. Now, it is done.

IKÚSANRÍ: Your mother?

ÌLÀRÍ: She too. In her grave where all the Olori lie.

It was my sister's bones that we did not know what to do with them. But Baba Awo asked us to return them to Ìjẹ̀kùn Odò... he says that we should bury her at the sacred ground set aside for the Arugba. But I...

IKÚSANRÍ: But?

ÌLÀRÍ: I disagreed with him. She was our Arugbá here in Ajagunṣèlú, not Ìjẹ̀kùn Odò. Definitely her bones were not theirs to have.

IKÚSANRÍ: CHUCKLES. Let it be. It was in Ìjẹ̀kùn Odò that she finally carried the calabash. In her white calabash, Ọ̀sun sent her message to us and resolved the matter. HE BEGINS TO MUTTER.
Ọ̀sun, Òrìṣà Odò Ògùgù,
Òrìṣà Odò Ògùgù
Ò-walẹ̀-walẹ̀-kÁjé sí
Ọ̀-padẹ-mọ́wọ́-padẹ-mọ́sẹ̀
Ó fidẹ ṣọlá
Ọ̀ lọ́mọ-wẹ́ẹ̀rẹ́-lágbàlá
Ọ̀sun, Òrìṣà Odò
Oore Òrìṣà Odò ò
Omi ò
Ọta ò
Ẹdan ò
Ẹri ò ò
Àgbá ò
Oore Òrìṣà Odò Ọ̀sun.
Two days to when she was to carry the Igbá Ọ̀sun here, she was forced into slavery. She was forced to commit suicide, to defend the sanctity of Ọ̀sun's purity, and it was in death

that she carried the calabash and thus resolved the problems of the two villages in one stroke. Òrìṣà Odò Ọ̀ṣun, it is you I greet.

ÌLÀRÍ: No wonder. In one brief moment as I lifted the calabash, I thought I saw her face smile. She too was there, with our parents.

IKÚSANRÍ: TAKES A SMALL BOWL OF KOLANUTS. Give this to the Apènà when you arrive. There are other gifts for the Ìjòyè. May Ọ̀rúnmìlà guide them as they pick a new King for Ìjẹ̀kùn Odò. Whoever is chosen must wash his body clean for three days with the water from the Ọ̀ṣun River in the middle of the night when the owl is awake.

ÌLÀRÍ: I have heard you Bàbá.

IKÚSANRÍ: And you? When do we expect our new king to sit on the throne of his fathers?

ÌLÀRÍ: Once a new king sits at Ìjẹ̀kùn Odò. Er Bàbá... I saw all the gifts Ọba Ògìdán sent. They are just the way, I brought them. Not one was touched.

IKUSANMRI: The gifts were used to open the gate of the world of the Òrìṣà. No Òrìṣà accepted them from me. Unknown to me was at the time Ọba Ògìdán sent them, he had perfected the opening of passages... and heightened the risk of confrontation among the Òrìṣà. Ṣàmù, aware that Ọba Ògìdán might kill him because he knew too much, set it all off. He dumped Ọ̀tún's daughter's body at the shrine of Èṣù. He in turn was livid with anger, thus decided to unravel the deeper truth of the matter. CHUCKLES. But the real joker was Ọba Ògìdán. Unknown to him was that he carried a curse which had to be fulfilled.

ÌLÀRÍ: A curse? Yes... I did not understand it when Ọṣun mentioned it.

IKÚSANRÍ: A dark curse spoken from the mouth of a young virgin... your late sister.

ÌLÀRÍ: I never knew. And I have remained with him from the time he was announced the heir to the throne... the son of the killer of my family. PAUSE. But despite all these, he was a good man. WONDERING. Except for...

IKÚSANRÍ: Except for his love for young virgins? That is what the gods used. The mark of the curse he carried. What will kill a king always lives within him. When the time arrives, the foolishness follows, and he dies a simple death... no matter how wise.

ÌLÀRÍ: Always I warned him that it would be his own downfall.

IKÚSANRÍ: Downfall? That is putting it mildly. It sent his headless body to a dampened crypt. Cocooned in the salty waters of Ìjẹ̀kùn Odò.

ÌLÀRÍ: I still can to believe it.

IKÚSANRÍ: Me too. I warned him. He could wait, until after the celebrations. But he would not hear of it.

ÌLÀRÍ: That is what I do not understand... even now as I speak. It must have been the work of Èṣù. You had promised that Èṣù's cloak would blur the sight of the onlookers. What happened Bàbá? Did Èṣù turn his back on us?

IKÚSANRÍ: Èṣù kẹ? He saved his damned soul. He would have had his whole body decapitated, not just his head removed. I tell you that it was Láàlú's eyes which saw far, from all sides of where he stood, it was him who saw the untold truths and set out to unfold them. He came here himself and told it all.

ÌLÀRÍ: You mean Èṣù is that patient?

IKÚSANRÍ: Yes. The inpatient animal is man. You and I. Always Èṣù unconcerned stays at the crossroads… it is man who goes to Onílé oríta. Ògún spurs man on too. CHUCKLES. Sadly, unknown to both you and your king, he was the sacrifice.

ÌLÀRÍ: A LOUD WHISPER. Sacrifice?

IKÚSANRÍ: Yes.

ÌLÀRÍ: Maybe that is why he accepted it that way. CALMLY. When we got into his room, with me carrying the calabash which my late sister had brought, I felt that I was the executioner. PAUSE. SLOWLY. He just resigned himself to his own fate. He was a willing olókùn ẹṣin… but my heart leaped when the white calabash was put on his head. The Apènà spoke to his spirits until his dilated eyes froze. He stretched his neck, as if ready. In one swoop, Ògún's cutlass did it. PAUSE. As his head rolled on the bare floor, I stretched to catch it. Not a move, the Apènà whispered. So, I froze.

IKÚSANRÍ: I hope you did not touch it?

ÌLÀRÍ: I wanted to, but my legs did not let me. Father, he was a king… and we killed him like a dog for Ogun's sacrifice. A common dog. HE BEGINS TO CRY. CROAKY VOICE. I don't want to be… no I don't want to.

IKÚSANRÍ: You don't want to be what?

ÌLÀRÍ: A king. I am comfortable being a shadow, which is able to melt when the sunlight rises and return when darkness falls. It is safer.

IKÚSANRÍ: Èèwọ̀! Is life safe? For whom? You were born to be a leader. Leaders are born to be used. Power itself crowns madness. CHUCKLES. It is a bad contrast. Either way, king or slave, there is always a sad story somewhere... for someone.

ÌLÀRÍ: Still... I don't want to be out spaced by issues I did not know anything about. Could he not have saved himself? I mean he was the king, second only to the gods. Is that not what the praise chant says?

IKÚSANRÍ: CHUCKLES. Save himself? No! This is why the tides of Ìjẹ̀kùn Odò, propelled by the anger of Òrìṣà Odò Ọ̀ṣun, urged on by Iyemọja, swept him off his weakened feet. For man, power corrupts even his scrotum, most times blurring his senses like that of your king. Indeed, the case of every man. We are like the banana shoots. One must die for the other to grow. This works even for kings. SOUND OF THUNDER. Ṣàngó's anger lingers. Hurry to Ìjẹ̀kùn Odò... the night approaches, and Olójú orógbó remains restless.

ÌLÀRÍ: But I have not finished.

IKÚSANRÍ: Nothing is ever finished... we just live our own and the others come along. SOUND OF THUNDER AGAIN. Still. HE TAKES THE LITTLE BRONZE BELL AND SHAKES IT TO A RHYTHM. Still mother of the river, I say still.
It is not in weeping for the night that we feel your anger.
Suppress the anger and let peace reign again.
Òrìṣà Odò... tell Ṣàngó to look away
There is no more sacrifice here for now.

I say still Òrìṣà Odò. SOUND OF RAIN FALL.
Oore Òrìṣà Odò o! Oore Òrìṣà Odò o!

DANCERS AND MUSICIANS, ALL DRESSED IN WHITE ỌṢUN WORSHIPPERS COSTUMES, COME ON STAGE. AS THEY DANCE.

    Lílé: Àwúrá olú onílé ikú o
          Amawomárò O mà kú ọlà
          Òrìṣà Odò káre ò ọlọ́wọ́ idẹ
          Àwúrá olú onílé ikú o
          Amawomárò O mà kú ọlà
          Òrìṣà Odò káre ò ọlọ́wọ́ idẹ
          Òrìṣà Odò dé
Ègbè: Ibi gbogbo lọnà
Lílé: Ọmọ Aládékojú
Ègbè: Ibi gbogbo lọnà
Lílé: Ònà kì ń dí mómi
Ègbè: Ibi gbogbo lọnà
Lílé: Ẹ̀wùjí mà dé o
Ègbè: Ibi gbogbo lọnà
Lílé: ALádékojú dé o
Ègbè: Ibi gbogbo lọnà
Lílé: Móremí mà dé o
Ègbè: Ibi gbogbo lọnà
Lílé: A-bé-wú-ṣọ-lá
Ègbè: Ibi gbogbo lọnà
Lílé: A-bẹ-sódo-sòrọ̀-ọmọ o
Ègbè: Ibi gbogbo lọnà
Lílé: Abiyamọ, A bòjá ńlá
Ègbè: Ibi gbogbo lọnà
Lílé: Ọlọ́já- gbọ̀ọ̀rọ̀- gbọọrọ o
Ègbè: Ibi gbogbo lọnà
       Oore Òrìṣà Odò ò
       Omi ò

    Ọta ò
    Ẹdan ò
    Ẹri ò ò
    Àgbá ò
    Oore Òrìṣà Odò Ọ̀ṣun.

SLOWLY, FINAL LIGHTS FADE.

                THE END.